DATE DUE

DEMCO 38-296

ABOUT ISLAND PRESS

Island Press, a nonprofit organization, publishes, markets, and distributes the most advanced thinking on the conservation of our natural resources—books about soil, land, water, forests, wildlife, and hazardous and toxic wastes. These books are practical tools used by public officials, business and industry leaders, natural resource managers, and concerned citizens working to solve both local and global resource problems.

Founded in 1978, Island Press reorganized in 1984 to meet the increasing demand for substantive books on all resource-related issues. Island Press publishes and distributes under its own imprint and offers these services to other nonprofit organizations.

Funding to support Island Press is provided by The Mary Reynolds Babcock Foundation, The Ford Foundation, The George Gund Foundation, The William and Flora Hewlett Foundation, The Joyce Foundation, The J. M. Kaplan Fund, The John D. and Catherine T. MacArthur Foundation, The Andrew W. Mellon Foundation, Northwest Area Foundation, The Jessie Smith Noyes Foundation, The J. N. Pew, Jr. Charitable Trust, The Rockefeller Brothers Fund, The Florence and John Schumann Foundation, and The Tides Foundation.

REOPENING THE WESTERN FRONTIER

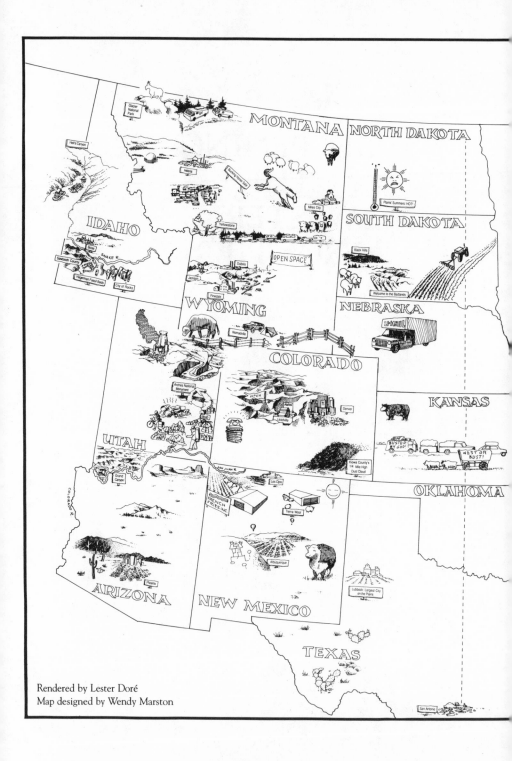

Rendered by Lester Doré
Map designed by Wendy Marston

From
High Country News

REOPENING THE WESTERN FRONTIER

Edited by Ed Marston

ISLAND PRESS

Washington, D.C. □ *Covelo, California*

This Island Press volume is the first book edition of four special issues
of *High Country News* that were originally published in the fall of 1988.
This volume includes some updating and minor revision of the newspaper issues.

Grateful acknowledgment is made for permission to reprint the following material:

Chapter Ten, in a different version, appeared in the *Chicago Tribune*
Sunday Magazine, November 22, 1987.

Portions of Chapter Twelve appeared in *Planning* magazine, copyright 1987
by the American Planning Association, and are reprinted by the Association's
permission.

Chapter Twenty includes material quoted from *The Economic*
Pursuit of Quality by Thomas Michael Power, published by
M. E. Sharpe, Inc., 1987.

Chapter Thirty-one contains designs and text from *Mimbres*
Mythology by Pat Carr, published by Texas Western Press, 1979, and designs from material made
available by the Western New Mexico University Museum in Silver City, New Mexico.

Library of Congress Cataloging-in-Publication Data

Reopening the western frontier / edited by Ed Marston.
p.   cm.
At head of title: High country news.
Contains modified material originally published as 4 special
issues of High country news in the fall of 1988.
Includes index.
ISBN 1-55963-011-6 : $24.95. — ISBN 1-55963-010-8 (pbk.) : $15.95
1. West (U.S.)—Economic policy—Environmental aspects.
2. Environmental policy—West (U.S.)   3. West (U.S.)—Economic
conditions.   4. West (U.S.)—Civilization—20th century.
I. Marston, Ed.   II. High country news.
HC107.A17R46   1989   89-2225
338.978—dc20   CIP

Printed on recycled, acid-free paper
Manufactured in the United States of America
10 9 8 7 6 5 4 3 2 1

Contents

Part Two
THE BUST

Part Three
THE IMPACT OF ENVIRONMENTALISM

Part Four
THE FUTURE

Contributors

Tom Bell founded *High Country News* in 1970. He now edits a history magazine in Lander, Wyoming.

Dennis Brownridge is a free-lance writer specializing in Western topics. He holds a doctorate in geography and currently lives in Orme, Arizona.

Colleen Cabot is a gardener in Jackson, Wyoming. For some years she was director of the Teton Science School near Grand Teton and Yellowstone national parks.

Peter Carrels is a free-lance writer and photographer who lives in Aberdeen, South Dakota. He is at work on a book about the United Family Farmers and South Dakota's Oahe Irrigation Project.

Jon Christensen is a free-lance writer based in San Francisco.

Lester Doré is an artist and conservationist in Madison, Wisconsin.

Bruce Farling is a free-lance writer in Missoula, Montana.

Pat Ford is a free-lance writer and conservationist in Boise, Idaho. He directed the Idaho Conservation League for several years.

DeWitt John is senior economist for the National Governors' Association in Washington, D.C. Before heading east, he worked for the state of Colorado.

John Leshy is a professor of law and an expert on mining law at Arizona State University in Tempe.

Bert Lindler lives and works in Great Falls, Montana, where he specializes in environmental and outdoor reporting for the *Great Falls Tribune*.

Betsy Marston is editor of *High Country News*.

Ed Marston has been publisher of *High Country News* since 1983.

Don Moniak, a resident of eastern Montana, writes an occasional free-lance article.

Deborah Epstein Popper is a graduate student in geography at Rutgers University in New Brunswick, New Jersey.

Frank J. Popper, Jr., chairs Rutgers's urban studies department.

Ed Quillen is a free-lance writer, columnist for the *Denver Post*, and resident of Salida, Colorado.

C. L. Rawlins is a poet and *High Country News's* poetry editor. He also works on acid rain studies in Wyoming's Bridger Wilderness.

Jim Robbins is a free-lance writer in Helena, Montana. He has written for the *New York Times,* the *Boston Globe,* and other major publications.

Peggy Robinson is a graphic artist and typesetter at *High Country News.*

Donald Snow ran the Northern Lights Institute for four years. He is now directing the Conservation League Study from Missoula, Montana.

Stephen Voynick is a free-lance writer and author of five books; he lives in Leadville, Colorado.

Raymond Wheeler trained for a career in journalism by working as a cab driver, bicycle messenger, and river guide. He now lives in Salt Lake City, Utah, and is writing a book about the Colorado Plateau.

Tom Wolf works for The Nature Conservancy in Sante Fe, New Mexico. A former literature professor at Brandeis University, he is currently working on a cultural geography of Wyoming.

Preface

MOST AMERICANS take pride in where they live—their nation, their state, and especially their hometown or home city. But they are usually humble about the time in which they live. They are proud of the *where* in their lives but not of the *when*.

Americans think that important times are either past or yet to come. As a result, this nation spends much time looking back with nostalgia, or forward with anticipation. In comparison with past and future, the present seems bland. Americans may speak of today's technological, and even social, miracles, but they do not believe they are on the edge of things.

This book begs to differ. Perhaps because the recent changes in the rural West have come so fast, and cut so deeply, the editor and writers of *Reopening the Western Frontier* know that the West will never be what it was. We know, as we watch century-old patterns disintegrating or being smashed, that a region that was frozen in time is again on the move.

There is nothing unique to the West here. The theme of traumatic change could be applied to many parts of America. New England has gone from textile mills, shoe factories, and granite-ribbed Vermonters to high-tech economies, ski colonies, and yuppies; the Old South has gone from being segregated and agrarian to a more open and urban way of life; and the nation of southern California has been transformed from a place based on citrus and films to one of the world's most diversified, dynamic economies and a polyglot population.

The major difference between the West and other areas is how long it has taken deep change to come to the West. It is the thesis of this book that the rural West has come to us, now at the end of the twentieth century, relatively intact from the nineteenth century. By comparison, change has been much more continuous in other regions.

In addition, the West comes ready-made with a metaphor for drastic change. Every region of the nation has been a frontier, but only the West is the subject of historian Frederick Jackson Turner's essay "The Significance of the Frontier in American History." Turner's description of the steady advance of civilization and democracy grabbed America's imagination, as did his conclusion that the frontier slammed shut in the year 1890. It grabbed America's imagination not because it was the first, or a unique, frontier, but because it was the last frontier.

This book picks up Turner's metaphor and runs with it. His analysis, of course, has not survived recent scrutiny. The settlement of the West was accomplished more by large concentrations of capital and by brutal treatment of Indians and the land than by broad-shouldered pioneers pushing democracy ever farther west.

But Turner's frontier image survives. The frontier may not have been quite as he described it, but there was a frontier—a space in place and time where two very different realities confronted each other. In the end, one was triumphant, and Turner's 1890 dates that triumph in the same way that 1776 officially dates the birth of the United States.

The extraordinary thing about Turner's thesis of a closed frontier is how long his frontier has remained closed, how long a way of life and ways of earning a living here remained in place. You can visit parts of the West where life is carried on today much as it was in the nineteenth century: cowboys herd cows from horseback, loggers go into the woods with saws (chain saws, it is true), miners walk into hillsides in search of gold and silver ore, farmers use shovels to lead water out of irrigation ditches and onto the land, and Indians live on reservations.

The West of wide-open spaces also survives, although it is interwoven with our modern age. The greatest danger on many Western highways is a collision between a speeding car and an antelope or deer, or horse or cow. And while the big sky is crisscrossed with jet contrails, the mythic landscape survives: the Grand Canyon, the Rocky Mountains, the canyon and desert country of Utah.

The landscape will continue to survive, but that nineteenth-century way of life, which was dominant only two decades ago, is now in massive retreat. In part it is in retreat because of a natural winding down of a way of life. And in part it is in retreat because the region was subjected to calamitous economic change brought about by national and global forces and the region's own collective miscalculation. Hence, the reopened frontier.

This tale of late-twentieth-century pioneering is told by a newspaper, *High Country News,* created by the rural West to describe itself. Conventional economic forces could not produce a newspaper to cover this 1-million-square-mile, ten-state landmass; so Westerners, with help from people outside the region who care about the West, seized on a crusading environmental biweekly newspaper started by Wyoming rancher Tom Bell. Thus far, "a paper for people who care about the West" has been sustained by its readers' subscriptions and contributions for nineteen years.

Tom Bell was provoked to start *High Country News* in 1970 by the dawn of the West's latest energy, minerals, and land boom. In the nineteen years following that founding, *HCN* has covered the events that have eroded the Old West and led to today's drastic change.

This book had its genesis as four special issues of *High Country News* published in the fall of 1988 with the help of reader contributions to the paper's research fund and with grants from several foundations. Members of the paper's far-flung network of free-lance writers were asked to write articles describing the changes they saw occurring in their corners of the West. Their thirty-odd articles and essays were assembled into the four special issues, and, now, with some modification and rearrangement, into this book.

Normally, HCN sticks to on-the-ground articles on logging, mining, water pollution, wilderness, endangered species, and national park management. But biannually it attempts to synthesize and unify. In 1986 it published four special issues on water under the title *Western Water Made Simple,* also later published as a book by Island Press.

Here, HCN attempts a larger synthesis, based upon two decades of covering Western booms and busts. It comes to you from a love of this immense, empty region, and out of a conviction that Westerners are living in what the Chinese call "interesting times."

Writer Wallace Stegner has said that all writing is regional—everyone needs a place to stand, a place from which to see the world. If Stegner is correct, this book should enable its readers to see a long way, for the American West has the clearest air, the highest peaks, and the fewest trees of any place in the lower forty-eight states. We hope you enjoy the view.

Ed Marston
Paonia, Colorado

Part One

THE
BOOM

CHAPTER ONE

A Shattered Region

Ed Marston

A RECURRING THEME of Western movies is the wide-open town. In hundreds of Westerns, decent folks hide in their homes while bad guys stalk the streets. Finally, the hero—Shane, the Lone Ranger, whoever—rides in and cleans house, plugging some hearts full of lead and breaking others. With the town clean, and the hero's personal mix of good and evil now out of place, he saddles up and rides toward the next bit of dirty work.

Those movies are about the West of a century ago—a West that raised cattle, dug gold, and tried to build communities. But they could also be about today, for once again the West is wide open. And it is wide open in precisely the sense of those old movie-set towns: law and order have been broken down.

In this late twentieth century, people are not shot in the streets and bullies are not swaggering past closed stores on semi-deserted main streets. Today's West is wide open in ways too subtle to depict in an episode of *Gunsmoke* or even in a feature-length film. But not too subtle, we hope, for this book, *Reopening the Western Frontier.*

The Western frontier "closed" at the end of the nineteenth century. Frederick Jackson Turner said census figures showed that the nation lost its last frontier—the West—in 1890. It lost the frontier partly because the land was settled, if one can speak of small towns and isolated ranches scattered over 1 million square miles as a settling. But the frontier was closed also because a question was settled around 1890: Upon what was the future of the West to be based?

The answer, as it was worked out in the last half of the nineteenth century, was cattle ranching, irrigated agriculture, mining, milling, and logging. Although no one planned it that way, ranching and irrigated agriculture were to be the steady part of the economy. Laid over this base was to be the unsteady part: the mining of gold, silver, coal, uranium, copper, and oilshale; the drilling for oil and gas; and the construction of dams and coal-fired power plants.

What the rural West was not to have, except on its vast borders, were large metropolitan areas—centers of industry, services, and communications—that are common on both coasts and in the industrial Midwest. What the West got instead were a few medium-size cities, like Denver and Salt Lake City, a few towns of 100,000 or so, like Boise and Billings, and thousands of communities that wouldn't fill an apartment house in a city or a subdivision in a suburb.

These small communities grew up around and were shaped by the West's dominant economies. On the plains and in the irrigated valleys were the agricultural communities, with their wide main streets and dusty, unpaved side streets. In the mountains were the mining towns, with their narrow streets and tiny homes built amidst railroad lines, piles of mine waste, and loading silos.

For the most part, the ranching towns were Anglo in character, populated by people whose families had probably come West from Appalachia or other rural Eastern areas. And the mining towns were generally populated by people with more recent European roots, or Hispanic backgrounds.

There are other ways to characterize the two kinds of towns. The West is usually rural, in the way it earns its living and in its values, below 7,500 feet of elevation, and urban above 7,500 feet, where mining and recreation dominate. There are a million exceptions to the above generalizations. Agriculture can boom and bust. Mining can be stable. Mining towns or power-plant or dam boomtowns can be found in the flats, in the territory we have assigned to agriculture. Ranching communities are found in the mountains. People recently arrived from Europe or people of Hispanic backgrounds own or work on ranches, and Anglos mine. So the above generalizations are useful not because they are accurate, but because they are catchy and memorable. A bad rule of thumb is better than no rule so long as its weaknesses are kept in mind.

With that escape hatch in place, we will say that from the 1890s to the early 1970s, the West consisted of a stable agricultural base overlaid with booming and busting extraction. Around this grew up two societies: a socially and religiously conservative one and a rooting-tooting one that, for example, gives Anglo youths in small Western communities a higher death rate from violence than youngsters coming of age in an urban ghetto.

For one hundred years, the West lived with this twin personality, finding stability in the instability. This generalization is especially true if the stable part of the economy is extended beyond agriculture to include retirement, recreation, government employment. Then, in the 1970s, all the switches were thrown at once, and the West boomed as it had never boomed before. Everything in the West was in demand, and no price was too high.

The oil crunch set off feverish energy activity in the West. Its oil, oil shale, uranium, coal, and natural gas were in great demand. The region was renamed America's Saudi Arabia, and out of Washington came billions of dollars and word that the West was now a "national sacrifice area." Its clean air and spectacular landscape were to take a backseat to the nation's need for BTU's.

The energy boom was accompanied by heightened demand for the West's molybdenum, gold, silver, soda ash, phosphate, and logs. The inflation diluting the nation's currency made the West's land and water and ski condominiums look like great investments. It was as if some global King Midas had touched all 1 million square miles of the empty West. Everyone was to be rich.

The boom, like all booms, fed on itself. The need for towns to house energy workers attracted construction workers, who in turn needed services, which attracted yet more people. A heavily settled area could have put its underemployed population to work or could have filled up half-filled facilities, but the West was empty. There was no fat to draw on. There was no slack to be taken up.

The resulting boom went on so long, and inflated values so much, that previously stable parts of the West's economy got sucked in. Not just ranching and irrigated agriculture, but small towns and school districts, resort operators, and others outside the minerals and energy areas. School districts and towns, for example, took on huge debt loads to build facilities for the future. Farmers and ranchers stretched themselves to buy neighboring land, or finally felt they could stop scratching and pinching pennies. Instead, they borrowed heavily on the value of land and water. Their assets were rising so quickly there wasn't any limit to what they could borrow.

Then came declining energy prices and the end of inflation. The boom, fifteen years or so in the making, collapsed in the few years following 1982. The underlying, stable part of the economy was caught up in the collapse. A deep economic collapse first consumes the weak, and then pulls down the healthy in the turbulent wake it creates. Agriculture, as we've broadly defined it, went down with mining and power-plant building. Towns and school districts couldn't provide services and pay off bonds.

Political and social establishments declined or collapsed with the economy. Presidents of chambers of commerce, Rotary Clubs, and agricultural cooperative boards were swept away. Not just an economic world collapsed, but also a world of dreams and aspirations. Thousands of small Western towns and their residents thought they had arrived. They thought their community was going to have the same things—schools with swimming pools, a golf course, paved streets—as the metropolitan areas their relatives lived in. Suddenly, that was all gone.

What remained was a question the West hadn't asked itself in a century: How is the region to earn its living? What new values would it have to adopt to accommodate those new economies? Who would end up inheriting the emptying communities? It is in this sense that the Western frontier has reopened. This book explores the internal reasons for the collapse, the anguish it caused, the global economic context, and the paths the West may tread as the twenty-first century draws near.

Readers should know that these issues lack what the Western movies always have: a dramatic ending. There is no such ending here. Instead, there are only possibilities and a central question: Who will inherit control of the new West? Will the existing population recover from the blows it has suffered and adapt to changed times? Will the Indian nations, many of which are resurgent, carve out larger, more dignified niches for themselves? Or will outsiders come in, as happened a century ago, and shove aside both the Indian culture and the culture established by those who pushed the Indians out of the way in the 1800s?

And then what? Will a different, but still distinctly Western, way of life be established? Or will the rural West succumb this time and become just another chunk of homogeneous America, yet another vast suburb on a featureless plain—New Jersey with bumps and fissures.

CHAPTER TWO

The Rural West Is Actually Very Urban

Dennis Brownridge

FEW PARTS of the world have experienced such explosive, sustained population growth as the American West. When the United States took it over in the latter half of the nineteenth century, the West was home to about 250,000 people. Now it has 50 million—an increase of 20,000 percent. If the rest of the world had grown at the same rate, we'd be staggering under the weight of 200 billion people. But in the 1980s, sizable areas in the Rockies, the Colorado Plateau, and the Pacific Northwest not only stopped growing, but began to lose population. In 1986 the states of Idaho, Montana, and Wyoming declined slightly. And for the first time in memory, almost as many people moved out of the West as moved in.

Does this mean an end to a century and a half of growth? Not likely. Even without in-migration, the West's young population, high birthrate, and huge metropolitan base would keep it booming. But population losses and economic decline in nonmetropolitan areas are bound to have an impact on the land. Few things have such a fundamental effect on a region as the number of humans who live there and how they make a living.

7

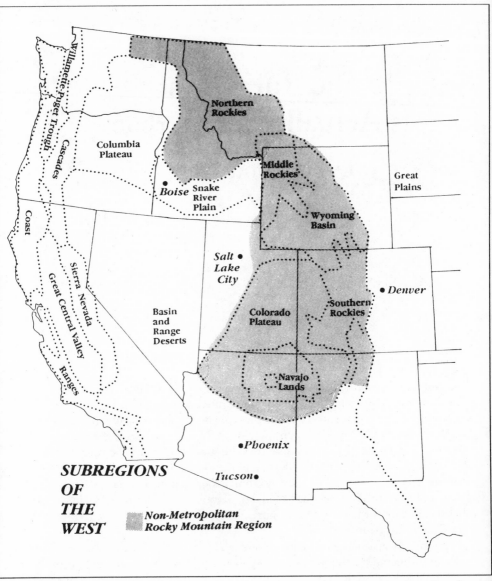

Willamette-Puget Trough

Cascades

Columbia
Plateau

Northern
Rockies

Boise
Snake
River
Plain

Middle
Rockies

Wyoming
Basin

Great
Plains

Coast

*Salt
Lake
City* ●

● *Denver*

Sierra Nevada

Great Central Valley

Basin
and
Range
Deserts

Colorado
Plateau

Southern
Rockies

Ranges

Navajo
Lands

●*Phoenix*

Tucson ●

SUBREGIONS

OF

THE

WEST

*Non-Metropolitan
Rocky Mountain Region*

Dennis Brownridge

What Is the West?

There are many Wests—the mythic West of cowboys and Indians, the geographic West, the Rocky Mountain West, the coastal West. This book is about what its editors call "the rural West"—that part of ten states that does not have major metropolitan areas. The states are Colorado, Utah, Wyoming, Montana, Idaho, the Dakotas, Nevada, and the northern halves of New Mexico and Arizona. By definition, the "rural West" excludes the Denver and Salt Lake City metropolitan areas and is north of the Phoenix-Tucson area. If one looks only at the core Rocky Mountain states—Colorado, Utah, Idaho, Montana, and Wyoming—there are fewer than 8 million residents. Exclude the Denver and Salt Lake City complexes, and you are below 4 million. As the maps show, this article covers the larger West of the geographer, including the three Pacific Coast states and the West's metropolitan areas, in order to provide a broader context for this book.

Where Westerners Live

When you look at a population map, the first thing that strikes you is how unevenly the West is settled. As historian Walter Prescott Webb put it, the West is an "urban oasis civilization," where clusters of people are surrounded by vast blocks of uninhabited public land. Both urban and rural populations are heavily concentrated along broad river valleys, where water and flat land are abundant. Metropolitan areas have grown up on plains at the foot of mountains. Except for some mining and resort towns, few people actually live *in* the mountains.

In the Rockies most folks live in the basins, parks, and valleys between the ranges. There are many such niches, since the Rockies are not a monolithic range like the Sierra Nevada, but rather a broken cordillera made up of dozens of discrete ranges. This pattern of settlement hasn't changed much since the last century. The withdrawal of public lands from settlement, starting with Yosemite in 1864, has helped keep new areas from being colonized. Half the West remains in public ownership as national forests, parks, monuments, recreation areas, wildlife refuges, military reservations, or unreserved lands managed by the Bureau of Land Management (BLM). These public lands have played an important role in making the West a distinctive region and, in some places, have perhaps prevented the dense rural population found in Appalachia.

We may speak of the "rural West," but the land west of the Rocky Mountain front has always been the least rural part of the country. Most Westerners live in cities and towns. The strong rural tradition of the Midwest, South, or New

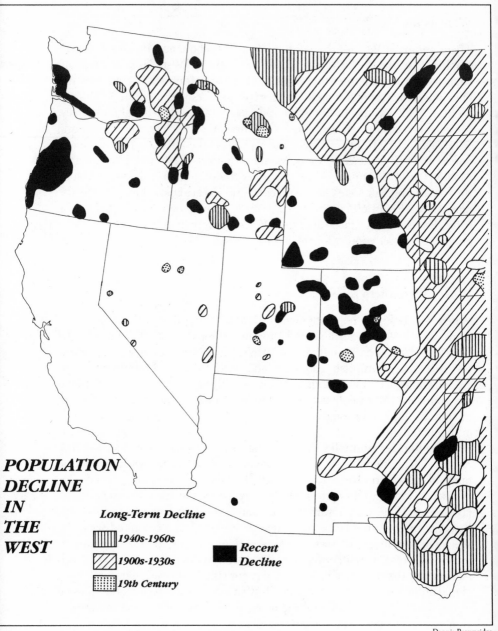

POPULATION
DECLINE
IN
THE
WEST

Long-Term Decline

||||| 1940s-1960s

/// 1900s-1930s

::: 19th Century

■ Recent
Decline

Dennis Brownridge

England—the dense network of isolated farmsteads and crossroads villages—is rare here. Tiny New Jersey, for all its cities, has five times as many rural inhabitants as Wyoming. In the West, full-blown rural settlement is limited to places like the Pacific valleys, the Columbia Plateau, the Snake River Plain, and smaller enclaves in the Rocky Mountain region. The West is "rural" only in the sense that so much of it has no people or has only small towns dotting immense expanses of land.

One notable exception is the two hundred thousand Navajos on the south-central Colorado Plateau. Their lands, the country's largest and the most populous Indian reservation, stand out on a population map. By tradition, the Navajos prefer to live in isolated homesteads rather than in the villages favored by their Pueblo neighbors. Normally, people cluster in arid lands to supply themselves with water and other services. But the Navajos are willing to haul water long distances in their pickup trucks—and then use it sparingly—to maintain a dispersed way of life. Still, this is changing, and as their population mushrooms, Navajos are increasingly concentrating in towns.

Usually, it is agriculture that settles large numbers of people, but most of the West lacks strong rural populations because it is too dry, cold, or rugged for farming. Although we may think of ranching as the quintessential Western livelihood, cattle grazing requires so little labor that it has never figured prominently in the Western workforce. The Rocky Mountain states have more insurance salesmen than ranchers. Mining, of course, got most Western states started, but it was soon eclipsed by other occupations. In the boom year of 1980, mining and energy extraction employed only about 1 percent of the people in the Rocky Mountain states. Georgia has more miners than Idaho does. The paucity of farming has saved the region from the long-term population declines that have hit almost every other rural region as agriculture became steadily more efficient. The Rocky Mountain front, the geographic boundary between East and West, shows up dramatically on the Population Decline map.

Rural populations in the prairie heartland of the Midwest peaked a century ago. The Great Plains, that vast short-grass belt between the Rockies and the one-hundredth meridian, have been losing population on and off since 1920. Drought, dust, and the Depression of the 1930s only accelerated the exodus. The Plains region was the country's last great agricultural boomland. Much of the land is marginal for farming, and historians place a good deal of blame on the government and the railroads for having encouraged more settlement there than the land could support. Ultimately, hundreds of square miles of abandoned Plains farmland were bought back by the government, replanted to grass, and returned to the public domain as national grasslands. Since then, the Plains region has enjoyed some local booms—fossil fuels in the 1950s and again in the 1970s, military installations in the 1960s, and some agricultural growth—particularly when the great Ogallala aquifer was tapped for irrigation. Most rural counties on the Plains, however, have half to three-quarters the population they had two or three generations ago.

The region west of the Plains escaped most of this. While most of the country was being ravaged by the Depression, the West was enjoying something of a boom. The lumber industry moved from the South to attack the rich virgin forests of the Northwest, and agriculture was given a boost by massive federal water projects. The only parts of the West that declined in the 1930s were areas of Plains-style dry farming (the wheatlands of the Columbia Plateau and Snake River Plain) and some of the old nineteenth-century mining districts that had been declining for decades, such as Colorado's San Juan Mountains and Butte, Montana.

The Rural Renaissance

For centuries cities have tended to grow faster than the countryside around them. Demographers have long regarded this rural-to-urban migration as the "trademark of an advancing society." In the 1950s and 1960s the flow to cities was so high that many rural areas—in the West and elsewhere—were stable or lost population. People were pulled to the metropolitan areas by jobs and a new way of life: the automobile suburb. It promised the best of both worlds: a quiet, countrylike place to live, with the jobs and amenities of a city close at hand. But as suburbs coalesced into sprawling, smoggy, congested metropolises and metropolises converged into still bigger megalopolises, the dream began to sour.

In the 1970s, for the first time, more people moved out of metropolitan areas than moved in. It was hailed as a "rural renaissance." For the first time greater New York *lost* population. A million New Yorkers moved away—a third of them going West. In the West almost every county experienced a boom. The main exceptions were copper towns in Montana, Utah, and Arizona, which had been declining for years as high-grade ores were exhausted and cheaper sources became available in Chile and Mexico.

Demographers were taken by surprise, at first dismissing the trend as a statistical aberration, and then as a counterculture fad. Environmental and back-to-the-land movements were factors, but it wasn't just the hippies who were migrating. It was retired folks seeking to escape the urban din and young families looking for cheap land and a good place to raise kids. These forces were much like those that had driven the previous generation from the cities to the suburbs. The new interstate freeway network and expanding air travel encouraged the outward flow by reducing the isolation of once-remote towns. By the mid-1970s few areas in the West were more than two or three hours' travel from a sizable metropolitan center.

This lifestyle boom was followed by a second, more traditional boom after the oil crisis of 1974. People flooded into the vast energy-rich region centered on the Rockies to exploit its oil, gas, coal, oil shale, and uranium; boomtowns sprang up from Texas to Montana. The two booms were distinct, but they coincided, and where there were both energy and scenery, they collided. There was concern about the impact both booms were having on the land and traditional lifestyles, but much of the concern came from outside the region; residents seemed content to enjoy their economic windfall.

The booms brought economic upheaval as well as prosperity. A frenzy of real estate speculation inflated land prices, and many ranchers, caught in the euphoria, went deep into debt to acquire neighbors' land and to expand operations. This happened as U.S. beef consumption was dropping 20 percent. When interest rates skyrocketed in the early 1980s—and land prices also fell—many longtime ranchers were caught between high debt payments and low income.

1980s Decline

When the "rural renaissance" first became apparent, skeptics said it wouldn't last, if only because places would fill up and lose the appeal that had attracted folks in the first place—a replay of suburbanization. Others thought the novelty of woodstoves and harsh winters would wear off or that the provincial atmosphere of small-town life would drive people back to the cities and suburbs, as it had driven their parents and grandparents.

Before any of those forces could come clearly into play, the global economy was hit by the worldwide recession of the early 1980s, followed by declining, and then collapsing, crude oil prices. The early stages of the recession treated the West rather gently, affecting mainly the logging states in the Northwest. Away from the timber areas, the overall boom in the Rockies accelerated into the 1980s. As late as 1983, demographers were predicting that Wyoming would lead the nation in rate of growth, even as plummeting crude oil prices (they bottomed in 1986) were causing energy operations to wane and laid-off workers were starting to move away.

Then, quite abruptly so far as the statisticians were concerned, the boom turned to bust. Since 1983, the Rocky Mountains and Colorado Plateau—excluding the metropolitan areas on their fringes—have lost about 30,000 people, down from a peak of 1.3 million. Growth in the Rocky Mountain states as a whole has slowed a bit but is maintained by increases in the big cities.

The Future of the Rockies

What is the long-term population picture in the West? The loss of a hundred families can mean a lot of empty storefronts in a town of ten thousand, but it is important to keep those numbers in perspective. There are individual cities in the "rustbelt" of the East that have suffered a greater loss than all of the Rocky Mountain West. How long the decline will continue is anybody's guess. Demographers are no better than economists when it comes to the future. History shows that areas tend to grow much faster than they decline. Once people move in, most find a way to stick. It is clear that in the Rockies most of the decline is due to the energy bust. That's likely to be temporary, since the world is still running out of oil. Much of the energy boom was built on speculation, exploration, and government programs meant to create a synthetic-fuels industry. But there are still lots of BTU's buried in the West. Someday, for better or for worse, they'll undoubtedly be dug out and sucked up.

The lifestyle-driven boom is a separate story. While it has waned since the 1970s, there is no sign of its reversal—another mass movement to the cities like that of the 1950s and 1960s. Urbanites still dream of escaping the metropolis, of living someplace where you can hike or ski out the back door. However, would-be émigrés are being more selective. The more appealing small areas are growing; others are not. College towns stand out among those with the most enduring growth. Places with the worst weather or bleakest scenery and those most remote from a good-size city are not doing as well.

The relentless growth of the metropolitan centers—Denver, Salt Lake City, Phoenix, and especially California—cannot be overlooked. California gains more new people *every year* than Wyoming *has*. This tends to push people out in concentric waves, spawning growth in satellite cities hundreds of miles away. Most of the people flooding into Arizona, for example, come from California, not from the frostbelt. Ultimately, even the farthest corners of the rural West are bound to be affected.

Unlike many developed nations, the United States is still expanding rapidly, adding more than 2 million people a year (1 million in the Western states). This growth is due partly to a high birthrate, the "echo" of the 1950s baby boom, and partly to heavy immigration. The United States takes in about two-thirds of the world's immigrants, who account for between one-third and one-half of our annual population increase (depending on which estimates you use for illegal immigration).

While the Rocky Mountain states get very little of that foreign immigration, they lead the country in the rate of natural increase. The Mormon domain of Utah and parts of adjacent states has a fertility rate (children born per woman) higher than any other part of the nation. Humans are the only creatures for whom constant population growth is regarded as "normal." Other animals' numbers may wax and wane, but in the long run are normally stable. Not so with mankind, whose numbers have grown geometrically, increasing by increasing amounts, for as long as we know. Someday, of course, we will have to learn how to get along with a stable population *and* a stable economy, since neither can expand forever. Perhaps the current Rocky Mountain experience will give us some practice in that endeavor.

CHAPTER THREE

Boom! Boom! Boom!
War on the Colorado Plateau

Raymond Wheeler

After the Party's Over

IT'S 5:00 P.M. on a lovely spring afternoon in Moab, Utah. The sun blazes in through an open doorway, pooling on the floor of the Grand County courthouse. It has been a long and tedious county commission meeting. I am praying for a quick end, but commission chairman Jimmie Walker has one last item. There is a problem at the Moab city dump. Things just haven't been the same at the dump since the chamber of commerce issued its now-famous nationwide challenge. Moab, declared the chamber, had the most scenic dump in the nation. The chamber's scenic dump photo contest had brought a flood of publicity from all over the country.

Unfortunately, notoriety entails obligations. Now that Moab's dump was more famous than the town, one had to maintain its image. The problem, explained Walker, was scavenging at the dump. One could find people scavenging there almost any time of day. Sometimes there would be two or three parties carefully sorting through the trash, pulling out aluminum cans, old clothes, furniture . . . perhaps even food.

As county commissioners go, Jimmie Walker is one of the best. He knows

16

his job, he knows his constituents, and he knows Grand County like the back of his weathered hand. This was a matter of civic decorum—nothing more, nothing less. The people of Moab were beginning to feel like strangers at their own dump, like visitors to a creep show. It was unnerving as hell to unload your garbage into the waiting arms of scavengers. Something had to be done.

Walker had a plan. The county commission would issue an ordinance requiring all dump scavengers to apply for permits. Along with the permit, a business license would naturally be required—"at an address zoned for that kind of commercial activity." Having met these requirements, scavengers would then pay a fee: "$25, $50, $100—I don't care what you make it." Walker leaned back in his chair, sucking contemplatively on a lifesaver. "Well?"

The other commissioners were smiling. You had to hand it to Jimmie—the man was a master. All the same, one commissioner seemed apprehensive.

"Jimmie, have you ever been up to the dump to see who it is up there doing the scavenging?"

"No."

"Well, you'd be mighty damn surprised to see who some of those people are."

"Well, I don't much care who it is, but I'm getting pretty darned sick of seeing people hauling stuff back as fast as we haul it up."

We all had a chuckle, but behind it there was an ache in the air. Those scavengers weren't tramps or latter-day hippies. Many were lifelong residents of Moab—people like Blackie. I heard about Blackie later that evening, while sharing a dish of ice cream with my neighbor Ruth Brown.

"Lots of people go up there to the dump every day," Ruth was telling me. "Like Blackie and his wife, Sandy—they used to go up there a couple of times a week."

Like many Moab residents, Blackie was a miner who had lost his job when the Atlas Uranium Mill shut down. Blackie was a good carpenter and handyman, but in Moab, where everybody is a carpenter and handyman, that didn't pay the bills. As a last resort, Blackie and his wife began paying regular visits to the Moab city dump.

"You know, his wife died last year," said Ruth. "And Blackie just ain't been the same since."

Blackie's predicament is far from unique. In just six years the town of Moab—and most of southeastern Utah—has undergone a metamorphosis most of us encounter only in history books. Since 1980, shot down by the simultaneous collapse of the oil, uranium, coal, and potash markets, southeastern Utah has banked into an economic tailspin unlike anything since the Great Depression. Between 1980 and 1986, Grand County lost more than a thousand jobs—30 percent of the county's nonfarm wage and salary employment. The official unemployment rate has soared to as high as 19 percent, and the county's population has plummeted nearly 20 percent. "We're looking at unemployment rates which are at depression, not recession, levels," says

University of Utah Bureau of Economic and Business Research director Thayne Robson. "We've had communities with 22 to 25 percent unemployment rates in the past few years."

Since 1982, southern Utah has been falling, out of control, into a seemingly bottomless economic black hole. "Every time we think we've bottomed out and reached a floor—as established by local (power-plant) consumption of our coal, with a few fortunate contracts with companies outside the area— then something happens, like the Wilburg mine fire, and we have even more loss, and more businesses closing," says Bill Howe, director of the Southeast Utah Association of County Governments.

Ruth and I finished our ice cream in silence, staring off across the city of Moab, watching the alpenglow die on the wall of rose-colored sandstone that soars above the Moab city dump. As day slipped toward night, I found myself slipping backward in time . . .

Just seven years ago Moab's economic and political future looked radically different. On the morning of the commissioners' meeting, tracking backward through the annals of the town's newspaper, the Moab Times-Independent, I was drawn, in Henry Adam's phrase, by "invisible lines of force," to a remarkable issue: that of November 20, 1980. On that third week of November, the town of Moab had achieved the pinnacle of its desire. Three front-page headlines told the tale: BLM Has Dropped over Half of Wilderness Study Areas in the Moab Area; Negro Bill Canyon Squabble Settled; S. Gene Day Will Transfer. Together they were a ticker-tape parade for the commissioners of Grand County. This was their finest hour, their V-J and V-E days rolled into one, their triumphant moment of victory in a battle that had taken seven years to win.

In a sense, it is timeless—this battle, this war for the land. This most recent phase began with the introduction in Congress in 1974 of legislation that would become the Federal Land Policy and Management Act. FLPMA, as it was called, brought a hailstorm of new regulations governing use of Bureau of Land Management (BLM) lands: mining regulations; grazing regulations; road right-of-way regulations; and, worst of all, the ultimate insult to southeastern Utah, a mandate to inventory, study, and designate wilderness. It was the wilderness study provision that was the last straw for the Grand County commissioners. That provision required the BLM to identify all lands with wilderness character and to protect them from development until Congress, in its wisdom, could pass legislation to designate wilderness.

About 80 percent of Grand County is owned by the federal government, with 90 percent of that land managed by the BLM. When BLM's first statewide wilderness inventory map was published in April 1979, the Grand County commissioners went through the roof. Between the Forest Service, Park Service, and BLM wilderness inventory programs, some two-thirds of south

The dump for Moab, Utah, has a view of the La Sal Mountains

eastern Utah was under review. When they saw that map, the Grand County commissioners realized what was at stake: a way of life.

"Frederick Jackson Turner was wrong," says Bill Booker, a battle-scarred veteran of the tempestuous BLM wilderness inventory. "He said we lost the western frontier in the 1890s, when the urban population of the West first exceeded its rural population. But in Utah we lost the frontier in 1976, with the enactment of FLPMA. Before FLPMA, these people could do virtually anything they wanted on the public lands."

"Back about that time I got thinking about something," Jimmie Walker recalls. "The thing that creates wars is a foreign intrusion that's trying to destroy a way of life. It's just that damn simple. The people here could recognize that, and as far as they were concerned, it was war."

When FLPMA became law in October 1976, it set off a battle that was to be waged all over the West under the name Sagebrush Rebellion. Nowhere was that battle to be as brutal—and public—as in Grand County, Utah. The county commissioners' strategy had the elegant simplicity of a sumo wrestling match. If the commissioners could not change the law, they would break it.

Bulldozer Wars

In July 1979 a Grand County road crew rammed a bulldozer through a barrier blocking vehicular access to Negro Bill Canyon, a 26,000-acre BLM wilderness inventory unit featuring 400-foot vertical walls of Navajo sandstone, slickrock domes and fins, stupendous natural bridges, and a clear, cold, perennial stream studded with waterfalls and swimming holes. With the barrier removed, a second bulldozer—piloted by a local miner—charged up the canyon for a distance of a mile and a quarter and carved more than 500 yards of new roadway across the floor of the canyon. Since neither the miner nor the county had a right-of-way permit, as required by FLPMA, BLM Moab District Manager S. Gene Day obtained a cease-and-desist order, and replaced the barrier at the mouth of the canyon.

Seven days later, a Grand County bulldozer again knocked down the barrier. BLM filed a lawsuit and once again blocked the mouth of the canyon—this time with a steel cable. Four days later, a Grand County road crew cut the cable. BLM manager Day was incensed. "The issue is whether any individual or group should have the right to preempt all others for private gain," he wrote in a letter to the editor of the Moab newspaper. Quoting Aldo Leopold's classic essay, "The Land Ethic," Day lashed out bitterly at the Grand County Commission. "Where do we draw the line on the right to explore for minerals? Must every square inch of this area, regardless of other clearly identified values, be sacrificed to mineral exploration?"

S. Gene Day

During five and a half years on the job, Day had earned a reputation as a hard-nosed, no-nonsense administrator. "Arrogant," some said. "Honest," said others. A feature on Day in the *Washington Post* labeled him The Most Hated Man in Southern Utah. In this war against FLPMA, Day was commander in chief for the enemy. "He was almost a zealot in defense of FLPMA," recalls Moab newspaper editor Sam Taylor. "Gene Day was a hard-core environmentalist," remembers Jimmie Walker. "He thought he was God. That's what power does to you."

Since his arrival in Moab in 1975, Day had been battling violations of federal law all over the district. With the nation in an energy crisis, uranium and oil exploration were booming, and the scramble for coal, tar sands, and oil shale had grown frantic. All across southern Utah boom-crazed exploration companies were penetrating roadless areas. In November 1976, days after the passage of FLPMA, Gulf Minerals launched a massive uranium exploration program, slicing thirty miles of roads and twenty-two drill pads into the heart of the 100,000-acre Mancos Mesa roadless area—a bighorn sheep lambing area and for nearly a decade the Moab District's number one candidate for primitive-area designation.

Though Gulf repeatedly promised, in writing, to reclaim all physical impacts, by 1979 it had abandoned the area, leaving the roads in place. BLM simply let the matter drop, blocking off the road with a barrier. Within weeks, a San Juan County road crew tore down the barrier. The Gulf Minerals roads, explained commission chairman Calvin Black, were now part of the county road system, and the county had an obligation to its citizens to keep the roads open. Not the least of those citizens was Black himself, who owned five thousand acres of mining claims in the heart of the unit.

In 1977 Cotter Corporation, a Commonwealth Edison subsidiary with a field office in Moab, launched an exploration program in the Dirty Devil River Canyon, blading more than fifty miles of roads and trails into the heart of a 400,000-acre wilderness inventory unit. BLM responded by accelerating its wilderness inventory, but carefully excluded Cotter's illegal roadwork by adjustments in the wilderness study area boundary. That was not accommodating enough for Cotter. Before the ink could dry on the wilderness study area map, the firm was at it again, blasting eleven miles of new road and more than 100 drill pads in the new wilderness study area. Once again, BLM went to court.

North of Moab, in the Book Cliffs, Anschutz, Tenneco, and Palmer Oil were carving new roads across wilderness inventory units. Uranium and potash exploration companies were slashing a maze of new roads through pristine canyons and mesa tops bordering the Colorado and Green rivers. On the San Rafael Knob—a splendid tower of bare rock at the crest of the San Rafael Swell—two uranium companies crowded thirty miles of roads into a 7,000-acre wilderness inventory unit. To the south, uranium and oil exploration companies swarmed over the benchlands around the perimeter of White Canyon and Natural Bridges National Monument.

The grand finale of the Bulldozer Wars came on the Fourth of July, 1980, when 250 flag-waving Moab residents celebrated Independence Day with a ceremony that by now had become local tradition—parading a bulldozer into the nearby Mill Creek Canyon Wilderness Inventory Unit. When Gene Day announced, several days later, that the bulldozer had mistakenly stopped short of the unit boundary, a Grand County crew hauled the bulldozer back to the site and extended the road until it crossed the boundary. This act was so brazen that the commissioners were convinced they would be jailed.

"Gene Day was our biggest obstacle," recalls Jimmie Walker. "He was going to have the federal marshals come in and take us all to jail. But we had (Utah Senator) Orrin Hatch back in Washington, keeping an eye on it, to make sure they wasn't going to mess with our constitutional rights."

Psychological Warfare

That was the physical dimension of the war—bulldozer scars, webs of seismograph lines, torn-up streambeds, drill pads, borrow pits, slag piles, and hundreds of miles of new roads spiderwebbing the nation's last great block of pristine high desert wilderness. But there was a psychological dimension as well. One week after publication of BLM's first wilderness inventory map for Utah, San Juan County Commissioner Cal Black stormed into a BLM public meeting. "I thought the man was drunk," recalls former BLM wilderness specialist Janet Ross. Her staff report on the incident is chilling.

"I'm not a violent man," Black reportedly said, "but I'm getting to the point where I'll blow up bridges, ruins, and vehicles. We're going to start a revolution. We're going to get back our lands. We're going to sabotage your vehicles. You had better start going out in twos and threes, because we're going to take care of you BLMers."

Later that same day, Black met with Utah congressman Gunn McKay. According to the *Moab Times-Independent*, "Black warned McKay that residents of the county are frustrated with the agencies and may resort to violent action." Said Black, "People might get hurt. There's going to be a lot of vandalism."

William P. Davis

Accompanied by supporters, a county employee drives a bulldozer onto public land near Moab, Utah, during the Sagebrush Rebellion of 1980

In a county where "outdoor recreation" means carving up canyon bottoms with bulldozers, ripping across fragile cryptogamic soils on off-road vehicles, and pulling apart thousand-year-old Anasazi Indian ruins in search of valuable artifacts, the vandalism threat must have seemed almost coy. But when an entire pictograph panel was destroyed by vandals near Moab in April 1980, it was as if Calvin Black's prophecy had at last been fulfilled. "An abrasive material was used to scour the thousand-year-old paintings from the wall of Wingate sandstone," marveled the *Times-Independent*. This was no high-school prank. It was a bold and deliberate act of war.

For five years the campaign of intimidation had been gathering momentum. For BLM employees and environmental activists, death threats were routine. In January 1978 Moab writer Fran Barnes listened with a sense of foreboding as his comments on an environmental impact statement were broadcast by the local radio station. Barnes had recommended, in a letter to the Department of Energy, that DOE terminate the operating license of the nearby Atlas Minerals uranium processing plant, since it was common knowledge that the plant was bleeding radioactive matter directly into the Colorado River. That evening the phone began ringing with the first of a series of death threats from Atlas employees. The calls ended only when Barnes identified the callers by means of a phone tap and promised them, in exchange for his family's safety, never again to speak out.

In May 1979 a bomb threat evacuated the BLM district office.

A typical BLM staff report of the period: "Melvin Dalton said that if cattle were not allowed to graze Red Canyon that he would make sure that bighorn sheep would not use the area. Melvin also said that a person could get shot going into Red Canyon. I mentioned to Melvin that he could go to jail for shooting a BLM employee. Melvin indicated that he would not be out that much if he was tossed in jail, when compared to the BLM individual he would shoot. I do not feel that Melvin constitutes a threat to my well-being, because Melvin has threatened me every other year for the past five years. However, I believe it is important to document his attitude towards bighorn sheep."

The ubiquitous nature of such threats was depicted in an August 1980 letter to the paper, from the wife of a federal mine safety inspector: "From the time of our arrival here, we have been under constant harassment. . . . We have been ordered to stay at home by the local law enforcement agency . . . so they could better protect us against the threats that were made upon us. We check our cars daily for bombs, have listened to phone calls of every nature (even to family death threats). Our children have been called everything in the book, harassed and intimidated both at school and socially because of the position held by their father. . . ."

This was jihad, a struggle not merely political and economic, but religious, moral, ideological. At its center was a philosophical question: Who really owns the public lands of the West? Do they belong to the residents of the nearest small town? Do they belong to the federal land-managing agencies? Do they belong to Peabody Coal, Exxon, Tenneco, Sohio? Or do they—incredible as it might seem—actually belong to the American public?

By 1979 the conflict had earned itself a name—the Sagebrush Rebellion. Ostensibly a campaign for legislation to transfer ownership of federal lands to the states, its real object was less quixotic: to defeat FLPMA—and, at all cost, to stop the BLM's wilderness inventory in its tracks.

"The focus of that movement was, of course, to restore federally owned lands to the state of Utah, but I repeatedly said that that was a very unlikely event," Utah Senator Orrin Hatch told me in 1983. The real purpose of the Sagebrush Rebellion, Hatch explained, "was to put pressure on. And it worked. It got national attention, and it did cause some of the most reprehensible overseers of Utah lands to back up and look at themselves and even caused some of them to be transferred."

At the time, sitting there in the senator's palatial Washington, D.C., office, I wondered just who were the "reprehensible overseers" who had been deported from Utah. Four years later, flipping through back issues of the *Moab Times-Independent,* I discovered the answer.

Carter/Andrus Sell-out

By the summer of 1979, the Sagebrush Rebellion had become a national cause. Two state legislatures had passed Sagebrush Rebellion legislation, and a parade of politicians, including congressmen, governors, and presidential candidate Ronald Reagan, were bragging that they, too, were "sagebrush rebels."

Back in Washington, D.C., the Carter administration was running scared. Carter's environmental agenda, once wildly idealistic, had created harsh political reactions. His "hit, list" against federally funded water projects, for example, had, in the words of Carter's Secretary of Interior Cecil Andrus, "put together a coalition that beat us." Hamstrung by OPEC, inflation, and the hostages in Iran, Jimmy Carter had begun his retreat. By 1979 the Carter environmental agenda was experiencing a sea change.

"I would go in to lobby with Rupe Cutler, the assistant secretary of agriculture," recalls Dave Foreman, then a top lobbyist for The Wilderness Society. "Rupe had been assistant executive director of The Wilderness Society at one time. And I'd get the argument from him, 'Well, the president's in trouble in the West—this senator, that senator—you've got to back off.' And we'd come out having made all the compromises and having been lobbied." The last thing Jimmy Carter needed, with Ronald Reagan breathing deregulatory fire, was the bad political press emanating from southern Utah.

In August 1979 BLM's Utah state director retired. His replacement, Gary

Wicks—handpicked by Andrus—was a man with a mission. Ten days after taking office, Wicks was barnstorming across southern Utah, preaching the gospel of the Sagebrush Rebellion to the converted. "Unlike some, I don't believe that the policies and the laws are immutable," Wicks told an astonished Moab Chamber of Commerce. "I believe that state and local governments ought to have some important say over the kinds of decisions that affect their lives."

"Wicks went on to say," reported the *Moab Times-Independent*, "that he dislikes confrontations and feels that alternatives can be worked out through cooperation between the BLM and local residents. 'My basic approach to the job,' Wicks said, 'is to eliminate as much as possible the criticism people have of the BLM, in Utah.' "

The significance of Wicks's visit was clear: The Sagebrush Rebels' strategy had worked. Violence talked—and the politicians had walked. "It's really kind of an exciting time to be living in the rural West," cheered editor Sam Taylor in an accompanying editorial. "A whole lot is going to be happening in the next few years to determine how vast amounts of public domain are going to be used in the future. There is little question in my mind that the rules, as now defined, are going to have to be changed."

Indeed, the rules were changing faster than the Sagebrush Rebels had ever dreamed. On October 25, 1979—about three months after the bulldozer had passed the Negro Bill Canyon barrier—Moab residents opened the *Moab Times-Independent* to a piece of astonishing news. Senator Hatch said that the war for Negro Bill Canyon was over. BLM State Director Gary Wicks had told him that "District Manager S. Gene Day had been instructed to resolve the dispute."

Demise of the Wilderness Inventory

By November 1980, when the BLM announced its final wilderness inventory decisions, the meaning of Wicks's remark was made plain. Negro Bill Canyon had been dropped from the wilderness inventory. Along with it, 1.25 million acres of pristine wilderness—a land area greater than that of all seven national parks in Utah and Colorado combined—had also been cut from the Moab District's wilderness inventory. In all, forty-two roadless areas had been wiped off the district's wilderness study map. Nearly half of the vanquished roadless areas had been identified as candidates for primitive designation in earlier. BLM documents.

On November 17 two BLM wilderness inventory team members appeared before the Grand County Commission to present copies of the agency's final decision on wilderness study areas. Day was nowhere in sight. Team leader Dianna Webb (herself a target of conflict-of-interest charges after routinely filing negative wilderness inventory recommendations on units containing mining claims owned by Cotter Corporation—her husband's employer) made a speech to the commission. Out of 229 roadless areas in the Moab District, Webb announced, BLM had eliminated 200 from the wilderness inventory. In all, nearly 60 percent of the district's roadless lands had been dropped.

The BLM employees had a second announcement: District Manager S. Gene Day would be leaving his post. The commissioners were delighted, but hardly surprised. "It was just a matter of time until Gene Day went down the road," explained Jimmie Walker. Ten days later the Negro Bill Canyon lawsuit was settled. According to the terms, the BLM would construct four hundred yards of new road up the bed of Negro Bill Canyon. Grand County agreed to maintain the new road.

By Thanksgiving 1980 the commissioners of Grand County must have been near exhaustion from counting their blessings. Their most powerful political allies—the OPEC nations—seemed destined to rule the world's economy through the turn of the century, ensuring a brisk domestic market for uranium, oil, natural gas, coal, tar sands, and oil shale. All across southern Utah the multinational energy companies were prowling for buried treasure, opening up offices, buying mining claims, building new roads, constructing new milling plants, and buying equipment.

The sole threat to this economic utopia—the wilderness inventory, which had thrown countless roadblocks in the path of exploration and development—had been resoundingly defeated, and along with it, the *hubris* of the federal land management agencies. The way was now clear to all-out development. This was it: this was the Big Bang, the boom to end all booms.

CHAPTER FOUR

The Rural West: An Artifact of the Nineteenth Century

Ed Marston

THE RURAL West appears to defy certain laws of physics. To board a plane in Bozeman, Montana, and get off in Los Angeles or New York makes one think that diffusion, entropy, even common sense, have been suspended. How could so much congestion, submersion of nature, smoggy air, bruising social interactions exist alongside so much emptiness, so much triumphant nature, such clear air, such easy public life? Why don't people diffuse out of areas where it takes an hour to creep-commute twenty miles and move into the rural West, whose small towns know only rush-minutes at the end of Friday evening high school football games? Why doesn't the smog infiltrate a region whose air is so clear it makes landmarks ten miles away look as if they were across the street?

For the most part, the West is a region without metropolitan areas. To rural Westerners the idea of spending an hour or more inching to and from work along a freeway is as inconceivable as queuing for an hour to buy a pound of meat. Residents of Los Angeles and Chicago have more in common with a Muscovite than with someone from Deer Lodge, Montana.

It is usual to blame, or praise, the West's mountains, canyons, aridity, and harsh climate for the emptiness and separation from the main American stream. It is said that a difficult geography and climate have diverted modern

27

development away from the rural West. The assumption is that in the course of time this almost accidental diversion will end, and the West will rejoin, in an economic sense, the rest of the nation. As a result, many Westerners are waiting for the West to happen—for it to become like the America they visit and see on television. The idea that the West has been on a separate track for decades, and may now be fundamentally different from America—and heading not toward a joining with America but in some other direction—is not considered.

The possibility that the West will remain separate from the United States seems unlikely if only because of its location: the region sits athwart America, between the coasts that dominate the nation. But thus far that location has led to only the loosest integration. Today America simply flows over the West, in air lanes and as television signals, and under it, as telephone and computer data communications.

Those from outside who pass through the West play hopscotch, jumping from enclave to enclave: first a foot in Denver, and then a long stretch to Salt Lake City, or a stretch and a jump from Denver to Phoenix, and then safe and familiar again in San Diego–Los Angeles. For tourists, the safe islands are Boulder, Aspen, Telluride, Jackson, Santa Fe. Between them lies nowheresville.

What is it that maintains this terra incognita? Certainly not mountains, deserts, and canyons; they are easily penetrated and are what today attract people to the West. But at one time they did isolate the land physically and therefore economically. In the shelter of those barriers grew up a way of life based on the West's economy of interlocking natural resources: grass for cattle, trees, damming water for irrigation and electricity, mining, milling, digging coal and burning it in power plants, building transmission lines to export the electricity, and excavating caves to accept the radioactive refuse from metropolitan-area nuclear power plants.

Upon this extractive economy has developed an extractive way of life—a culture anchored in small communities, extended families, traditional religions, and an education system designed for the procreation of that way of life. It is a way of life that until recently was seamless, with strong inner and outer fortifications. The West is about half public land, and the outer fortifications of the region are the federal laws governing the use of the public land—what law professor Charles Wilkinson calls the "lords of yesterday." Those laws guarantee free access by prospectors and mining companies to minerals through the 1872 Mining Law; low-cost access to oil, gas, coal, and oil shale through the Mineral Leasing Act; subsidized access to grass and trees for ranchers and loggers through an array of laws; subsidized water through the Bureau of Reclamation and the reclamation laws; and markets for the West's uranium through a federally created nuclear power industry and the national defense business.

This economy is maintained by a shifting bloc of twenty U.S. Senators from Western states whose economies are based on the land. In round numbers, 6 percent of the U.S. population has 20 percent of the U.S. Senate. The senators are backed by a cohesive array of state legislatures, county commissions, thousands of boards, and countless ranching, farming, and water groups. This, then, is the outer ring: laws often dating back to the nineteenth century and defended by one-fifth of the U.S. Senate.

The inner defense is the extractive culture itself. It is so pervasive within its sphere that it deters outsiders from putting down roots in the region, like plants that produce a chemical to block other species from establishing themselves. This culture is the product of a century of a low-level, fluctuating— sometimes wildly swinging—economy in an isolated, often beautiful, and always difficult landscape.

The result is a region harder to penetrate than the fabled small towns of taciturn Vermont. At the extreme of impenetrability are Utah's small, theocratic communities. A non-Mormon family in such a community will literally have no one to associate with because all activities center around the church.

In any small Western town, if Rotary, Kiwanis, or the Elks is not your cup of tea, or if you prefer hiking or skiing to snowmobiling and jeeping, or if you are a woman with an independent streak, you will find yourself short of groups to join. This may not be a high barrier to self-sufficient adults, especially if there are other newcomers. Even a family with kids will be fine through, let's say, the sixth grade. Parents from an urban background may be startled when their fourth grader comes home with a copy of the Bible, presented to every child in class personally by a member of the Gideons. But that's not a major problem. Nor is it important when your kid comes home after taking the Iowa Basics test to say the other kids didn't care about the test, that they said, "We're going into the mines and make more money than the principal."

It is harder in high school, especially when the biology class votes overwhelmingly in favor of creationism. You will be surprised that evolution is a voting matter. You will be even more surprised that the biology teacher was among the majority voting for the creation myth. "Who voted with you?" you ask your teenager. You may or may not get an answer. Teenagers love to fit in, and yours is furious that you have brought him or her up to have beliefs so at odds with the community.

High school reveals more than just religious differences. The rural West makes its living from the ground. There is a little manufacturing, and away from tourist towns, fewer service jobs. For generations the way to survive has been by farming, ranching, logging, or by digging under the ground. As a result, if a school inculcates a thirst for higher education in its children, that almost guarantees that they will move away, not merely geographically, but also in terms of values. It is not only Native American and Hispanic families

Ed/Betsy Marston

*Senior citizens of Cedaredge, Colorado; from left: Mae Himes, Alice Stoffel, Virginia
Porterfield, Margaret Robinson*

who fear losing their children to an outside world and an alien culture. It is
also many Anglo families—who have been in America for generations—in
thousands of small Western communities.

The result is predictable. Grade schools in small towns usually do an
excellent job. But high schools are likely to be relaxed, with sports taken far
more seriously than academics. Attend a monthly school board meeting for a
rural district in the spring, when hiring is being done, and you are likely to
hear the head of hiring tell the board: "This is a clean-cut young man who
grew up in the nearby town of X, and went away to Y (the local teachers'
college). He will coach football this fall, and teach math and French." The
lack of a beard or a hippie appearance, the local origins and in-state teaching
diploma, are guarantees that the new teacher will not be out of step with the
community. The combination of math and French comes from a small district's
need to hire coach-teachers. The pressure is always there to get the "coach"
first and then figure out what he or she can teach. The reason is simple: failures
on the athletic field are far more public and felt far more deeply by the
community than failures in the classroom.

After high school, it is acceptable for youngsters who don't want to mine to go to agricultural or teachers' colleges—they can come home with that. But additional or different education is likely to separate a young person from the family and town. Compare that attitude with the typical urbanites, who want their kids to have credentials, preferably Ivy League credentials, and who expect the public schools to provide the motivation and courses to give those sons or daughters a jump on life.

If you consider the schools, social organizations, and churches as a whole, a small town presents a formidable presence to a person moving in from the "outside." A mountain climber would say it presents few handholds. During the 1970s energy boom, when large firms transferred thousands of engineers and executives into the region, one often heard wives complain, "There's no shopping here." Undoubtedly, the lack of large malls and specialty shops bothered them. But the "no shopping" complaint was also code for a more difficult set of complaints, one their corporate positions wouldn't let them voice. They were complaining of a lack of social niches for people like themselves. And when the energy boom collapsed, they were gone as quickly as they had come.

The existence of astounding real estate prices in Aspen, Santa Fe, Jackson, and Telluride, for example, provides other evidence of the strength of the West's defenses. Why would people spend fortunes to shoehorn themselves into a Santa Fe or Sun Valley when there are scores of much, much cheaper traditional towns that are just as spectacular in terms of scenery, and far more Western? The easy answer is glamour, but actually many former urbanites moved to a resort town despite the glitz, rather than because of it. The answer is that non-Westerners buy into the West's Aspens because that is where they feel at home, even though those towns are far less friendly on the surface than a traditional small community.

There is something else that discourages many people who move into the rural West: money doesn't talk as loudly here as it does elsewhere in the country. You can't buy your way into a typical Western community unless your money is matched by a clever folksiness, in which case the money isn't needed.

It is not so much resistance to money as a general lack of it; for example, there almost surely won't be a country club to join. If there is one, it will have been jury-rigged. Perhaps some newcomer built a large house with a swimming pool and tennis court, a place that would fit in in any well-to-do suburb elsewhere in America, but which will be a white elephant in most Western towns. Should the family then discover that it has settled in the wrong place and put the home up for sale, it will prove exceedingly hard to sell. At that point a creative realtor might assemble a group of families and sell them a "country club."

Show and pretension—even the kind called "good taste"—are rare here. People live in unpretentious houses, although they may be able to afford more impressive homes. Their passion and money, and tendency to show off, go to the outside: spectacular flower and vegetable gardens, a nice barn and fences, a hobby ranch for those able to keep cattle as pets.

Money has another handicap in the rural West. Planning and zoning are seen as something bordering on communism. Even where a developer has tried to create an upscale island by adopting restrictive covenants, you will find homes with travel trailers, boats, snow machines, and even four or five cars cluttering the yard of an otherwise nice-looking ranchhouse. Occasionally, there may even be a 4-H lamb in the backyard. The covenants are there, but enforcing them would go against the Western grain.

These are all general impressions taken in during a fourteen-year sojourn here rather than by survey and analysis. But there is one set of statistics, beyond the price of real estate, that bears on the question of the West's resistance to mainstream America. The data show how different the rural West is and perhaps also show why that difference can no longer be maintained. Many residents of small Western towns say they are great places to raise children. Perhaps, but not in terms of life expectancy. A study by three New Jersey academics, published in the spring 1987 issue of *The Public Interest,* showed that young people in the rural West are more likely to die a violent death than young people in an urban ghetto. When broken down by category—suicides, murders, accidents—the rural West was more dangerous than the Harlems of America. The high death rate in the rural West isn't due to one large factor, such as dangerous rural roads, but holds across the board. What it implies is a reckless, violent undercurrent to life. Perhaps that violence, like the region's gentler defenses, is part of how the West has maintained its insularity deep into this century, confining the virus we call modern America to a few mountain tourist towns.

Today that insularity is threatened. The social and political defenses of the small Anglo communities we have been considering (the nature of the West's Native American and Hispanic communities would be another book) are still in place, but their economic bases are crumbling. As a result, the West faces a question that is complex in its details but simple in outline: Will these communities be able to devise a new way of earning their living within the existing way of life? Or will the economic demands of the twenty-first century require such large changes that the underlying social base will be altered beyond recognition?

CHAPTER FIVE

Good Fences Make Good Calluses

C. L. Rawlins

No stigma attaches to the love of money in America, and provided it does not exceed the bounds imposed by public order, it is held in honor. The American will describe as noble and estimable ambition that our medieval ancestors would have called base cupidity.

Alexis de Tocqueville

NEARLY EVERYONE had them the first week, even with the good leather gloves I supplied. Usually, a big blister at the base of the thumb and a matching set on the little pads where the fore and middle fingers join the palm. A double-bitted ax doesn't rest easily in the modern American hand.

After the second week, we were all rednecks from the sun at eighty-five hundred feet, welted with mosquito bites, but the blisters were gone. The crew had learned to brush and buck and hew, notch and fit, toprail and brace. Instead of disappearing into the tents after dinner with an exhausted mumble, the mix of college kids, ranch kids, and drifters would saunter off for fishing or a look at the beavers in the big pond up the slope.

In the cook tent you could see the new shape of someone's forearm as he reached for the coffeepot. A broadening of the muscle into a nice bulge below

WATCH OUT FOR BOB WARR

My friend was from Utah. A ranch out of Tooele. He had a rural Utah drawl broader than the salt flats and a cowhand's laconic style; a sentence is composed of four words or fewer. Besides a respectably filthy Resistol hat, he wore a pair of down-at-the-heel Tony Lamas, faded jeans, and a lime green cowboy shirt with cuffs and collar buttoned. Across his cheek, from lip to ear, was a piratical-looking scar which I assumed was the mark of some late-night battle. I asked him about it.

"Bob Warr done it," he said.

My friend was a tough character, and I figured Bob Warr to be at least six-five and built like a bull. Definitely a natural hazard. Since we were en route to Tooele for a weekend of carousing, I wanted to avoid Bob Warr; there might be lingering hard feelings.

"Is he going to be around?" I asked.

"Huh? Who?"

"Bob Warr," I replied.

He gave me a glance that questioned my sanity, parenthood, and right to be breathing the same air. He sighed. "Got bucked off. Into a fence. Bob Warr fence."

My feelings about barbed wire haven't changed much since. It won't pull a knife on you outside a bar, but it is dangerous, miserable stuff. Rips holes in jeans and skin. Puts deep cuts in horses and cattle. Degenerates into a rusty, ugly tangle. But it shaped the West because it has two strong points: it's cheap, and it works. A pair of competent ranch hands can string miles of wire in the time it takes to put up a short stretch of timber fence, and for a quarter the cost in money, sweat, and thought. It doesn't take imagination or craft to stretch wire.

Timber fences are another story. A well-built buck-and-pole fence, as it settles and weathers, becomes part of the landscape. To build one requires a knowledge of wood, axmanship, applied physics, and a canny eye for the land. You have to judge where the deep drifts collect in winter and where the ground is soft in spring. If you throw one up in a hurry, it will fall down just as quickly. Timber fencing is a dying craft. The accumulated knowledge of farmers from America's colonial times onward included an array of techniques to fit many different purposes and landscapes. A litany of types: stake-and-rider, buck-and-pole, ripgut, log-and-block, post-and-rail, worm. Using basic tools and local materials, the expanding agricultural empire fenced livestock in or out, protected crops, enclosed pastures, and marked boundaries. A farm's or ranch's fence was its signature.

When farms were abandoned, the old timber fences groaned and sank to ground level, becoming tracks of decomposing wood with a few rusty spikes disappearing into humus, hidden under saplings and brush. Like the trees they came from, they returned to the soil and enriched it.

Most visitors to the West will notice one kind of fence: barbed wire. The total length of wire along

highways alone would probably stretch several times around the earth. Long, straight runs of wire— rusty or new and glittering—have altered the sweeping views, changed patterns of game movement, and made ranching, as practiced today, possible.

Still, there are enclaves in the high country of the West where timber is the preferred material, mostly in places where lodgepole pines grow thickly and heavy snows and wandering moose turn barbed wire into galvanized hash. There you find timber fences and people who know and appreciate the craft, even though most of the old-style fences are built to enclose summer homes and tourist traps, to lend a rustic look.

Having built miles of buck-and-pole drift fence in the Upper Green River country of Wyoming, I've become a collector of fences. I return from a trip to the piñon-juniper mesas of Utah or the Stanley Basin of Idaho with sketches and notes on a particular ripgut fence or a six-rail-buck horse pasture. The details of material and method fascinate me, and I gaze at a well-balanced pole gate or finely braced corner with relish and recognition, like an artist judging the brush strokes of another.

Rails must be just right: too long and they bend under snowload or their own weight; too short and they make a fence more work than it should be. Notches should be clean and angled to drain water, or the wood rots. Spikes should be driven to work with the pull of gravity and the weight of snow, and braces set with a keen eye for stress and slope. If the rails are too far apart, itchy cows will rub and knock the fence down, or the calves will slip through.

A poor fence can be worse than none. It won't hold the stock and will take more work to maintain than it's worth. On a recent ride I saw a fence built by a private contractor for the BLM. From a distance it looked all right; close inspection revealed trouble: the notches were chain-sawed at the perfect angle to collect water and start rot working around the joints. The spikes weren't spikes—they were skinny little nails. The braces, uphill and down, were set at the same spacing and angle, insuring that the fence will some day fold like an accordion and flop like a dead sheep.

The fence had weathered a single winter, and already rails had fallen and bucks twisted with the movement of snowdrifts. It was more an extended problem than a fence, built from a general idea of fences rather than from any specific knowledge. The apparent object was to slap up something that resembled a fence, collect the money, and run. The result is several miles of headache.

Although we like to think of this as the age of high technology, the means and methods of our ancestors were neither low nor crude. Given their limitations in materials and tools, their sense of fitness and ingenuity often surpassed that of the present day. There are plenty of modern miracles, but there are also cars that flip at thirty miles per hour, dams that crack, buildings that fall down, and chemicals that are discovered to be toxic beyond any benefits they yield. It turns out that any technology, so-called high or low, needs patience, judgment, and an observant eye to give us fences or spaceships that don't crash.

C. L. Rawlins

the elbow and the first suggestion of cords under the skin above the wrist. The work was re-forming our bodies: the clever wrist flip that pops a chip out of a hewn notch, the deep knee-bend to heft a rail into place, the long swing of the sledge driving a 60-penny nail into air-dried lodge-pole. Work changes us, in ways both evident and invisible. As the hand grows calluses to accommodate the ax handle, so the mind takes the shape of necessary tasks. Such is the economy of the human spirit, that the hunter is fascinated by deer, the potter by the soft coherence of wet clay, the banker by the hard edge of money. Many of us hate our work, and that shapes us too.

As our work changes us, so do the tools we choose. A double-bitted ax strengthens the forearms and wrists. A computer gives the sense of yes/no control in a chaotic world. A legal brief tries to justify a certain preference or right in terms of a contrived reality. A cost-benefit analysis reduces the world from its bright, wet, salty, rocky, sandy, snow-covered, floral, shaggy grace to columns of digits that don't have even the virtue of being real money; economists call these *projections* rather than fantasies; they should call them spells.

Buck-and-pole is good fence. Elk and deer can jump it, antelope can scoot under it. It won't stop anything but a cow. It looks good, in the way that a log house looks better than a pink, prefab, plywood rollerskate rancho. Since it's mostly untreated pine, given time it falls down and decays into a nice mulch, as any decent human construction should.

Barbed wire, on the other hand, is cheap. You can line a fence fast, especially with power augers and post pounders. It's meanly functional stuff that regularly butchers wildlife and horses. It looks like hell. When the posts come down, it leaves a vicious mess. Stockhands hate it; ranchers claim to hate it, but it's quick and cheap and easy. Barbed wire is shaped like a certain attitude toward the world; it lends a taut-strung control over a large area. It works because it derives maximum cruelty from a minimum of material. In brutalist-modern terms, it's cost-effective. Like many other elements of our culture, it is hated almost as widely as it used. Why use it? The commonest answer would be, "Everybody does," or "I can't afford not to."

> *Maybe when the people have outdone themselves, then maybe the stars will fall upon the land, or drops of hot water will rain upon the earth. Or the land will turn under. Or our father, the sun, will not rise to start the day. Then our possessions will turn into beasts and devour us whole.*
>
> The Zunis, *Self-Portrayals*, translated by Alvina Quam

How is money part of our work? In recalling my time as foreman of the buck-and-pole fence crew, money is the least vivid image. The sunburnt faces and voices of co-workers; the big, flapping canvas tents in which we slept; the sticky perfume of bruised lodgepole and the long curves of our log fences; the wild alternation of mountain weathers; the heat of stew in a handheld bowl and the crunch of frybread: it seems now that these are what the work was about, even though I recall toting up my hours on an index card and figuring my paycheck to the penny.

How much did I make? What did I do with the money? God knows. Generally speaking, I spent it. The money did what money ought to do: it was a medium of exchange, by which ten daily hours of ax and back work were converted to rice, beans, and beer. I cared more for what I did than for what I bought.

I liked the work. It was tangible and sensual, full of pine and sweat, sharp tools, small challenges that could be met, the righteous fatigue that flavors food but doesn't grind the spirit to bluntness. The money went fast, but I could *keep* the work, since it became part of me—physically and mentally—in ways that the money never did. Work came before money in my reasoning, just as it did in the world.

There was also the need to be in a certain stretch of country. One winter I gave guitar lessons, taught high school as a substitute, fed hay to cows, and, like the Shoshone, damn near starved by late spring. I worried about money, quite often as I recall, but I never quite gave in. I needed to see the green come back and watch the cottonwoods make leaves.

He was alone. At Sage Junction in the late afternoon, he waved me down with a look of distress so compelling that I had to pull over. He was bald, layered in ancient clothes: striped, once-white slacks, battered après-ski boots, and a coarse wool coat faded to asphalt gray.

I got out and opened the shell so he could throw in his trashbagged bundle. He smiled, but said nothing. As I pulled onto the road, he rasped something that sounded like "Kemmerer." He had no voice. Laryngitis? Throat cancer? He chainsmoked Camels all the way, but his eyes were clear. He didn't seem to be a casualty. I let him out a block before the Safeway, and he turned, pen in hand, and pantomimed writing. I found a scrap of cardboard.

I AM VERY GRATEFUL. COULD YOU HELP FURTHER WITH SOMETHING FOR FOOD?

Neat, block capitals and, considering the circumstances, a polished writing style. "I'm not that far from broke myself," I said, feeling the simple power of speech in the face of this silent man. He scanned the truck—sixteen years old with rust blisters starting under the blue paint and my bedroll and camping gear stacked in the bed—and then looked at me directly. The comment was clear: You're rich; you can make choices. I gave him a five, and he hastened south toward the Triangle and God only knows what sort of a night. He was right, in a way. I turned north toward Pinedale, five dollars poorer, feeling for the moment wildly fortunate and vaguely guilty.

My friends Bruce and Patty, and their sons Matthew and Chris, just moved out of town. As Bruce, a building contractor, put it, "We're getting out of this dead-ass place."

As we shuttled beds and dressers to storage in Bruce's mother's garage, he said that he'd learned to survive in Pinedale, but that he was sick of surviving, living on a shoestring between contracts, scratching for a decent way of life. Barely getting by was as bad as falling behind.

He'd found a job near Chicago; the big Ryder truck was filled and ready in the drive, stuffed with a household—all the pots and chairs and toys that become sad out of their home context, like uprooted trees after a storm.

Amazing, though, that four average persons, not rich, not even comfortable by the prevailing standard, can acquire so much and be so attached to it, as if more of them resided in their possessions than in their bodies—so many things that moving is awful, but abandoning them is like leaving the largest part of ourselves.

What would be accounted success in most countries can seem like black failure in America. Ireland had a potato famine; all we've had are stock-market crashes. These are crises that come not from physical reality, but from our notions of value. The blight, now, is not on our crops but on our hearts.

Some of us—native and pilgrim—will stick, dig in like badgers, and change jobs with the seasons: waitress, river guide, carpenter, clerk, cowhand, key-punch. In order to stay with a particular place or particular people, we'll let money be a frequent worry, something heavy that we drag on our way. We won't let it be our grail or conscience or soul. We won't let it decide for us *how* to live, except in extremity. Though there will be extremity, here and now, in trying to live such a life. The truest luxury today is not good credit, but to have one's choice of adversities.

Society cannot exist unless a controlling power upon will and appetite be placed somewhere, and the less of it there is within, the more there must be without.

So wrote Edmund Burke about the way in which greed and gluttony shove a society toward despotism, or biological disaster. The grass still grows and the sun still shines; we can survive, but most of us have the unshakable conviction that it is not enough simply to maintain ourselves in terms of our need for food, water, and shelter. What seems to matter now is not whether we can live, but whether we can live with hope. In any argument about what is missing in American institutions, in education, for instance, the frightening conclusion is that we have lost hope, for which money alone is a bitter substitute.

My friends, in leaving Pinedale, took with them enough to equip a small village in Peru, yet they aren't rich. Somehow, enough was still lacking that they felt they had to go, not where the mountains are higher or the air clearer or people kinder, but where the economy—that alone—was in better shape.

While this is not precisely a call to poverty, since that would be unthinkable today, it is a call to revolution. We are dominated not by the power of religion or the fear of armies, but by our desire for much more than we need. It is through our own inflated wishes that we are most rigidly controlled.

If we can shake the burden placed on us and on our land by the false equation that *life is money*, then we may find a life worth living beyond this one, which makes us enemies to our own home ground and half the world. Can we reclaim our land? God knows, but we might at least reclaim our hearts.

CHAPTER SIX

During the Boom, Idaho Succumbed to Good Sense

Pat Ford

LEST YOU think that the entire West succumbed to the hypnotic beat of boom, boom, boom during the 1970s and early 1980s, here is an account of how the conservative state of Idaho behaved conservatively—resisting the lure of a coal-fired power plant that was to carry the state to the land of milk and honey.

In 1988 Idaho's richest man stepped confidently into a time machine: potato king J. R. Simplot announced that one of his companies would build a string of coal-fired power plants along the Snake River—two 1,000-megawatt plants a year, for year after year after year.

Fourteen years dissolve. It is 1974, and the official construction schedule of Northwest and Northern Rockies electric companies is based roughly on two thousand megawatts per year. Big coal and nuclear plants are rising or about to rise in every neighboring state—Colstrip in Montana, the Craig trio in Colorado, several each in Wyoming and Utah, Valmy in Nevada, Boardman and Trojan in Oregon, and, in Washington, the flagship of the power-plant boom, the five-plant Washington Public Power Supply System (WPPSS) nuclear complex. And these are only the first wave. Idaho is poised for its usual role—follower. Idaho Power Company announces it will build a 1,000-mega-

41

watt coal plant, called Pioneer, near the Snake River south of Boise. Idaho's business, agricultural, and political establishments embrace Pioneer; conservationists and low-income advocates violently attack it. Wall Street stands ready to float the bond offerings.

The Simplot proposal, however, draws neither embrace nor attack—only silence—for it is 1988, and Pioneer was never built. Idaho, the only state without a commercial coal or nuclear plant, enjoys the lowest electric rates in the nation and has a surplus of electricity into the next century. Its establishments no longer speak with one voice on energy, its citizen groups have real threats to occupy them, and Wall Street is otherwise engaged. Yoked to the past, Simplot says that rejecting Pioneer was "the biggest fool thing that anybody ever done for the state of Idaho." Strike "fool," and you are nearer the verdict of events.

Idaho Power's public relations name for its coal plant has become, fourteen years later, a fitting name for the broader story, an economic and environmental success story in which Pioneer's foes did the pioneering. How Idaho's people said no to Pioneer is half of the vivid tale of grassroots democracy. The other half is something we don't much believe in—wise and courageous government. Fourteen years ago the Idaho Public Utilities Commission (PUC) foresaw the future and chose to lead rather than follow.

The Snake River's crescent fall across southern Idaho is a magnetic field, gathering land and water, people, settlement, development, and power. Three-fourths of Idaho's people, three-fourths of its largest economy, all but one of its biggest industrial plants and employers, and its dominant religion and politics are all on the Snake River Plain. This creation has a mantra: The Snake is a working river. Had Faraday never wired the dynamo, the Snake would still have been worked. But the marriage in our century of electricity to the river's own current makes the landscape and economy of southern Idaho what they are.

In 1901 Idaho Power Company's corporate parent built Swan Falls Dam in the Snake River canyon south of Boise. Stand within its old stone powerhouse, hear and feel the intimate throb of its horse-size turbines just steps away, and you can grasp, at the human scale, the elegance and craft of hydroelectric generation in a way the giant dams won't allow. You can understand the growth of skills and pride in generating power from this river, and how they could lead—as bigger dams produced ten, twenty, then eighty times what Swan Falls can—to skills and pride in wielding power over this state.

Idaho Power built dams on the Snake River—sixteen of them along 465 miles—for sixty-five years. Most of that hydropower was on the cost curve of computers today. Economies of scale, relatively stable costs, and free fuel made the electricity cheaper with each new dam. By 1969 that system produced a kilowatt-hour for less than half a cent. Idaho homes and businesses joined their Northwest neighbors, similarly blessed with Columbia River hydro, in

Swan Falls Dam

the highest per capita electricity use in the world. Energy-intensive industry was lured by the low rates; three phosphate-processing plants near Pocatello used up to 30 percent of Idaho Power's total supply.

But farming was the pivot of hydro's sweep. Irrigated agriculture has dominated Idaho since the 1890s, when, in Idaho writer Ed Chaney's words, "pioneer alchemists first created gold by mixing desert soils with water." That was Snake Plain soil and Snake River water. Idaho Power's dams generated energy, but they also strung irrigation reservoirs across arid southern Idaho.

After World War II, a Rupert farmer drilled the first deep irrigation well into the Snake River aquifer, lifting the water with an electric pump. Fifteen years later a Nampa farmer first used electric pumps in series to high-lift water from the Snake canyon several hundred feet to dry benchlands above. Soon almost every farm—whether it used reservoir, aquifer, or flowing river water—had electric sprinkler systems spraying the fields. Farming and hydro on the Snake River exploded for twenty-five years. Green fields, once found only near the river and canals, now shot miles into the desert. In 1949 nineteen hundred pumps watered 132,000 acres. By 1975 fourteen thousand pumps watered 1.6 million acres. A million acres of sagebrush and range had become cropland. The summer-only electricity involved was enough to supply every home in Idaho, and then some. It was cheap, and it got cheaper the more a farmer used.

Early in this surge, in the 1950s, Idaho Power took on the federal government and Northwest public power for the biggest prize on the Snake: dam-building rights in Hells Canyon. (Those opposed to any dams, no matter who built them, were a weaker third voice.) Persuaded that a federal dam could threaten state-granted water rights, Idaho agriculture and, with it, the Republican Party, from Governor Len Jordan down, swung to the company's side. Republicans won the White House in 1952, and, soon after, Idaho Power had a federal license for three Hells Canyon dams. Built over fifteen years, they generated almost one thousand megawatts at four-tenths of a cent per kilowatt-hour, doubling the company's size and making it the largest all-hydro utility in the nation.

Hells Canyon symbolizes Idaho's postwar economic burst and the political ligature among its parts. Agriculture, industry, population, commerce—growth in any served all, with electric energy seeding and lubricating the whole. Save for the Mormon church, Idaho Power was the most powerful institution in the state.

That is how they came at Pioneer, "like they came at everything, like Idaho was named for Idaho Power." When Bob Lenaghen—the words are his—arrived at the Idaho Public Utilities Commission in 1973, its meager staff was under orders not to audit any utilities. There had been one exception. In the late 1960s another new commissioner, looking for an apartment in Boise, stumbled upon an Intermountain Gas Company "guest house," stocked with liquor and, occasionally, women for important customers and contacts. An audit found it on company books under the name LIDO. Gas customers had been paying for it for years.

"That's how the PUC ran in those days," Lenaghen says. "All the utilities were used to getting their way. I broke the back of that."

He was perfect for the job. Bob Lenaghen is stocky, solid, gruff, gravel voiced—a tough man. Born and raised near Boise, he was working at a Boise store after World War II when a retail clerks' and meatpackers' union local got started. He was picked to lead it, and twenty years later he became the president of Idaho's AFL-CIO. He became a proud Democrat in a Republican state, helping run Cecil Andrus's losing try for governor in 1966, and then his victory in 1970. He ran the state Department of Administration for two years before Andrus appointed him to the PUC.

Lenaghen's growl has an edge when he talks about Idaho Power. "When I ran for the legislature [1958], I'd be out putting up campaign posters, and company crews would follow right along tearing them down." He was a public

One of three Hells Canyon dams

Idaho Power Company

power man, and had fought them on the Hells Canyon dams. Idaho Power's political judgments are usually acute, and they judged him an enemy. He isn't sure how they failed to keep him off the PUC—"ask Cece Andrus"—but his appointment was confirmed by one vote.

New commissioners were traditionally given the least, and dullest, of PUC jobs: trucking regulation. Lenaghen refused, "Andrus said he appointed me so consumers would have a strong voice. I took him at his word." By the end of 1974, joined by Andrus's second appointee, Karl Shurtliff, Lenaghen went to work to double the PUC staff and quadruple its spine.

It was a crucial time. The utilities were on the cusp of great change. From 1961 through 1973, the three-member commission granted electric, gas, and water companies, truckers, railroads, and telephones a total of $25 million in rate increases. When Lenaghen left in 1979, the PUC was deciding single rate hikes for double that 13-year total. Total yearly requests were several hundred million dollars. The energy crisis, the end of the hydro era's economies of scale, instability, and inflation—these mid-seventies forces gave the PUC sudden influence on an economy driven by electricity.

Take Idaho Power. The 1970s began with the fastest growth Idaho had ever seen, with electricity demand in the company's service area rising 7 percent each year. The big hydro sites were gone. With every expectation that rapid growth would continue, Idaho Power bought one-third of a coal plant, Jim Bridger, going up near Rock Springs, Wyoming. Bridger seemed a step in a familiar progression—big coal following big hydro. But Bridger's first output cost triple that of Hells Canyon's. The company's share of Bridger wasn't big enough to affect rates, but that tripling marked the end of an era.

In 1974, 121,000 acres of land newly irrigated by electric pumps put an additional large load on Idaho Power's system. Reports began appearing about a possible coal plant near Boise. (The PUC didn't know any more than the newspapers.) When the *Twin Falls Times-News* revealed that the coal supply contract was already signed, Idaho Power confirmed the news. In November the company formally applied to the PUC for a license to build a 1,000-megawatt plant called Pioneer.

Idaho Power had learned a lesson about boomtowns from its participation in the construction of the Jim Bridger power plant in Rock Springs, the West's most notorious boomtown. With Rock Springs in mind, the company proposed Pioneer for a desert site twenty-six miles south and a bit east of Boise. That way, it said, the huge swings of workers, children, public services, headaches, and taxes would be manageably absorbed by Idaho's biggest community. But there were problems. Dr. Robert Holdren was a respiratory specialist who already had too many patients during Boise's winter inversions; carbon monoxide was trouble enough without sulfur and nitrous oxides from a coal plant. Bill Smallwood was a pilot from nearby Mountain Home; visibility into Boise was already bad, and now his town's airport would be in the wind path from Pioneer's stacks. Jeff Fereday ran the infant Idaho Conservation League, formed to fight cascading assaults on Idaho's air, water, and land. Cliff Bradley was a young biologist living in Nampa who had just hooked up with Fereday. Ken Robison had gone from copyboy to editorial page editor of the *Boise Idaho Statesman* in ten years, becoming a passionate conservationist on the way. These men started asking publicly what a lot of Boiseans silently wondered: Could there be a worse place for a coal plant than next to a fast-growing city in the weather-holding bowl of the Boise Valley?

Despite Idaho Power's protestations that Pioneer would meet all air quality standards, the site guaranteed much automatic opposition and doubt. Natives had watched Boise quadruple in twenty years, with much of the growth caused by newcomers who were trying to escape ills like air pollution. It wasn't a matter of meeting standards. Boiseans new and old were already disturbed by the city's gray-brown haze, variably thick but never absent.

A month after the Pioneer application was filed, Lenaghen hired a new attorney, Conley Ward, who had grown up twenty-five miles from Boise and who had returned home after having gone to college in New York City and law school near Denver. He found himself one of the few PUC staff members who didn't think Pioneer was a fine idea. In 1975 he became staff attorney for the PUC in the Pioneer proceedings, midway through the case.

As these men—Smallwood, Robison, et al., in the public sphere, and Ward within the PUC—looked deeper into the project, they began to see that more was at stake than Boise's air. At first, Idaho Power said that $400 million would build Pioneer. Two months later it was $600 million. About the time Ward took the case, Lenaghen's insistent questioning forced a final estimate—$828 million. Ward said, "Well, my God—at that time the net value of their entire system was $648 million. And Pioneer was only half their 10-year construction program. By 1986 they planned to spend $1.6 billion on a new plant." Pioneer's power would cost seven to eight times the hydropower in place. The result, in the company treasurer's quotable phrase, would be "prompt, frequent, and substantial rate increases." More precisely, power rates would probably triple in a decade. That got attention, and not just in Boise. Low-income activists, led by a War on Poverty veteran named Al Fothergill, joined the opposition, and public doubts grew.

The first man to grasp the full meaning of the numbers was John Peavey. One of Idaho's biggest ranchers, third generation in a powerful Republican family, himself a Republican state senator (replacing his mother when President Nixon named her director of the U.S. Mint), he was also a maverick. For example, just days before Pioneer was filed, Idaho voters had overwhelmingly enacted the "Sunshine Initiative," requiring campaign contribution reporting and registration and reporting by lobbyists. Peavey had led the petition drive that put Sunshine on the ballot, defying his party's leaders and the corporate phalanx the initiative was aimed at.

Peavey saw Pioneer's grim message for Idaho farmers. The agricultural boom obscured how marginal most Snake Plain farms were—irrigation-dependent, far from markets, helplessly riding global price swings. The cheap hydro they used so prodigiously was their biggest advantage, but, on the flip side, their biggest dependence. What Peavey called the "hydro base" had made these farms. Its loss would break them. Peavey saw that the hydro base would be destroyed by more irrigation. First, newly irrigated land would require more power than was presently being produced, which in the coal era would drive rates up, not down. Second, it would shrink existing hydrogeneration by draining water from the Snake before it could pass through the turbines of the Hells Canyon dams. That lost hydro would have to be replaced with coal, driving rates up further.

Idaho Power and the agriculture establishment were too fixed in the go-for-all growth past to comprehend this new reality: the biggest threat to southern Idaho farms was now more farms. Calculations confirmed what Peavey had already sensed by instinct. Add the power demand from the company's projected new irrigation in the next decade to the hydropower lost when the required water was pumped out of the river to those new acres. The total was Pioneer's output. Eaten from both ends, the hydro base would become an ever-smaller part of Idaho Power's system. As it shrank, so would southern Idaho agriculture, triggering what the 1980s would know as a death spiral—fewer and fewer customers paying higher and higher rates for unneeded power plants.

In early 1975 an organization called CAP (Citizens for Alternatives to Pioneer) gradually coalesced. Smallwood became president, and Cliff Bradley the staff; Fereday and Peavey raised some money. CAP was classic grass roots—vital, quarrelsome, Manichaean, learning on the fly, utterly consuming of its leaders. Smallwood had never written a letter-to-the-editor before; now "I just gave nine months of my life [unpaid] to Pioneer. I had to. We had to beat that plant." In public meetings all over southern Idaho, on radio talk shows, in letters, in talks at grange halls and with single farmers, and most visibly in Ken Robison's columns and editorials, CAP pressed its case.

Idaho Power's own grassroots network was equally active. Local managers in every town gathered endorsements from businesses and leaders. Local Farm Bureau leaders ridiculed Peavey's ideas—how could farming be bad for farming? Company chairman Al Carlsen and chief executive officer Jim Bruce hit the luncheon circuit; paid ads repeated their arguments. Allies and fence sitters were flown to Jim Bridger and came back saying the plant was clean and the air clear. Both sides organized for the PUC's many public hearings on Pioneer. The biggest, in Boise, drew five hundred people.

CAP also joined the applicant, the PUC staff, and seven other intervenors in the PUC's formal proceeding. This was a world of its own—deliberate, paper-heavy, attorney- and expert-oriented. In the company's corner were the Idaho Farm Bureau and Water Users Association, Lenaghen's old friends in the state AFL-CIO, the Idaho Association of Commerce and Industry, and the Idaho Association of Professional Engineers. With CAP was the Ada County Medical Society (Dr. Holdren), the Idaho Citizens Coalition, and Idaho Consumer Affairs.

Idaho Power's case took months to assemble and present—witnesses, exhibits, cross-examinations, motions, and rulings; the intervenor and staff cases took more months; and then came the company responses and revisions. The process rewarded money and experience; CAP's Bradley and Fothergill, with neither, scrambled to make a dent. Conley Ward's late entry kept him scrambling too. The staff's fairly meek case, its witnesses and analysis, was largely set when he took over, so his only way to influence the record was to cross-examine mostly hostile witnesses. "I did a lot of 'Let me read to you from a recent study on energy conservation and ask your reaction'—backdooring into the record."

Idaho Power's strongest argument was need: prompt, frequent, and substantial rate increases were unfortunate, but the alternative was brownouts, blackouts, and economic chaos. The company forecast growth, 6 to 7 percent per year, through the next decade, and its forecasts were supported by recent history, national policy and forecasts, industry and agriculture, expert opinion (including the PUC's own independent consultant), and most of the PUC's own staff. CAP doesn't mean citizens for alternatives, the company charged, but citizens against Pioneer. What is the alternative?

Idaho Power's first public polemics for the plant, in 1974, countered the options they thought people would raise—nuclear, solar, and geothermal, and purchased power from other companies. Conservation wasn't even mentioned. Idaho Power had spent seventy years single-mindedly encouraging electricity use. That cutting use was even possible, much less good, fell outside of its experience and instincts. To its foes conservation was an ethic, part of the profound change needed if a habitable earth were to endure. They fervently urged it as the effective, low-cost, and right alternative to Pioneer. Idaho Power's response was strategic (conservation is okay, but it's small potatoes). But deep down Pioneer's advocates saw conservation as a profound change— backward, threatening the growth ethic. This ideological clash awoke the fiercest passions on both sides.

Conservation was a crucial practical issue for the PUC. Idaho Power's growth projections took no account of price-induced conservation. But for Ward, it was common sense that tripled power rates would provoke farmers and others to reduce power use. At 7 percent annual growth, even a small conservation effect could put off the need for Pioneer a year or two. A CAP witness, University of Montana economics professor Tom Power, was helpful as a live expert who agreed. He planted another seed. The PUC couldn't mandate conservation, but it could reform rates. Like every utility, Idaho Power had a raft of rate schedules, all designed to encourage use. The more electricity used, the less paid per unit. Power said that rate design reflected a past era. The company's rate makers were horrified when he suggested collapsing and flattening those schedules, putting more of growth's cost on customers responsible for it, and probably inducing some conservation as well.

The public and PUC combat ground on into 1976. CAP's leaders were sure they spoke for most Idahoans, certainly most Boiseans, but the PUC was conducting an evidentiary hearing, not a plebiscite. Then the decisive strategy walked through CAP's door in the person of Jon Robertson. Robertson was a self-proclaimed socialist—young, intense, and ideological—who made pipes in his father's Boise tobacco shop. His goal wasn't new—a popular vote on Pioneer had been suggested in 1974, and as quickly rejected by county officials. (Idaho Power's Al Carlsen made a fateful remark at the time: People were not informed enough, and couldn't become so, to vote on such a complex issue.) But Robertson proposed a petition drive to force the Ada County Commission to hold a vote.

Before CAP could quite decide if it made sense, Robertson and a few helpers were on the sidewalks downtown, calling themselves Campaign to Put Pioneer on the Ballot. They rephrased Carlsen's remark: Don't sign if you agree with Idaho Power that you're too stupid to vote on Pioneer. When Robertson had five thousand signatures, he went to the county commission. They said no; Idaho Power was working them hard from the other side. Back to the street corners, now with a lot of help, and in a few weeks he was back with ten thousand. Again they said no. But halfway to fifteen thousand, with no end in sight, the commission caved in. Pioneer would be an advisory question on the May 1976 primary ballot. Neighboring Canyon and Elmore counties followed suit.

On March 15 the PUC held its penultimate hearing on Pioneer, allowing next-to-last licks for all the parties at the mountainous record begun sixteen months before. The day's drama was the last public witness in the case. The PUC's long, narrow hearing room was jammed to hear Cecil Andrus speak on Pioneer. Governor Andrus was extremely popular—he would shortly win a second term with 70 percent of the vote. He had appointed two of the three men he addressed. He had watched the petition drive catch fire and knew the people would render their advisory verdict in fifty days.

"Mr. Chairman and members of the commission, I am adamantly opposed to the construction of a coal-fired power plant at the proposed site, and I strongly urge you to deny Idaho Power's application." Those present remember the words, and the wild applause and the rapping of Lenaghen's gavel that followed.

His testimony mixed arguments. There was "no question Idaho will need additional electricity," but the air and health concerns of a site so near Boise argued against Pioneer, as did the effect on power bills. He ran through Peavey's agricultural arguments and called Pioneer a dangerous growth switch.

He explicitly left the door open to support a plant at another site. He reflected both the growing public certainty against Pioneer and the uncertainty about what would come next.

What leaps out today is his antigrowth rhetoric: "Pioneer is in one sense a 'growth switch.' If the switch is turned on you will be committing Idaho to a significant increase in population and industrial activity. . . . We have already been discovered by the industrial country clubs. . . . To knowingly destroy the very things that make Idaho unique for the sake of all-out growth would be foolhardy." (This conviction, shared by all the leaders against Pioneer, although not a major factor with the people at large, is inconceivable from Cecil Andrus today, back again as Idaho's governor. Today his administration's top priority is to turn on that growth switch.)

"Our decision would have been the same whether Andrus testified or not," say both Lenaghen and Karl Shurtliff. It certainly upped their leverage on the lone pre-Andrus holdover, Ralph Wickberg. Wickberg had already told a reporter that "there's no hiding I'm in the minority here" on Pioneer.

These were tense times at the PUC. Public exchanges between Lenaghen and Idaho Power witnesses were testy, and privately he and Al Carlsen were at each other's throats. The staff was bitterly divided. Most saw Karl Shurtliff as the man in the middle. He most vividly remembers the workload—Pioneer's 20-foot-high record came on top of rate cases from every major utility—and the equation that raced daily through his mind: Need-cost, need-cost, need-cost.

The two months before the public vote were angry and loud. Idaho Power helped some supporters, businessmen, engineers, and a few economists organize "Pioneer Spirit—dedicated to rational analysis of the proposed plant and to communicate the true picture to the people of southern Idaho." Here is the analysis of a chief spokesman, given to the Caldwell Chamber of Commerce and then to the people in the morning paper: "If you are accustomed to looking ahead, you'd better buckle up for the crash-landing of inadequate power and brownouts, of interruption of industrial and agricultural power supplies, of serious economic distress, sometime in the early 1980s. . . . The opinions of reputable, qualified professional and technical people as to future growth in energy demand and as to environmental impact of Pioneer are being thrust aside by a little group of misguided, crusading, amateur zealots who want to turn society around and point it in the direction of India."

"Experts know best" was a constant theme. Idaho Power brought the Northwest's most visible energy expert, Bonneville Power Administrator Don Hodel, in to lobby. Hodel's standard speech, given a hundred times since 1973 to convince utilities and their customers to buy into the WPPSS nuclear plants, applied equally to Pioneer. Its peroration was the indissoluble link, akin to a physical law, between energy growth and jobs: "Energy means jobs. No energy, no jobs." Pioneer Spirit spent some $15,000, largely on apocalyptic newspaper and radio ads: "If we say no to Pioneer, what do we say to our children? Do we say 'We're sorry, you'd better get out of Idaho. There's no future for you here. We planned it that way'???"

CAP relied largely on public meetings, conversation, free media, and Ken Robison's columns. Letter-to-the-editor pages were thick with Pioneer. In the Boise Valley the real primary—voters were picking candidates for president, Congress, governor, and the legislature—was a clear subplot to the advisory vote on the plant.

Turnout was heavy on May 26. In Ada County—Boise—56 percent opposed Pioneer. Thirty-two percent favored it, and 5 percent favored it, but somewhere else. Sixty percent opposed it in Canyon County, and 80 percent in Bill Smallwood's Elmore County. The unqualified citizenry rendered a pretty unqualified verdict: the results cut across party lines, and the three counties contained more than half of Idaho Power's customers. The company did have one victory that day. In the Republican primary in the twenty-first legislative district—south-central Idaho, where Pioneer was not on the ballot—a challenger handpicked and well funded by Idaho Power beat John Peavey for his state senate seat.

The next months would have been lively if the PUC had been on a different course than the people, but it was not. Lenaghen, Shurtliff, and Wickberg began seeking common grounds for disapproval. Idaho Power tried to salvage something by proposing the PUC approve a plant but leave the where and what-size decisions till later. Stop trying to paint us into a corner, Lenaghen responded.

Conley Ward drafted the PUC's order, and the commissioners issued it with one major change on September 17, 1976. (Ward deliberately wrote to a citizen audience rather than lawyers or utility experts.) The end of the cheap hydro era, the economic implications for Idaho and especially its farmers, and the senility of conventional utility thinking were crisply argued years before the electric companies and most of their customers caught on.

The decision itself was narrow. Idaho Power claimed it required new generation by 1980 or 1981; the commission found the need would exist by 1982 or 1983. (This was the change from Ward's draft, which admitted no such need.) Pioneer was then denied because of potential "impact on air quality and human health . . . in the state's most populous and fastest-growing region." Shurtliff's insistent need-cost equation was put off a bit and left explicitly unresolved. But Pioneer was dead.

It would take another story, as long again, to record the echoes and aftershocks, some of which are rumbling yet. What follows is a bare and partial summary. Idaho Power struck back where it could. When a drained Karl Shurtliff left the PUC three months after Pioneer, Andrus's replacement, Matt Mullaney, was promptly rejected by the 1977 legislature. (The company couldn't get at their real target yet; Lenaghen's term didn't end until 1979.)

The legislature also directed the PUC to study alternative sites for a coal plant and to choose one—what Ward calls the "build anything, build anywhere, but build" order.

Idaho Power, however missed a big one that same session. Days after appointing Mullaney, Cecil Andrus left for Washington, D.C., and four years as Jimmy Carter's Secretary of Interior. New Governor John Evans wavered for six weeks, then bowed to Lenaghen's insistence and appointed Conley Ward to the PUC. On the session's next-to-last day, three Republican senators crossed Idaho Power and their caucus, and Ward was confirmed 18 to 17.

Three months later the company reapplied for a coal plant, this time at one of three isolated sites in south-central Idaho. Opponents called it Son of Pioneer, and a smaller version of the same battle began. Peavey charged back in, new foes sprang up near each site, business and agricultural leaders rallied in support, public meetings and PUC hearings resumed. At one site a company air-monitoring tower was acetylened to the ground.

But Ward and Lenaghen moved crisply out on a course of their own. Call it Ward's vision, Lenaghen's will, and their common populism. In the next two years they turned Idaho utility regulation inside out. Lenaghen completed his expansion and spinal transfusion of the PUC staff, making it the most talented assemblage in Idaho government. They essentially ignored the legislature's find-a-coal-plant order. Working through the rate cases each utility was filing—so fast there would be at times three cases in various stages from one company—they ended promotional rates and mandated a clutch of conservation programs.

Big irrigators and businesses, big all-electric homeowners—all hooked on the old "use more, pay less" rates—and, of course, the utilities, howled and fought. "For a while there, it seemed like every legislature was a PUC lynch mob," says Ward. "They made it about as hot as it can be in public life." Legislation reversed PUC actions (for instance, inverted rates—use more, pay more per unit—were banned). The utilities appealed every PUC decision, and the Idaho Supreme Court reversed many.

In mid-1978 Idaho Power withdrew Son of Pioneer to avoid the rejection they saw coming. The PUC instead approved a few least-risk projects, like hydro upgrades and shares in joint ventures. Gradually growth rates came down, to 5, then 3 percent. Conservation took hold as rates rose. When the recession hit in 1979, growth essentially ended. Beginning that same year, the PUC used a new federal law, the Public Utilities Regulatory Policy Act, to start building a robust nonutility electric generation industry in Idaho. Today small hydro and cogeneration are able to supply any new in-state power needs through the century's end.

The PUC's goal was to bring the hydro base through the thermal plant binge sweeping the West in those years. The state's electric rates today are proof of their success.

John Peavey also made a modest post-Pioneer contribution. Since 1975 he had wanted a more direct solution to the core problem of which Pioneer was a symptom: draining the Snake River for new irrigation. Spurred by his defeat at Idaho Power's hands, Matt Mullaney began excavating hydro law for Peavey. Each Idaho Power dam had a legal right to a certain level of river flow, but these rights were expressly "subordinated"—the state could allow future upstream diversions, even if they diminished the water rights at the dams. This subordination language reflected agriculture's preeminence in Idaho water law; it was routine in every hydro water right. But Mullaney discovered that Idaho Power's oldest water right, at Swan Falls Dam, had quite accidentally never been subordinated. It was for 8,400 cubic feet per second of Snake River flow, but seventy subsequent years of irrigation diversions had reduced actual flow at Swan Falls to some 6,000 cubic feet per second. Twenty-four hundred cubic feet per second were out irrigating farm fields, illegally, instead of generating power in the river.

In August 1977 Peavey, Mullaney, and thirty friends filed a petition with the PUC asking that all the hydro system's lost potential, from failure to defend the Swan Falls right, be removed from Idaho Power's rate base and refunds made to customers. The wedge to break the Idaho Power–agriculture alliance was driven. The issue was soon in court, but not before the PUC ordered a moratorium on new irrigation hookups. Idaho Power's potential financial exposure forced it to begin defending that part of its water right still intact— forced it to begin resisting new diversions from the river. Gradually, its forced defense became a willing defense, as it realized that protecting the hydro base was good business. Gradually, though the company never quite said it this way, Idaho Power realized John Peavey was right. They became allies against new diversions, and in 1984 joined to enact legislation severely limiting future consumptive withdrawals from the Snake.

Bob Lenaghen knew he would be a one-term commissioner from the day Pioneer was decided. In the two and a half years left him he took most of the heat, out on point, for the great and greatly misunderstood service he and Ward were rendering their state. In 1979 he was rejected for a second term on a party-line vote. It gained Idaho Power little but revenge. It did not slow the achievement the PUC was building, guided now by Ward, who was in turn guided by his friend's example: "Bob told me, and showed me, that 'you can do anything in this job you are big enough to do.'"

Today Lenaghen works mornings for Cecil Andrus and plays some golf in the afternoons. Last year he was at a little meeting that Jim Bruce, now retired from Idaho Power, also attended. As talk ranged off the main point, Bruce told the group that if it hadn't been for Bob Lenaghen's shutting off Pioneer, his company would surely have landed sooner or later in financial trouble. Lenaghen's growl can be unexpectedly cheerful, "That made me feel pretty good!"

Ten years after the Pioneer proposal, Boise was still experiencing serious inversions. During one, the same gray murky cloud hung over Boise for twenty-two straight days. Most of those days the sun was shining on the mountains just north of town. In town you couldn't see the mountains; you could barely see the town, but you could clearly see the air. Children and old folks, among others, stayed indoors. The city council voted itself authority to prohibit woodstove use and invoked that authority several times that winter and this past one. From my home in Boise last winter I talked long distance with Bill Smallwood. "Can you imagine," he asked me, "what you'd have there today if they'd built Pioneer?"

CHAPTER SEVEN

Choosing a Future
for the Rural West

DeWitt John

In the 1970s economic development seemed the enemy of conservation—crash programs to mine, dam, or log the West, or fill it with condos and ski lifts. Economic development was also often colonial, thrust on the West by the federal government and large corporations. Today things are different. In the 1980s and probably into the 1990s, economic development has become something the rural West must compete for, not something that will be forced on it.

That means the West now has choices. Should the rural West compete for development? Or should it stand pat and let events take their course? If the rural West lets current trends rule, then it will gain jobs and income at about 80 percent of the rate of the metropolitan West through the year 2000. That projection is higher than it was from 1979 to 1986, when rural areas produced jobs at only 40 percent of the metropolitan rate. And the projected rate for the West is higher than comparable rates for the rural South (66 percent) or the Midwest (78 percent).

A broad trend does not mean every rural county will fare the same. Some towns will prosper; others will not. The reasons are elusive. Momentum counts for something (size, a better-educated workforce, higher per capita income, faster growth in the recent past). Help from outside counts for something (a university, an interstate highway, a nearby metropolitan area, or getting more than the county's share of federal economic aid). But these count for less than one might expect—only 17 percent of the variance in job growth, according to a study of rural counties in the farmbelt for 1979 to 1984.

The study, A Brighter Future for Rural America?, published by the National Governors' Association in 1988, suggests that a community's choices are as important as what it has to work with. If a community unites, pursues economic growth, works with neighbors, taxes itself to invest in people and infrastructure, and shares risks with local businesspeople, then growth is possible for all but the smallest, most isolated places. Is economic growth worth that kind of effort? The answer depends on values and on the type of growth one is talking about. The thing to remember is that life is flexible. Economics sets limits, but within those limits, the choices are up to the West.

The region has five broad strategies to choose from. Payoffs from two traditional Western strategies—federal aid and commodities like cattle and coal, wheat and timber—will not be good. Payoffs from three newer strategies—scenery, moving indoors, and self-reliance—may be better.

The Subsidy Trap

For decades the rural West's economy has been helped by federal subsidies— dams, rural electrification, land-grant universities, agricultural price supports, military bases, and low-cost use of public lands. These are less helpful today. Subsidies tend to keep people in place, producing the same crops or products. But staying in place is no longer a recipe for survival; the world is changing too rapidly.

Every day, for example, billions of dollars are moved around the world. Scientific and technological information are also shared widely. Industry has become international, with firms able to shift production from one location to another. In addition, it is increasingly difficult for any nation or group of nations to manage exchange and interest rates, which are fundamental to all prices and thus to the distribution of wealth. Professor Daniel Bell says, "The nation is too small for the big problems of life and too big for the small problems of life." The nation-state lacks the tools to address the biggest problems, which are global. And it is too remote to help communities and companies compete in the turbulent global marketplace—a turbulence which arises because it can't manage the big problems.

Federal subsidies are still important. But to compete, communities and states will have to increase their nimbleness by investing in better education, upgrading their workforce, revamping universities, or encouraging new relationships between labor and management. This may sound good, but actually no one knows how to organize the investments, except that they should attempt to address the diversity of local conditions. That means a client relationship with the federal government won't help. If a community or region or firm wants to prosper, it must help itself.

Cattle and Other Commodities

What global and national conditions must the West take into account as it charts its course? First is the changed market for commodities. In the 1970s the traditional Western rural economy based on cattle, oil, coal, minerals, grain, and timber was comparatively prosperous. Energy prices jumped, and a long-term rise in all commodity prices seemed reasonable. In fact, *The Limits to Growth*, a report on the Club of Rome's Project on the Predicament of Mankind, predicted that increasing world population would put an intolerable burden on the world's farmland, natural resources, and environment.

Environmentalists saw the report as bad news; others saw opportunity. As late as 1981, the yearbook of the U.S. Department of Agriculture asked, "Will There Be Enough Food?" and encouraged farmers to expand. The $88 billion federal synfuels program, widespread oil and gas exploration, the opening of new coal mines, and the construction of new power plants were all part of the expected boom in commodities.

The Club of Rome report may yet turn out to be right about the environmental effects of growth. But global warming and depletion of the ozone layer are not reflected in prices. Rising energy prices in the 1970s were the exception, not the rule. Looking at the period from 1950 to 1986, we find that the prices of nonoil commodities declined by about 40 percent. We are using more commodities, but prices have not risen because technology has helped locate more deposits, produce more efficiently, recycle, and substitute. In mid-1987 world commodity prices did jump about 20 percent. Some Western mines reopened, and the farm credit crisis eased, but over the long haul, commodity prices are likely to stay flat. As a result, the West's traditional natural resource industries cannot stage a sustained comeback.

Scenery for Urban Cowboys

Although cows are out of style, cowboys are not. Commodities may not be due for long-term growth, but the interest of the outside world in the romantic, wide-open, rural West is undiminished. Rural Western towns can turn the attraction of the outdoors and the myth of the cowboy to advantage. In roughly ascending order, as measured by local spending per visitor per day, studies show the most lucrative tourist activities are backpacking, car camping, hunting and fishing, bed and breakfast at working ranches and farms, commercial rafting, skiing, and conventioning at resorts. The impact of tourism on a rural community is somewhat hard to assess because profits from larger resorts may flow out of the community and because the retail and service jobs in tourism are low wage and seasonal.

Retirement often goes with tourism. Nationally, only two kinds of rural counties—recreation-retirement centers and government-dependent counties—have kept pace with metropolitan areas in the 1980s. To compete for retirees, rural towns may want to invest in improved health care. States and counties can also push tough environmental policies.

In Europe and parts of New England, there is talk of subsidizing farmers in order to keep the countryside cultivated, and therefore attractive to tourists. Westerners, however, may be repelled by the idea of maintaining the myth of the cowboy in order to build a tourist economy. The self-image of the rural West, as of most rural communities, is based on wresting a living from the land with hard, physical toil. As a Vermonter said in a public hearing last year: "Rural is not a place; it is an activity. It's people doing stuff with the land, with trees, with animals. I don't see much 'rural' around here any more."

Moving Indoors

Manufacturing might be a tolerable compromise to some traditional Westerners. It is inside work, but it involves making something. And the short-term prospects for manufacturing are good. The drop in the dollar boosted U.S. exports of manufactured goods by 17 percent in 1987. But over the long haul, U.S. employment in manufacturing has been stable for almost forty years. Most new jobs have been in service industries, which brings us back to recreation and retirement. That doesn't mean manufacturing won't work for certain towns or areas. Some niches will be found in "value-added" manufacturing—turning logs into furniture, durum wheat into spaghetti, and soggy Powder River coal into high-BTU fuel. The United States currently exports $1.4 billion of raw timber and imports $4.2 billion of finished wood products. If some of that lumber (or other commodity) were processed in the rural West, reducing bulk and adding to the value of the commodity, it would strengthen local economies.

There may also be niches for entrepreneurial businesses using advanced technologies. However, there are good reasons why rural manufacturing has been concentrated in low-skill mass production. When products are first created and are changing rapidly, they are often made in metropolitan centers, where information and technical expertise are close at hand. When the product becomes stable, production can be moved to areas that lack specialized skills but where wages are lower. In the 1960s and 1970s, many rural areas in the South and West gained low-wage manufacturing "branch plants." In the

1980s, as the United States moved squarely into the global economy, hundreds of thousands of these jobs were lost to automation or to nations with lower wages.

The prospects for rural manufacturing growth may be better in "footloose" industries—those that are not tied to specific natural resources, do not need to be near markets, can function well by using the U.S. mail and the telephone, and might be attracted by the cowboy image of the West. Publishing, "back-office" data processing, software programming, and handcrafts are often cited. There are also less-obvious examples: lightweight, made-to-order, prefabricated steel buildings, mobile homes, and shuttle buses.

The classic way to attract "footloose" firms is to offer tax breaks and other subsidies. However, these burden local taxpayers, including other businesses. And once the benefits are used up, firms may move on. A more enduring lure would be high-quality recreational amenities, a skilled labor force, and a community spirit that appreciates businesses and responds quickly to their needs.

Self-Reliance

A fifth strategy would emphasize self-reliant communities. Rural residents might hunt and garden, exchange products with neighbors, practice energy conservation, shop at the locally owned store instead of at Walmart, and "Buy Montana." Mainline economists are skeptical here. During the 1960s and 1970s, many Third World nations tried "import substitution" with tepid success. Mexico is a prime example. The success stories all came from export-driven economies—Japan, Taiwan, Korea, Hong Kong, Singapore, and now perhaps Thailand.

Self-sufficiency shelters an area from external disruptions. The drawback is that larger, global markets can often achieve lower costs and lower prices. Initially, a nation or a town may reap savings by weeding out high-priced imports, but subsequent savings are difficult, so further efforts to reduce imports just make consumers poorer. Although self-sufficiency has limits, organizing a community around economic well-being makes excellent sense. Each part of the rural West will have to work out its own economic future. The answers will be as diverse as the communities in the West. They will arise from local discussions involving a broad cross section of the community.

In spite of the current economic crisis, the West has long-term advantages. Its natural environment and romantic appeal are world class. And the West is inside the biggest market in the world. Although the playing field is tilted against them, rural communities can prosper if they understand their potential, mobilize a long-term development effort, and make risky investments of time and money to help struggling businesses. Should they do so? That depends. The costs of growth, in terms of the kinds of people attracted to an area and the loss of traditional values, will be too high for some towns. Money, after all, isn't everything.

Not So Dismal

Thomas Carlyle called economics "the dismal science." Most economists operate with assumptions conservationists will reject as mean-spirited and self-defeating. Economists of all schools honor the discount rate. They believe a dollar earned a year from now is worth less than a dollar today, because one can put a dollar in the bank today and have a dollar plus interest next year.

Conservationists have a different sense of time. They value today as much as they value tomorrow. They care about preserving the (nearly) pristine air of the Utah desert until 2050 and beyond. Many ranchers and farmers feel the same way about their land. And parents and grandparents feel a tug of stewardship for the future.

For economic reasons, many economists also have misgivings about the high U.S. discount rates—they encourage immediate consumption and discourage saving. The disillusion is often expressed in concern about the low savings rate in the United States and the economic success of Japan, where individuals are more willing to postpone consumption.

Economics, including a degree of callousness about long-term consequences, drives business decisions, which in turn influence individual decisions and determine the life chances of everyone. Thus, economics sets constraints for communities and individuals. Perhaps, then, it is fortunate that the predictive power of economic models, especially of models that address the location of economic growth, is so weak. Since economics is an inexact guide to social engineering, the dismal worldview implicit in its tenets can serve as a dose of pragmatism rather than a prediction of destructive behavior.

Part Two

THE
BUST

CHAPTER EIGHT

Global Economy Turns "Lite"

Ed Marston

THERE IS a school of economic thought that believes all wealth comes out of the ground—as mined ore, as grown food, as logged trees, as grazed forage. It is a belief adhered to most fervently in rural areas. Farmers, miners, ranchers, and loggers all believe they are the underpinning of the U.S. economy. A majority of Americans appear to share that conviction. How else explain the billions of dollars given willingly to the 2 percent of Americans who live on farms.

Now comes the well-known author Peter F. Drucker, Clarke Professor of Social Science and Management at Claremont Graduate School in California, to declare that we have been worshiping at the wrong shrine. Drucker sets himself in opposition to the theory that wealth comes out of the ground. In fact, he maintains, commodities are increasingly irrelevant to wealth. In the careful language of the economist, Drucker wrote in the Spring 1986 issue of *Foreign Affairs:* "The raw material economy has thus come uncoupled from the industrial economy."

Those who make their living in the rural West have already experienced Drucker's thesis. They have watched the prices of silver, oil and natural gas, uranium, coal, and food plummet and take the region's economy down with them. Such collapses are not new. But the lack of reaction to the collapse is: "If there was one thing 'proven' beyond doubt in business cycle theory, it is that a sharp and prolonged drop in raw material prices inevitably, and within 18 to 30 months, brings on a worldwide depression in the industrial economy."

Drucker dates the nonoil commodity price collapse to 1977. In the energy-rich West the collapse came in the very early 1980s. Whatever the exact date, there clearly has been no national or worldwide depression. Instead, the economic gulf between the urban and rural parts of the United States has widened, creating the so-called bicoastal economy—the rich East and West coasts sandwiching an increasingly poor interior.

Drucker does not think the situation is a fluke. "The primary-products sector has become marginal where before it had always been central." He has no general theory for this enormous change. The theory will come, he says. In the meantime he cites example after example to show how commodity prices have been hammered down. Moreover, the declining prices haven't created short-ages and resulting price increases. The cycle that commodity producers have

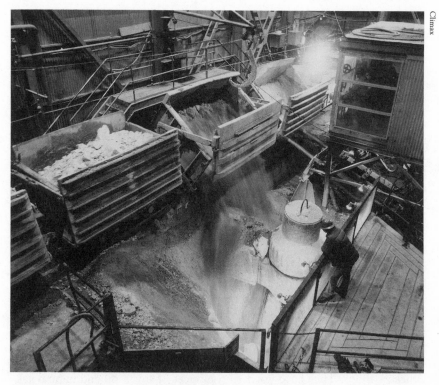

Crusher used at Climax molybdenum plant near Leadville, Colorado

depended on for hundreds of years has apparently been broken. The break has two sources: an economy that uses fewer and fewer raw materials, and technological advances that allow commodity producers to be ever more efficient.

His most dramatic examples of why commodity prices are in permanent decline surround what we and the underlying productive economy consume. The center of consumption after World War II was automobiles, trucks, and buses—products whose cost was 40 percent steel, copper, rubber, and other raw materials.

Today center stage is occupied by the computer, television sets, VCRs, Sony Walkmans, and the like. At their heart is the microchip, 3 percent of whose cost is raw materials. When you carry a Zenith VCR or an Apple Computer out of a store, most of your $300 to $4,000 has gone for intangibles—research, interest on investment, software development—all things that rural areas most assuredly do not specialize in.

Telecommunications is another boom area. In the old days the growth in communications and data flow would have required enormous amounts of copper. Today it requires enormous amounts of sand. It takes no more than one hundred pounds of fiberglass cable to carry as much information as two thousand pounds of copper cable. Savings cascade when you look at the energy. Copper cable requires twenty times more energy to process it than the equivalent amount of fiberglass.

Drucker scoffs at the theory that the United States is being deindustrialized. Industrial output, he says, is holding steady, but industry is producing the same output with ever fewer blue collar workers. Steelworkers, miners, millworkers, and mechanics are going the way of the family farmer. Production has shifted from the assembly-line worker to the laboratory researcher, the computer software writer, and to a hundred other "service" jobs that are actually part of the production process.

Commodities, and the rural areas that produce them, are being squeezed from both ends. On the consumption end, consumers of all kinds are making do with fewer and fewer raw materials. On the supply end, the same kind of information revolution is allowing mines, mills, farmers, and wood-products firms to produce more with fewer workers, thinner ores, and less energy.

There is more in Drucker's article—a great deal about the flow of capital and production from nation to nation, the national strategies that work best in the new global economy, and so on. But his discussion about the increasing irrelevance of commodities bears most heavily on the rural West. If Drucker is correct, the West is not experiencing a bust—it is experiencing the painful beginning of a long-term decline. One hundred years of boom-bust have been replaced by a future made up of bust and more bust. The West's commodity producers have entered onto a steadily accelerating treadmill. No longer may they dream of striking it rich. Instead, they are galley slaves who will always be selling into a weakening market. Companies can think only about how to cut costs, how to reduce the workforce, how to reduce the wages paid to that workforce. All the talk of marketing in the agricultural and other commodity sectors means simply that too many producers are chasing too few customers.

The change comes just when the United States is no longer able to shelter the West. In today's global economy, it is every region for itself. The federally built dams, the made-in-Washington market for the region's uranium, the cheap loans or grants to electrify the rural areas, the heavy military spending, are no longer supportable by the rest of the nation.

Instead, the rural West is being thrown back on its resources. It enters this global race with more handicaps than strengths. Its extractive culture, its desire to continue to work the ground, its lack of interest in education, its sparse population, its lack of a progressive middle class, are all handicaps. But it has a major advantage: the most compelling landscape in the world. Miraculously, and despite great damage, that landscape survives. The air is still clear; large stretches of land are unpopulated; wildlife—even grizzly bears and wolves—survive or could be reintroduced. Whether the West remains in decline or figures out how to reverse its present situation depends on only one thing: how it chooses to use the land.

CHAPTER NINE

The West Lacks Social Glue

Ed Marston

BUST FOLLOWS boom in the West as night follows day. Busts are interesting as studies in human suffering, fractured communities, and immense real and paper economic losses. Even more interesting is the question: Why does the West set itself up for a bust by allowing a boom? Conventional wisdom has it that the West boomed in the 1970s and early 1980s because of President Jimmy Carter's panicky, $88-billion Synfuels Corporation response to OPEC, because the oil companies had a vast flow of cash and a minimum flow of good sense, and because inflation of the dollar inflated the West's land and minerals.

The West likes that answer. It places responsibility outside the region—in the White House, in Congress, and in corporate boardrooms. But the West is not a helpless colonial nation. Its twenty U.S. senators are a formidable group, and the region can and has used its power to stop booms. Take Utah and the proposed MX "racetrack" project. On the surface it was a made-for-the-West project. Enormous amounts of dirt would have been moved, rivers of concrete would have been poured, armies of semiskilled and unskilled labor would have had jobs, and approximately $100 billion would have been spent placing nuclear weapons on railroad cars, or, in a later plan, on large trucks, so that they could be shuttled to and fro in the event of a crisis. Then the Mormon church put its foot down, deciding that the project would threaten the state's way of life. As a result, the conservative Republican Utah and Nevada delegations to Congress stopped the project in October 1981, and those military dollars flowed elsewhere.

Although the West can resist or stop booms, it almost never does. The most you can say of the 1970s energy boom was that the states required "mitigation": upfront funding by energy companies of schools, sewer systems, town halls; siting regulations; the establishment of trust funds to cushion the public sector when the bust came; and an influx of social service people to hold the hands of isolated or battered wives, alcoholic boomers, and dislocated local residents.

There was no attempt to preserve the rural West, its environment, and its way of life. They were considered expendable. During the boom, the larger America—its values and its cash—was in the saddle. The few resisters—such as Boise, Idaho, in the Pioneer power plant episode described earlier—were rare exceptions.

In addition to Boise, there was Meeker, an isolated cattle- and sheep-raising community at the center of Colorado's oil shale country. At the height of the boom, Meeker-area elected officials told the oil companies that the town and county wanted no part of the oil shale construction mancamps and the problems that went with them. It may be that the residents of other small communities also wanted to hang on to their economy and way of life, but Meeker was almost alone in having a leadership that resisted the boom.

Grand Junction, Colorado, on the fringe of oil shale country, was typical. Some agricultural people in surrounding Mesa County have charged that the county commissioners engaged in a rural form of blockbusting, placing subdivisions and commercial development in the heart of Mesa County's orchard area to destroy fruit growing. That may or may not be, but it is certain that Mesa County participated joyously, recklessly, in the boom. Even after oil shale's climactic event—the spring 1982 closure of Exxon's Colony Project—Mesa County chose to spend the proceeds of a $35-million bond issue on roads and other improvements. The county commissioners' goal was to keep the heated economy hot until a new private-sector boom came. The strategy failed. The $35 million was a drop in the bucket (Exxon alone had been spending $1 million a day at Colony). Six years later, after numerous bond refinancings, Mesa County remains in serious financial trouble.

The rural West in the boom period can be understood as a local example of the same policies that have resulted in Third World debt to U.S. and other developed nations' banks. The difference is that in the West, national wealth was sunk into home soil. A large chunk of money was lost directly by energy and mineral corporations. But their spending set off a secondary housing and commercial development boom that has put many banks in the region into the hands of the federal insurance agencies. Lending and investment policies that, abroad, left Brazil, Mexico, and other nations owing foreign banks billions, have, in the West, left the financial insurance agencies—FDIC and FSLIC—holding an immense bag of debts.

The losses were suffered by institutions of all sizes. Small-town bankers, accustomed to making their big loans to people buying late-model used cars, and their small loans to people buying freezers and dryers, suddenly found themselves "participating" with large, distant banks on projects that destroyed them or that they now carry on their books at astronomical values. During the early days of the bust, when the outflow from the region was at its height, one banker said of his former borrowers: "The nice ones drop off the keys to the house and car and snowmobile before they leave town. The rest take the keys with them. Here I am, almost sixty-five, and I'll have to spend the next five years getting rid of other people's property."

Was the boom a wealth transfer mechanism from banks and energy corporations to individuals. Was it a Robin Hood episode? Some firms and individuals, mainly those outside the region, did well in the boom and escaped the bust. They were mainly bond salesmen, architects, consultants, construction and engineering firms, and construction workers. So long as they didn't invest more than their time in the West, they did well. Main Street businessmen and ranchers who sold out during the boom for cash also did well. But most local people were burned. Ranchers who made a killing on paper selling land and water to developers often got the property back a few years later. The payments they had received may or may not have covered the cost of restoring the ranch—repairing fences, getting weeds out of the field, digging silt out of the ditches. People who sold a 40-acre pasture to a construction firm for a storage and parking area may have got it back covered with gravel or asphalt—wonderful land in a city, but not of much use for cattle.

The boom went on so long it got to the heart of the communities. Usually the guy who works for close to minimum wage at the lumberyard or who delivers milk for the local dairy will stick with his job through a quick boom. But if it goes on, he's likely to try to get on at the mine, the mill, the power plant building project. In many cases he would rather not change jobs. Most likely he doesn't think he should be making high wages. And he's not sure he wants to move out of a protected world into the boom.

But a boom is like war: "What's an able-bodied man like you doing selling paint for $4 an hour when you could be building a power plant for $12 an hour?" So pretty soon he has quit and reluctantly joined the army of boom-town laborers. To go with his new status, he may buy a new car, or even a house—something that may wash him out of town when the boom turns to bust. His boss is no better off. The boss may raise what he pays his help, but still be unable to compete with construction pay. He also raises prices, making him even less competitive with the new K-Mart out on the highway.

By any scale, the latest boom hurt the West. Most of the wealth flowed through the region, ending up elsewhere. Where the "wealth" remained in the

West, it did so in the form of sunk resources: Exxon's semi-abandoned Colony Oil Shale Project; Unocal's inefficient oil shale project; thousands of miles of roads built to reach now-abandoned oil and gas drill sites; scores of closed coal mines; unneeded town halls, police stations, new housing, shopping centers, recreation centers, platted subdivisions.

Where a boom-time investment worked out, it was often by mistake. Exxon built a subdivision—Battlement Mesa—to house its oil shale workers in western Colorado. They did such a nice job that when the region went bust, they were able to market the homes and apartments to the so-called active retirees that became the area's alternative economy.

Why weren't there more Boises, Meekers, Utahs? In part the blame rests at the local level. Mayors; boards of county commissioners; state legislators; water, rural electric, hospital, and school district executives; and the rest of the rural West's establishment didn't have the foresight to resist. Despite talk at the national level of making the West a "national sacrifice area," the leaders either couldn't see the need to resist, wanted to cash in on the blood that would flow from the "sacrifice," or didn't know how to stand up to the city slickers who flooded the area.

But there was more to the West's failure to contain the boom than lack of leadership. The thinly populated, far-flung West lacks resources that developed parts of the United States take for granted. It is especially hurt by a lack of communication. No single newspaper or radio or television station speaks to more than a tiny part of the lightly populated region. Only Wyoming, a state that lacks a city, has a true statewide newspaper—the *Casper Star-Tribune.* Denver's two dailies concentrate on the metropolitan Front Range. The Salt Lake City papers are only a bit more aware of rural Utah. Taken together, the West has nothing that approaches a *New York Times, Los Angeles Times, Atlanta Constitution,* or *Boston Globe.*

Nor can the West see itself in the national media. *Newsweek, Time,* the *Wall Street Journal,* the *Christian Science Monitor,* typically cover the ten or so Western states with one reporter, usually based in Denver, but sometimes in Dallas or San Francisco. They're almost always competent, but they're also invariably on their way to somewhere else in one to three years.

When the boom came, then, there was no way for the West to talk to itself. Each area was left alone to face national and global interests that were cohesive and had a clear sense of direction. Even if the West had had a regional medium of communication, it would have been handicapped, for it lacks two other institutions. The first is a university—a Harvard or Berkeley or Stanford—that could talk authoritatively about Western issues. Instead, the University of Utah, the University of Colorado, the University of Wyoming, and their fellows look outward, competing with the nation's other large schools for grants and recognition based on national and international academic standards. The University of Colorado provides an excellent recent example: it has spent much time and money attempting to attract the Superconducting Super Collider to Colorado. If the university succeeds, it will increase cash flow, but make no other difference.

Original ideas on the West's water, grazing, energy, economics, wildlife, and land management almost always come from outside colleges and universities—from Allan Savory's Holistic Resource Management Center, from Amory Lovins's Rocky Mountain Institute, from the Greater Yellowstone Coalition. There are outstanding individual exceptions within all the institutions of higher learning, but only the University of Colorado's Law School stands out as consistently interested in Western issues.

This lack of an authoritative, regional institution has major implications. When forest fires hit the West in the summer of 1988, there was no Western academic center to which the media could turn for answers. When other issues arise—dams or grizzlies or timber management or elk infestation of Yellowstone—there is no academic home at which issues can be discussed and no widely circulated newspaper to communicate that discussion. The lack of a firmly grounded regional sense reaches from top to bottom. The West's many schools of education—part of a closed loop that sends young people back to teach in the system they graduated from—do not produce teachers or curricula that have a sense of place. At most, local schools in rural communities have their kids memorize the state's counties and learn a smattering of local history.

It has remained for outsiders—for Outward Bound, the National Outdoor Leadership School in Wyoming, the Teton Science School near Yellowstone, prep schools such as the Colorado Rocky Mountain School, all catering largely to urban youngsters—to design education rooted in the West. Local rural Western school districts act as if they were in Ohio when it comes to adopting textbooks and curricula.

The rural West is missing one last social element that much of America takes for granted: a citizen reform movement, a.k.a. "do-gooders." The Northeast early on developed a movement against child labor and unhealthful housing and labor practices. The South more recently had the civil rights movement to bring it into modern times, with the help of the national media and a few courageous regional papers. But citizen reform groups and accompanying media are missing in the West. As a result, when the boom hove onto the horizon, most small communities had to cope without the help of questioning, critical citizens. It is difficult enough for a community to deal with threats if there is diversity and discussion; without them, it is hopeless.

The West did have a fledgling reform movement. Almost every community had at least a few environmentalists, and some had local groups. But grassroots environmentalists in the West were then focused on wilderness and wildlife. Often environmentalists were new to the region, or at least new to their small towns, as part of the influx of the 1970s, and were unable to understand the economic and social issues. In addition, the boom seemed so massive and so irresistible, so eternal, that neither local nor national environmentalists were thinking of the big picture. They were trying to save only pockets of land and clean air here and there.

The lack of these three forces—a communications medium, a major Western university, and a strong citizen reform movement—sealed the fate of the rural West. When the boom came, the region's institutions proved incapable of understanding it or of standing up to it.

CHAPTER TEN

Discouraging Words in Montana

Jim Robbins

APPROXIMATELY ONE century ago, in the wake of the forced passing of the bison and Indians, the cattle industry was established on the northern plains of Montana. At the heart of this vast country lies Miles City, a community of ten thousand that has spent one hundred years living and breathing ranching. Today Miles City and its region are experiencing traumatic change as economic and other forces shove the family ranch off the Western stage. The scene is an American archetype. A couple of hundred head of bawling red-and-white cattle half-gallop across the yellow center line of an abandoned highway, trampling clumps of sagebrush and range grass grown through cracks in the broken asphalt. Three shouting cowboys on horseback, leather chaps flapping against their legs, push the animals down the two-lane. A bullwhip whirs through the air and cracks with authority at the end of its arc.

Ray Sprandel, general manager of the 100,000-acre Diamond Ring Ranch just east of Miles City, Montana, surveys the scene through aviator glasses, a $200 custom-made cowboy hat on his silver-gray head. He nods toward the horizon. "It's about twenty-three miles from here to the other side of the ranch," he says matter-of-factly. "Just about everything you can see from here is Diamond Ring."

When the blizzard of 1886/1887 swept through the northern plains country and killed cattle by the thousands, it forced an infant livestock industry to rethink and restructure. The big absentee-owned corporate ranches fell victim to the weather, and the realization came that smaller, family-size units were the kind that would survive. Now, a century later, the dark clouds of economics have gathered over the industry, again forcing change in the way business is being done. This blizzard, however, is reversing the trend established a century ago. The family ranch is being pushed aside by economic realities. Some people blame a changing world; others blame a refusal by ranchers to adapt. Whatever the case, people are migrating out of ranch country, and the land is either not being utilized or it is concentrating into fewer hands.

The severe drought of 1988 exacerbated the situation, and many ranchers, including those on the parched earth near Miles City, are liquidating their herds. The primary problem is that the ranch economy has twisted out of its usual proportion, and overhead costs have risen at a much faster pace than the price of beef. Cattle and sheep can simply no longer pay for the land and interest. The past ten years, full of drought and a market that seemed to have no bottom, have been bad ones. As a consequence, there's little new blood in ranching. "The only way to get into ranching," said one rancher, "is to marry it or inherit it."

If they're not bought by corporations or wealthy individuals, family ranches are being used for other, more profitable ventures. Some ranches are dug up for coal, covered over by subdivisions, or leased as hunting preserves or dude ranches. In many cases the land is not being used to full capacity. Cowboys still gallop across the Western range, like these three punching cattle on the 100,000-acre Diamond Ring ranch near Miles City, but they're far fewer in number, and usually they are working for someone else.

In 1940 there were 44,000 farms and ranches in Montana, averaging about 1,350 acres in size. By last year that number had dwindled to 23,600 farms and ranches averaging nearly 2,600 acres each, a pattern repeated across the West. The family rancher, the backbone of the ideal of Jeffersonian democracy and the subculture that spawned the elemental notions and myths of freedom, independence, brutality, and grit, is riding into the sunset.

"If we lose this round we're going to lose the family farm structure," said Helen Waller, a farmer and rancher near Circle, Montana, and chairman of the National Save The Family Farm Coalition. "Land is being turned over to a few companies. We've gone from an owner/operator to an owner/peasant structure, and that's wrong. The owner needs to live on the land."

Miles City, a town of around ten thousand, came into being in the 1880s just before the era of the open range. Placed at the heart of ranch country, surrounded by the fecund range grasses of the northern plains, it is one of the last of the true Western cowtowns. The muddy Tongue River empties into the Yellowstone on the edge of town. A canopy of tall cottonwood trees gives Miles City the feeling of an oasis on the treeless plains. It is the seat of Custer County, a rambling chunk of almost thirty-eight hundred square miles with a population of thirteen thousand.

It's difficult to comprehend just how big this country is, or, to put it differently, how tiny other places are. Rancher Julian Terrett, talking about a recent trip to New York City, says, "The island of Manhattan is about thirty-six square miles. That's about the same size as my ranch. Well, actually my ranch is about forty square miles. I could never understand why they put so many people and buildings in a place so small."

The wooden sidewalks and muddy, rutted main streets of the once-robust cowtown are long gone, replaced with pavement and concrete. But it's still the kind of burg where you expect to see Glenn Ford or Randolph Scott walk out of a store on Main Street in a Stetson and sheepskin coat and throw a roll of barbed wire in the back of a pickup truck. In the lounge of the Olive Hotel on Main Street recently, during a ram sale that drew sheepmen from around the region, numerous white-straw cowboy hats seemed to float above the bar in the dimly lit atmosphere. A faded poster in a saddlery window advertised tapes by lantern-jawed Paul Ledoux, the Singing Bronc Rider, for five dollars. Horse trailers, with the long, straight tails of two roans hanging out the back, often stood guard in front of the neon lights of the Log Cabin and Range Rider bars. The peculiar Western culture, while not thriving, survives.

Miles City is the center of the universe for the hundreds of ranch and farm families scattered across the big country fifty or one hundred miles away. But because there are fewer ranchers, stores on Main Street that serviced the livestock industry are disappearing one at a time, blinking out like the neon tubes in the sign at the Bison Bar. In their stead are jobs at K-Mart, Wendy's, and Motel 6, businesses that cater to tourists on Interstate 90. The change shows up in numerous ways. "It used to be that one in five men you'd see had a cowboy hat," says Bob Barthelmess, former rancher and now curator of the Range Riders Museum in Miles City. "Now you're lucky if you see one in fifty."

When Lewis and Clark traveled through this country in 1805 on their way to the Pacific, it was home to immense herds of bison, and to the Indians who lived off the bison. For several decades it appeared that whites would use the plains—the Great American Desert—only as a passageway to Oregon. But the discovery of gold in Western Montana Territory in the 1860s brought mines and a demand for Western beef to the region. And although most of eastern Montana had been designated Indian Territory by the Treaty of 1868—a plan that was to allow the Indians to hunt the buffalo "for as long as the grass is green and the sky is blue"—when gold was discovered in western South Dakota's Black Hills, the center of Indian territory, there were clashes between the Indians and the fortune seekers. Despite the 1876 Indian victory over General George Armstrong Custer at a spot one hundred miles southwest of Miles City, the Indians were the ultimate losers.

Among the forts put up to protect settlers was Fort Keogh, built in 1876, after Custer's last stand. It attracted a ramshackle and seamy assortment of tents, shacks, and open camps that was to become Miles City. The first cattle were brought to Miles City the following year, prompting General Nelson A. Miles, who chose the spot for Fort Keogh, to remark, "When we get rid of the Indians and buffalo, the cattle and sheep will fill this country." They got rid of the Indians in eastern Montana in June 1881. People in Miles City gathered to watch as sixteen hundred Sioux under Chief Rain-in-the-Face were loaded onto government steamers bound for a reservation in Dakota. Preparing for their move, the Indians had camped along the river. A witness wrote, "For two days and nights, the Indians and, more especially, the squaws kept up their dismal howlings on taking farewell of their beloved home and hunting grounds."

Bison were to follow. As the shaggy, lumbering creature disappeared elsewhere, many buffalo hunters followed the remainder to their northern range. The last phase of the slaughter began here near Miles City, and the "harvest" of the bison followed past patterns. Thousands of the docile animals were killed in a matter of months. Hides were stacked like cordwood on the prairie in preparation for shipping. Carcasses were left for predators. In 1882, 200,000 hides were shipped. About 50,000 were shipped in 1883. In 1884, the last year hides were shipped out of Miles City, there were only 300. Hides went out by railroad, the arrival of which in 1881 had sealed the fate of the bison and Indians by assuring access to the East for the burgeoning cattle industry. It was the era of the open range; the federal government allowed the ranchers to use the public domain for grazing and, under the Homestead Act, to claim what land they wanted for their homes.

The Terrett Ranch, owned by Julian Terrett and his family, is some twenty thousand acres, roughly thirty square miles. Eroded hills rise up like islands from the oceans of prairie grass. Rolling hills are carpeted with pine forest along Beaver Creek, a tributary of the Tongue. In this dry country, people are still identified by the creek they live along. Rock outcroppings of subtle shades of red and pink break to the surface on hillsides here and there. The gravel road that winds through the hills to the white Terrett house is made of this rock and resembles a pink ribbon laid gently over the hills. On one side of the house lie rich, verdant alfalfa fields. Julian's grandfather, W. W. Terrett, came to the Tongue in 1881, during the era of the open range. This land, some sixty miles south of Miles City, appealed to him, and for several hundred dollars he bought out a trapper living on the land.

Back then, cattle belonging to a number of owners were turned out onto the range to run wild. Calves were gathered in the spring for branding and for sale in the fall. W. W. Terrett was a member of the Pumpkin Creek pool of ranchers, who lived along Pumpkin Creek, a large, year-round tributary of the Tongue. Come spring, after the cattle had calved, cowboys in the pool would ride out to gather up the stock. They would be joined by "reps," or representatives of different ranches outside the pool, who would cut out any of their livestock that had strayed into the Pumpkin Creek country and drive them home. The spring roundup was for branding, and the brand of each ranch was seared into the hide of the new calves.

One of the unwritten rules of the ranching industry was respect for the brand. "It was customary," says Julian Terrett, "that if you picked up somebody's cattle a long way off, you shipped them to slaughter and sent the money to the owner." While the open range is gone, some customs important to survival continue, although as ranches pass into the hands of absentee owners or become coal mines, there has been a further breaking down of the social structure.

By 1886 most of the land in eastern Montana was being ranched by out-of-state corporations. Investors were drunk with the promise of large profits from the open range, and capital from Chicago, Boston, New York, and London poured into Montana and Wyoming. Control of the commons was a free-for-all, and the well-heeled, well-connected cattlemen were ruthless, driving the small operators off the public domain land through the use of force. In Miles City and elsewhere, powerful cattlemen formed vigilante groups with the stated goal of clearing rustlers out of the country, but also keeping away small ranchers who dared claim their portion of the open range. Granville Stuart, a formidable rancher from central Montana, headed a group that came to be known as "Stuart's Stranglers." They left as many as two dozen "rustlers" swaying in the trees, often with a sign attached to their clothing as a warning to others.

By the mid-1880s the boom had gotten out of hand; there were too many cattle for the grass to support. Though the cattlemen had cleared the range of anything that might threaten a cow, they couldn't control the weather. The blizzard of 1886/1887 is legendary. Thousands upon thousands of cattle died. Some places lost 95 percent of the herd. The storm changed the infant industry. Ranchers realized that turning cattle out into the wilds and rounding them up in the fall wouldn't work during a bad winter. Cattle needed to be fenced so they could be fed during bad winters. Crops such as alfalfa or corn were needed to feed cattle during mean seasons. A balanced operation—part ranch, part irrigated farm—was needed. In response to this pressure from the land and climate, tracts of open range were slowly carved into smaller ranches. The out-of-state corporations began dropping out. The cattle baron was becoming an anachronism.

Each baron was replaced by scores of family ranches. The order and cohesion the baron had enforced through ownership of huge tracts of land and

Mike McClure

employment of many people were now achieved through custom and cooperation: the pooling of cattle, respect for brands, and the sharing of equipment
and labor. A way of life grew up around family ranching: small towns, rural
schools, supportive local politics, and businesses catering to the cattle trade,
and—over it all—the tradition of independence.

That nearly century-old economy and way of life has had its ups and
downs—including dust storms and depression—but in many ways the present
period is worse than anything in the past. These bad, perhaps fatal, times were
ushered in by a boom. During the 1970s, when land and cattle prices were
rising, many ranchers felt the boom was permanent. Urged on by the banker,
they borrowed money—lots of it, at double-digit interest rates on the inflated
value of their land—to buy adjoining property. They bought new machinery,
expanded herds.

Then in the 1980s a slump hit the industry like an electric cattle prod.
Cattle prices dropped to as low as fifty cents a pound—a record low. Land
prices plummeted. Ranchers who had borrowed heavily with the inflated value
of their land as collateral could not make payments to the bank. Drought
occurred several years in a row, and grasshoppers struck much of eastern
Montana, shriveling the gama and needle-and-thread grasses that fatten

cattle. People were forced to sell off their breeding herds to stay alive. Record numbers of ranchers couldn't meet their payments and went out of business. The ones that survived were the family-owned ranches, like the Terretts', with their land paid for and their practices sound, or the large ranches owned by corporations and wealthy individuals. The 1980s saw not just another slump in a cyclical market; it was a pivotal period that shook out many small operators. "There's a fundamental restructuring of agriculture going on," said Keith Kelly, director of Montana's Department of Agriculture.

One ranch that has weathered the storm is the Diamond Ring, whose foreman is Ray Sprandel. (It's owned by Dan Brutger, a wealthy Minnesota businessman.) Sprandel, a lean man, takes care of the ranch as if he owned it, often getting up at 3 A.M. to do the books, beginning outside work at first light. The price of this, he says, was his first marriage. Now he's trying to cut back some on his work.

Sprandel was raised on a dairy farm near Miles City, a 400-acre parcel of land his grandfather came from Germany to homestead. He grew up working on ranches in the area, and later bought a farm on the outskirts of Miles City to raise sugar beets and corn. A hailstorm just before harvest one year cost him $80,000 and the farm.

After working for a couple of other ranches, Sprandel took the job with Brutger. It's one of the better ranch jobs around. Sprandel earns $40,000 a year, plus a home, a beef, and fringe benefits. His boss often flies to Miles City in his Citation jet to pick up Sprandel and take him to another Brutger property near Livingston, Montana. They've also gone fishing in Ontario. "It's a different kind of ranching," Sprandel says.

Good ranch land in the Miles City area now sells for $35 to $70 an acre, down from $130 to $140 an acre in the 1970s boom. Brutger paid $90 an acre for the majority of his property, $140 for another spread, and in one year paid $660,000 in interest. "There's no way to make that kind of money running cattle," Sprandel said. While the economics of ranching make life tough even for outfits like the Diamond Ring, especially with the change in the tax law that does away with tax shelters, they play hell with the small-scale rancher. Sprandel knows how tough it is for the average rancher to make it pay. "I get three or four calls a week from people who are looking for a job," Sprandel says. "Two of my neighbors who have lost their ranches are working for me now."

New family ranches are as rare as two-headed calves. Lending institutions can't or won't lend a young rancher—now a contradiction in terms—the money he would need to buy a ranch. To put together an outfit, says Keith Kelly, a rancher needs a 500-cow breeding herd—the mother cows kept to raise the calves sold to market. At $600 per cow, that's $300,000. He would also need at least ten thousand acres at, let's say, $50 per acre. That's another $500,000. A pickup truck, a tractor, and odds and ends add another

$150,000. Roughly $1 million to start a ranch. Annual interest payments at 10 percent would be around $100,000. Yearly operating costs—gas, oil, feed, and the like—are another $62,000. On the other side of the ledger, annual gross income based on calf prices of the last ten years or so would be $110,000 to $120,000. The numbers just don't work out. "We're frozen in time," says Kelly. "We've flushed the bottom end out, the young people. And the older ranchers can't sell out. There's no transition." The average age of a rancher in Montana is fifty-one.

Bob Barthelmess is a big man, his body tired and sore from a lifetime of ranch work riding a horse behind a herd of cattle, building fences, and throwing hay over the side of a pickup to feed cattle. Comfort, he says, is the reason he wears running shoes these days instead of a pair of leather Western-style boots. A thick slab of foam lines the back of his wooden rocking chair. He still wears a cowboy hat, even in his new job as curator of the Range Riders Museum, a jammed-to-the-rafters museum stuffed with chaps, spurs, saddles, photographs, and other paraphernalia from the open range days near Miles City. And he still works rancher's hours, getting to the museum at first light and staying until the visitors stop coming.

Barthelmess, a third-generation resident, flicks on the light in the museum's Pioneer Hall. Hundreds of black-and-white portrait photographs of residents who settled and developed the ranch country around Miles City are hung on the wall. Many resemble old publicity stills of Gene Autry and Sky King. In a black metal tube attached to each photo is a scroll with a history of the person. Miles City is a town very much aware—and proud—of its past.

As an announcer's voice at a team roping event in a small arena across the street echoes in the distance, Barthelmess explains that he recently ended a lifetime of ranching. But not by choice. The ranch he was leasing was broken up by the owner and sold to neighboring ranches. It just wasn't big enough to make enough money to satisfy the owners, Barthelmess says. It's part of the trend toward bigger ranches and fewer ranches. "If the old-timers that have been dead for twenty years ever came back," he says, "they'd have a fit the way people are doing things."

Barthelmess is particularly displeased with the crumbling of relationships between neighbors. "There's one man who came from the East with a 'don't trust anyone' position," Barthelmess said. "Hunting season came, and he dragged big rocks across the road. He closed the road to anyone, whether they're hunters or people who've come to fight a prairie fire on his land. You can't do that here," where a prairie fire can destroy a season's worth of grasses.

Family ranchers are involved in the community, Barthelmess believes, unlike the corporate ranchers. "These big outfits don't sit on your school boards," he said. "They buy their supplies wholesale in Texas or Oklahoma and don't help the local economy." As a result, stores and implement dealers close their doors, and the labor pool drifts away. Towns like Billings end up with the

John Moore

Rodeo at Miles City, Montana

trade. "The ones that stay," said Keith Kelly, "are going to have to drive 140 miles to buy anything."

The economies of scale favor the big outfits that can buy in big lots. And the profit margin on cattle is so small that it takes a large number of animals to bring in any kind of profit. Julian Terrett says, "I remember when one hundred head of cows was a pretty good living," he says. "Now a family can't live on one

LIFE WITHOUT FANCINESS: GETTING BY ON THE PLAINS

It has never been as easy to find a comfortable job in the Rocky Mountain West as in the more settled regions of the country. But there has always been a stream of migrants leaving the coasts and agricultural heartlands of America for the rugged beauty of the West. And despite the return stream of Westerners seeking the high-brow culture and education, or high salaries of the more settled regions, there have always been Westerners whom hardship could not displace.

For those individuals, it was better to get by in the West than to get ahead somewhere else. Henry David Thoreau expressed the idea in *Walden,* a book written during a 2-year retreat from the commerce of the city. He compared the jobs of those living "lives of quiet desperation" to making and selling baskets: ". . . instead of studying how to make it worth men's while to buy my baskets, I studied rather how to avoid the necessity of selling them," he wrote. Lloyd Oswood has taken his advice.

When the thermometer drops to 35 degrees below zero and winds whip off the Sweetgrass Hills to sift snow through the cracks of his homestead shack near the Canadian border, Lloyd Oswood turns up the fuel oil burner in his converted woodstove. "It's not the best goddamn thing," he said as he took another sip of Milwaukee's Best. "It's the same as the Pilgrims had."

When the electricity was out during one winter storm, Oswood's shack filled with neighbors cooking steaks on the old stove, which also has propane burners for cooking. "Ain't got no fanciness," Oswood said. "People don't need that fanciness."

Oswood's jeans were shiny black above the knees, where he wiped his hands on them. He had a beer in one hand and a cigarette in the other, though he insists he never inhales. A Zane Grey paperback, *Wanderer of the Wasteland,* was lying open, face down, on the wooden kitchen table. The mattress on the bed alongside the wall was water-stained, topped with faded covers. "This is my mother's homestead shack," Oswood said. "I haven't gone up to the split-level stuff, have I? No, I haven't. No, I haven't."

With the exception of a 5-year hitch in the army during World War II, Oswood has spent 72 years in the foothills of the Sweetgrass Hills twenty miles from the paved road near Chester, Montana. His father came to the United States from Bergen, Norway, homesteading the small ranch along Corral Creek in 1912, when promises of easy living on the prairie drew many settlers to Montana. The promises held out as long as the rains. But since the 1920s, it has taken more than a few hundred acres of grassland to make it in Montana. Still, Oswood has held on.

He worked odd jobs until his father died. Then he ran a few cattle to support his needs. Now he leases his land. "A little place like that you can't run over fifty or sixty cattle,"

Oswood said. "You can't make any money, and you sure as hell can lose." His entire herd died during one winter storm. "I just hauled 'em into the nonprofit pile," he said. "There's no use crying about the damn things. You can't bring 'em back to life."

There's no power on the place other than the generator Oswood bought a year ago to run a few electric lights. "Expensive son-of-a-gun," he said. "And a lot of work. You've got to pack gasoline to it." Food and beer are stored in the dirt cellar beneath the house. The food's in cans, or "airtights." "Well, if they aren't airtight, you got damn trouble," he explained.

Along one wall of the entryway to the house are a washpail and a "stomper," an upside-down metal funnel on a wooden handle. On infrequent washdays Oswood fills the pail with water and a little cold-water soap and agitates his snap-button cowboy shirts and jeans with the stomper. He has taken his clothes to the laundromat a few times. "But, I

Bert Lindler

Lloyd Oswood

tell you what," he said, "a laundromat is damn tough on clothes."

In the rocks above the house are three rattlesnake dens. When the snakes need thinning in the fall, Oswood heads to the dens with a stick. He flips a few out, hits them with the stick to injure their feelings, and then steps on their heads with his boot heel. "You got to be kind of damn fast on your feet," he said. "I don't do it by myself now."

Once he skinned a snake right after he killed it and stretched its skin over the cantle of his saddle, where it remains today. Rattlesnakes have got natural glue if you skin them right away, he said. Oswood has never been bit. "A rattlesnake isn't so bad," he said. "They don't go for you. They go away from you, don't they?" Someone once suggested he dynamite the dens. "They stay up on the hill," he protested. "They don't bother anybody. Why eliminate everything?"

Oswood used to spend a lot of time in the saddle. "I've been stacked up, walked on, and kicked on," he said. But no matter what the circumstance, he wanted his horses to stay with him. When a horse would run off, he would catch it, wrap a rope around its front foot, and tie the rope to the saddlehorn, flipping the horse on its side. After the horse had a chance to learn its lesson, Oswood would let it get up.

In recent years Oswood has spent more time in the hospital than in the saddle. Last winter he was treated for a bad case of the water belly. That, he explained, is cow country talk for a prostate operation. The nurses could make his hospital bed bend up and down like a bucking bronc, but still he couldn't wait to get back to the faded covers of his bed in the Sweetgrass Hills. "I think if you're not sick, you've got everything," he said.

"I don't see why people weep and wail and cry the blues, because they got everything," Oswood said. "People ain't got it too bad. They're eating three squares and buying drinks. I think people is just too damn fancy. I can't see all this stuff. Air-conditioning. If it's too hot, roll the window down. If it's too cold, roll the window up."

In the evenings Oswood enjoys going to the Lamplighter Bar, where he dances with the ladies and whistles with the band. When he accompanied me to my car as I was leaving, Oswood opened the door of his pickup and turned on the radio. Soon he was accompanying the band, his whistling as pure and sweet as the chirping of a bird. "Some days you're up," he told me. "Some days you're down. Some day you're going to be deep in the ground. No use crying."

Bert Lindler

---

hundred head. If a family of four wants to have a decent standard of living, four hundred head is minimal. Absolute minimum." But that's about the limit; getting any larger would be too much for one family to handle, and they can't afford a hired man.

Not everyone thinks the high failure rate of ranches is beyond the control of the rancher. E.O. "Nibs" Allen, a 79-year-old rancher near Volberg, Montana, south of Miles City, recently sold most of a ranch he spent a lifetime building with blood and sweat equity for several million dollars. A bank director and sun-to-sun worker, he believes that if a rancher looks for a deal he can work into, he can still win. "The people that tend to business and manage, they're going to make it," the weathered rancher said over a procession of cups of coffee at his home. "Those people who have to have new cars and play with racehorses, they're going to have a tough time."

Another man who doesn't believe the downward spiral is inevitable is Allan Savory, father of the controversial rotation-grazing approach to ranching. "They're leaving the land because of poor management, but it doesn't need to be that way," he says. "The condition of the land is declining. So input costs (for example, supplementary feed) increase. And the stocking rate goes down, and the capitalization costs are spread over fewer and fewer animals." To survive, he says, ranch families must "plan in detail what they want from their land." Integral to that planning, Savory says, is the use of cattle as tools to achieve their goals. Cattle must not be seen simply as meat machines, he insists. "American ranchers should not be going out of business," he says. "The prices they receive are some of the best in the world, and the input costs are some of the lowest. The Amish are not leaving the land because they think more holistically."

One of the ways ranchers are trying to get out from under the banker is by using the land for things other than raising cattle. Bob Barthelmess's son has forsaken ranching for outfitting hunters on leased acreage. A Hamilton, Montana, man has taken the idea further and proposed that ranchers in a large area just north of Miles City, known as the "Big Open," give up ranching altogether. By selling off livestock, tearing down fences, and introducing bison, antelope, and deer, ranchers could create a 10,000-square-mile wildlife preserve similar to Africa's great Serengeti. Ranchers would profit from hunting fees. The idea has not gone over well, but some are listening.

Such an idea seems radical to a world dominated by cattle, but the countryside around Miles City has been home in the past to other ways of life. For a while it ranked among the world's horse capitals. Miles City's moderate altitude produced horses with strong limbs. The grass was rich and diseases were rare in the cool climes. It was, according to some, superior to the bluegrass country of Kentucky. But the style was different. The horses on the plains were raised on large ranches, and they weren't all raised to ride. The last of the horse ranches, the CBC, raised them for meat. Tens of thousands of CBC horses grazed millions of acres between the Yellowstone and Missouri rivers, a country bigger than many states.

A vestige of Miles City's era as horse capital is the Bucking Horse Sale. Each May, rodeo stock buyers travel to Miles City to watch a rite of passage as young men from the area climb on bucking and snorting animals, letting the buyers see what the horses are made of. The Bucking Horse Sale is Miles City's biggest annual event, a boisterous affair, when bars do a land-office trade and the spirit of the Wild West rides again.

A less compatible use of the land was that of the homesteaders, or honyockers: immigrants lured to the region just after the turn of the century by the railroad's promises of free land in a western Eden. Their main tool, barbed wire, was a cheap, easy way to fence cattle out of 160-acre homesteads, which were later increased to 320 and then to a still-insufficient 640 acres. Conflicts arose with both large and small ranchers. With the exception of bottom land, the northern plains didn't respond well to the honyocker's plow and seed. Drought was periodic in the teens and twenties, and the wind was constant. One by one the homesteaders dried up and blew away, just like the soil they had turned over.

Cattlemen also made use of the Homestead Act, but not to farm. They and their hired hands filed on the land around springs. He who controlled water, controlled land in that arid region, and "homesteads" helped cement the ranchers' hold on the country.

When the Great Depression came in the 1930s, it dealt a final blow to those who had managed to cling to the land. It also dealt a blow to many ranchers. Dust devils would swirl across the landscape, carrying dust from barren ground into the sky and giving sunlight an eerie, brownish cast. Flourlike dust blew into drifts several feet high, and blew through doors and windows, coating furniture and inhabitants. "During the thirties was the only time I saw Dad cry," recalls Barthelmess.

The rains came in 1938 and brought prosperity back to eastern Montana, a prosperity that was to last through the war. For the most part, it came too late for the homesteaders. With their disappearance and the appearance of better roads and faster automobiles, many little towns were abandoned. Ranchers began bypassing the smaller towns, going to the larger ones, especially Miles City, for supplies. Children began taking buses into modern, central schools, rather than relying on one-room schoolhouses. Empty buildings blew down, or were pulled apart for their lumber, or burned down. Some of the buildings have weathered the years in places like Powderville and stand like memorials on the plains. In some towns a family or two may still be there, living among the abandoned buildings.

Depopulation continues. While Miles City's population has remained stable, smaller towns decline. Carter County, in Montana's southeastern corner, was the state's top sheep-producing county last year but is among many declining counties. In 1930 it had 4,136 people; the 1980 census found only 1,799. Forty-one of the state's fifty-six counties lost population during the 1960s, and twenty-one mostly rural counties lost people during the 1970s—a decade in which many other rural areas experienced a "rural renaissance," a gain of population and business.

Just as there's no sure way to forecast the weather or markets, there's no sure way to tell what the future of this lonely and rigorous land, and those who live here, will be. Keith Kelly says that the "psychic income" that has sustained many ranchers through lean times is no longer enough. "It's the old 'love of the land that surpasses mistresses and wives' line," Kelly says. "Younger people are saying, 'Baloney, I need to make money,' or 'I want to live near a city, where I can go to the movies,' or whatever."

For the rancher whose family for generations has grown up on and been shaped by the land, the prospect of being the last of a breed, of watching neighbors leave, of seeing homes stand empty, and of seeing your way of life as no longer relevant, is eerie and unsettling. And damned unfair.

"I don't know," said Julian Terrett, doffing his cowboy hat with thick, reddened fingers. "There may come a day when they don't need this land for cattle anymore. They'll figure out a way to grow them inside or something. I don't know what will happen to the land then."

CHAPTER ELEVEN

A Nomad with Deep Roots

C. L. Rawlins

In arid country, resources are never stable from one year to the next. A stray thunderstorm may make a temporary oasis of green, while only a few miles off the land remains parched and bare. To survive in drought, therefore, any species must adopt one of two stratagems: to allow for the worst and dig in; to open itself to the world and move.

Bruce Chatwin, *The Songlines*

WIND SLAPS the brush, with the soft weight of a spring rainstorm pushing it, raising the odor of sage and the sweet-sharp aroma of cottonwoods in bud. Inside, I waterproof my boots and add an extra sweater to the pack. Rain in the valley will be snow or hail up under the divide, and sixteen miles in wet boots can put anyone in a bad state of mind. The talk on the radio about the mood of Wall Street and the temper of the Federal Reserve doesn't make the best sense to a person heading into the mountains, knowing that in Wyoming June rain is cold, and the wind makes it colder, that June snow is wet and sticks to everything.

Living and working outside puts you in two worlds. One is the world of immediate consequences, in which your eyes and nerve endings tell you the same thing that a coyote's senses tell him: it's going to rain. The other is a constructed world, made of language: a world of culture where meanings are shared and voices come over the radio. In this second world the economy has become as real as rain. To some of us, more real. Like Cyndi Lauper sang, and made a lot of it, "Money changes everything."

Living in Palo Alto on the north marches of Silicon Valley, I felt exposed to the lurching progress of the military-industrial high-tech beast. At rush hour the population of the Bayshore Freeway between any two exits was higher than that of Sublette County, Wyoming, from where I'd come to study at Stanford for a year.

The weather during that period in Palo Alto was unassertive. Nobody noticed it much, unless they had plans for a ball game or the beach. The radio smugly delivered endless details of stock splits and financial drama involving high-tech companies, fitting in with the fact that a tract house with a nice little atrium full of ferns and no windows on the street cost more than a small Wyoming ranch. The whole time I was there, I felt vulnerable to a thousand decisions made out of sight and earshot, any one of which could wreck me on the freeway, put poison in my food, or drive me howling into poverty. People, even within the charmed circle at Stanford, seemed scared. One thought circled my feelings from grim amusement to horror: No wonder they're frightened; they believe all this.

In the world of weather, where your feet actually hit the dirt when you walk, it all seems a bad dream. You shake your head, look at the clouds, smell the breeze, hear a magpie squawk. Maybe it is a bad dream, but there are a lot of people dreaming it up. Almost everyone owes money, talks money, worries about money, loves money, marries money, lives for money. Where does this balloonful of dreams we call The Economy come back to earth?

In the arid West, open water is a rarity in vast, dry space. Forage is seasonal and varies in abundance from year to year. Large grazers like buffalo and elk, and browsers like pronghorn and mule deer, need the ability to move long distances quickly. To be restricted to one place is to die of starvation or thirst. The people of the coldest, driest portions of the West—Ute, Shoshone, Paiute, Navajo, Apache—were moving peoples because they had to be. The Great Basin Shoshone followed seasonal resources: camas roots in spring, piñon nuts in the fall, hunting rabbits, antelope, and birds. Scarcity spread them out during the growing season into single-family bands.

The piñon nut harvest brought them to the best groves to harvest and store, each family having by custom an area suited to its ability to gather the cones before they fell. In winter relatives camped within visiting distance, living on their stored food, sharing it. In spring they often shared starvation.

According to anthropologist Julian Steward, the Shoshone concept of economics and property rights was both simple and functional: "In most parts of the area, natural resources were available to anyone. The seeds gathered by a woman, however, belonged to her because she had done the work of converting a natural resource into something that could be directly consumed. If a man made a bow or built a house, these were his, although prior to making objects of them, the trees he utilized belonged to no one. . . . This principle of property rights was essential to survival." Small wonder the Anglo settlers saw the Shoshone as thieves, while to the Shoshone the settlers seemed insane with greed.

The specialization of farmers in an arid region can be compared to the specialization of perennial plants: grow deep roots, conserve moisture, save up for years of drought. The ethic of settlers in dry country is one of endurance, stoicism, and community, such as the traditional Hopi survived with for more than a few centuries. The deepest settledness in the interior West is probably that of the Pueblos and the agricultural tribes of the lower Colorado, followed by the Spanish-speaking villagers of New Mexico. More recent comers to rootedness would be the Mormon farmers, who dug their first irrigation ditches late in the 1840s. The common element of sedentary culture is irrigation, which was the only way to achieve a dependable food supply while staying put.

The land-loyal nomadism of the Navajo is based on the needs of livestock. A traditional Navajo outfit would move upcountry in the spring as the plants greened at higher elevations. Many families had a home in the mountains and a home in the lower desert, where sheep could browse winterlong. Many Anglo ranchers follow a similar pattern, with grazing in the mountains for summer and lower elevation ranges for winter. Those with irrigable land grow hay for winter feeding and keep their stock at the home ranch in the snowy months. Being herders as well as farmers, they work both sides of the Neolithic revolution, relying once on the horse and now on the pickup to bridge the gap between nomadism and settled life.

The specialization into farmer and nomad created some problems that didn't occur to hunter-gatherers like the desert Shoshone. The two groups had different interests and needed to have different attitudes toward the land. Irrigation, with its ditches engraved along the contour, implies boundaries based on labor. Herding is best conducted with few restraints. The farmer needs repetitive traditions that suit a single place. The nomad needs to be an opportunist: it is dry here, yet it rained much in the northern hills, and there we shall go. Strike the tents.

The farmers must protect fields from animals during the growing season. After the harvest, sheep and goats clear stubble and manure the ground. Such biological facts led to an uneasy accommodation between villager and nomad, along with the desire of each group for the produce of the other: meat and hides in trade for grain and wine. Today the uneasy alliance is kept up between rancher and townie.

The Western heart is split between the instinct of the settler to dig in and tough it out and that of the nomad to move on to greener pastures. The twin impulses were outlined by J. Hector Saint John Crèvecoeur in his *Letters from an American Farmer*, which idealized the settler as the best in American character: hard working, familial, lawful, loyal, cheerful, perhaps even thrifty, brave, clean, and reverent.

The nomad didn't fare as well, living on the fringes of society in a tent or shanty with a litter of brats and dogs. His diet, the meat of wild beasts, disposed him to uncertain temper. He was liverish and lickerish and prone to disappear over the ridgeline at the approach of preacher or bailiff. Crèvecoeur, like most civilized persons since, was quite put out that this brute fancied himself free. In the grip of hunger or desire, the nomad could be a raider of settlements, a coyote among the prairie dogs. Modern nomads in the West, construction boomers, seismic crews, and oilfield hands, are seen by settled people as wolfish and dangerous. They often are.

The new nomads tend to be young, as the forty-niners were, aggressive and rootless. A recent change is that they often arrive with wife and children or soon acquire them in the flush of prosperity, along with a monster truck and a twelve-wide. When the job shuts down, divorce may follow, and the nomadic male roars off mad in the pickup, leaving half a family marooned in a remote little town where poverty equals disgrace.

This is the nomadism of raiders. Unlike hunter-gatherers, who travel to wild food, or herdsmen, who move to fresh grass, the raider heads for easy pickings. The life may involve hard physical work—the riders of Genghis Khan put in a lot of mounted overtime—but confers no loyalty except to the traveling band. One plundered village differs from another only in the degree of fight and the amount of booty. The raider thinks of locales as incidents within a life, equating time and place.

In contrast to boomers are ranch hands who work in the same spot year after year, heading south when the calves are shipped. Some have a near-feudal attachment to one ranch; others are loyal to a certain valley or river basin. Guiding and the seasonal round of Forest Service work have nourished a gentler sort of nomad, writer Ed Abbey for one, who heads for some college town to winter out.

The hunting tribes of the Western plains had a dedication to wide sweeps of country and matched their movement to the buffalo and seasons. No one aspired to own a single, small piece of land. To most the notion was repugnant, since immobility meant starvation, disease, and death. A chief—I recall the anecdote and not his name—was conducted to Washington for a meeting with the president. He was unimpressed with the White House. "Your Great Father," he said, sweeping his hand across the city, "lives in just this one house? Ha! I would live in them all!"

Another group of nomads are the farm workers—Latino and Asian—who spread out for the harvests and then retreat to urban ghettos or families across the border. Where they manage to gain enough foothold for family life, they form communities, often subject to suspicion and harsh treatment from local establishments.

What makes modern nomads different is that their movement is no longer strictly in response to land and climate. The new nomad moves to greener pastures, but the green is dollars. Thus, boomtowns heave up in response to a power-plant job, a pipeline, or a strip mine. The land and existing towns are overwhelmed with the roars of D-9 Cats and new pickups, beer cans, and dust. When the job's done, the horde moves on, leaving a few stragglers and steady types behind to settle in and scratch.

Like the rest of our society, the process of nomadism has come unstuck from the rhythms of the land, which may be one of the reasons it seems so ugly to writers like Wallace Stegner, even when it wears a white collar: "Habits persist. The hard, aggressive, single-minded energy that politicians say made America great is demonstrated every day in resource raids and leveraged takeovers by entrepreneurs; along with that competitive individualism and ruthlessness goes a rejection of any controlling past or tradition. What matters is here, now, the seizable opportunity."

Each successive human try at adaptation to the arid West seems to be overwhelmed by a further wave of invasion: the Indian by the stockman, the stockman by the homesteader, the homesteader by the miner, the miner by the oilman, the oilman by the technocrat. Each boom is an explosion; each bust creates a hungry human vacuum.

The "year-round resort community," so called by real estate sharks, is a rising Western phenomenon. Erstwhile ranching towns, like Jackson, Wyoming, or mining towns, like Park City, Utah, have become "lifestyle" colonies. These towns have a small hard core of longtime residents, a soft core of rich summerhome types, a seasonal flood of tourists, and an unstable, debt-haunted petite bourgeoisie: the stickers, the screwers, the cruisers, and the scratchers. These towns, despite their relative affluence, draw squinty looks from neighboring communities. New Mexico novelist John Nichols, an émigré himself, is particularly scathing in his send-up novel, The Nirvana Blues: "The Chamisa Valley was like a slave market, or a whorehouse. An entirely new breed had taken over the town and its once outlying, now incorporated, communities. Despite its pseudo-hip ecology-conservation rhetoric, when this new breed assessed landscape, all it saw was dollar signs. They rationalized, pretended, lied through their teeth, paid lip service to the Sierra Club, and brought in the backhoes."

These towns, with their pressure-cooker economies, exude a glamor that ranching and mining can't match. The combination of striking scenery and easy money works magic, but the souls of such towns burn uneasily between the lures of settlement and sellout. Transience is as attractive to the transient as it is wearing to the settler. In places like Jackson, I've heard complaints that no one sticks around for long; you make friends and they disappear. After a few seasons, the glow thins out, but land is costly and your labor's cheap. Too many new faces; you're feeling older. Time to find a real home.

This tension often works out as a series of "settlings" in different places. At each stop the ground is staked: a house, a yard, an address, a phone number, church friends or drinking buddies. Each place, it seems at first, will be The Place. But after a while the itch sets in. Co-workers aren't as nice as we thought they were; there's a job open in another state; the neighbors are insane; we're sick of the noise of trucks on the interstate; it snows eight months of the year.

When my father, his brother, and his sisters sold the family farm, it marked the end of a long tie to one place. My great-great-grandparents were Mormon settlers in Cache Valley, Shoshone land in the 1860s when my ancestors left

Clem Rawlins, Sr., and grandson Chip in Lewiston, Utah, 1949

the Salt Lake Valley on their mission-call to take it, plow it, and plant it. They multiplied and prospered. At one point my grandfather had fields of grain, hay, and sugar beets; ranches in Utah and Wyoming; ten thousand cattle and twenty-five thousand sheep. In 1921 he lost everything but the original place when a drop in livestock prices caught him in heavy debt. My grandparents farmed that land until just before he died, but their five children scattered.

My father ran off to Los Angeles, drank whiskey with John Wayne, became an engineer with Lockheed, flew to England during the war. Afterward he came back to Salt Lake City, where he met my mother on a blind date. They moved to Laramie, ran a radio station, and followed the football team, hip flasks, and hot times. I was born, and the business district burned, cutting off radio ads.

We moved on: Vernal and Ogden, Utah, and Albuquerque, where he got into the atom business, and I got a brother and a sister. Then to Tonopah, Nevada, for the building of a test range, and to Las Vegas, where he built the towers and dug the pits for atomic tests, lost his job in a takeover, sold real estate, retired to gardening and breadbaking, and died of a heart attack, riding a bicycle. He hated farming, hated riding after cattle, herding sheep, hated snow and cold of any sort. Or he claimed to hate those things. We always had dogs, cats, and horses, and he spent his happiest hours planting, mowing, and harvesting in a succession of yards.

The radio station woody;
Laramie, 1948

My mother's father was a mining engineer, the son of a Norwegian woman converted to Mormonism and a sailor, who either died at a distance or deserted her. He got his first real job in the rush at Goldfield, Nevada. He married, and the children were born in mining towns. My mother was born in Anaconda and named Helen, perhaps after Helena. Her elder sister was named Montana. They moved where the ground was red, yellow, or green, to places like Sulfurdale, a remote camp near the present junction of I-15 and I-70 in Utah. The kids grew, playing on tailings piles and breathing a rainbow of dust. With four children they finally settled for real. He started an engineering company in Salt Lake City, photographed landscapes, wrote chapbooks of verse for his friends. He outlived his first wife, remarried in his sixties, and died of Parkinson's disease a wealthy man.

My mother graduated from the university, where she was a yearbook beauty, learned to paint in oils, and worked in an ad agency until she met my agricultural-refugee dad. There is a constant thread in this narrative of women following the restless movement of men. Mormon history is almost exclusively one of paternity, yet much of the actual burden of both movement and successive tries at civilization was on the women. If men's history is colorful, like dye, then women's history is surely the fabric.

Since graduating from high school, when I fled Las Vegas for the home valley in Utah to start college, I've been a nomad. In the summers I've gone upcountry to the mountains as a campjack, horse packer, fence builder, range rider and, recently, a hydrologist. Winters I've shrugged through school or holed up in a cabin eating antelope and brown rice or fed cows on a ranch. Having a mixed heritage, I'm regularly torn between the need to dig furrows and the unrest that rises when seasons change. I've lived, if not entirely chosen, a nomadic way, assisted by the lack of land or money, moved by an inaccessible urge.

Like the Shoshone, I range the same places year after year: Cache Valley, the headwaters of the Snake, and the Upper Green. I lack neither a terrible love for the land nor the need for familiarity and community. I do lack the desire to own land, pile up debts, acquire much of anything except what I can use: good books and good tools. It's an old way of life, and it still works, even as money changes everything. Economics, in the long run, is exactly that: a landscape and what works.

CHAPTER TWELVE

The Fate of the Plains

Deborah Epstein Popper and Frank J. Popper, Jr.

The Plains, while less stunning at first sight, last longer, fill the esthetic sense fuller, precede all the rest and make North America's characteristic landscape.

Walt Whitman, 1879, after a trip to California

AT THE CENTER of America, between the Rockies and the tall-grass prairies of the Midwest and South, lies the shortgrass expanse of the Great Plains. The Plains extend over large parts of ten states, are endlessly windswept, nearly treeless and semiarid, and get less than twenty inches of rain a year. Three times white civilization has attempted to settle the arid, windy Plains—a land mass that includes one-fifth of the contiguous United States. Three times the settlement efforts have largely failed. The nation and the region should learn from the failures, including the 1988 drought, and help the land revert to a buffalo commons—to the state the land was in before the coming of the whites.

The country is rolling to flat in the north, flat in the south, and has occasional buttes. It is lightly populated: a dusty town with a gas station, store, and home is sometimes fifty or more unpaved miles from its nearest neighbor, another three-building settlement amid the sagebrush.

San Antonio and Denver are on the east and west edges, respectively, of the Plains, but the largest city actually in the Plains is Lubbock, Texas, with a population of 174,000. The population of the Plains—5.5 million—is less than one-fortieth of the American total—that of Georgia or Indiana—but spread over one-fifth of the contiguous United States. The Great Plains are America's steppes. They have the nation's hottest summers and coldest winters, largest daily and weekly temperature swings, worst hail and locusts and range fires, fiercest droughts and blizzards, and shortest, most perilous, growing season.

The Plains are the land of the Big Sky and the Dust Bowl, one-room schoolhouses and settler homesteads, straight-line interstates and custom combines, prairie dogs and antelope and buffalo. The oceans-of-grass vistas of the Plains offer enormous horizons, billowy clouds, intimations of infinity, and the somber-serene beauty that captivated Whitman.

During America's pioneer days and again during the Great Depression, the Plains were a national concern. But by 1952, in *The Great Frontier,* the Plains' finest historian, Walter Prescott Webb, described them as the least-known, most-fateful part of the United States. That description applies today. We believe that over the next generation the Plains region will lose almost all of its people. Then a new use for the suddenly-empty Plains will emerge, one that is in fact so old that it predates the American presence.

A Remnant American Frontier

In the shape of a tilted leaf half the size of the United States east of the Mississippi, the Plains run from the curling east wall of the Rockies to roughly the ninety-eighth meridian. The eastern Plains consist of four-fifths of the Dakotas, two-thirds of Nebraska and Kansas, and half of Oklahoma and Texas. The west is three-quarters of Montana, half of Wyoming and Colorado, and a third of New Mexico. The entire arid Great Plains—1,100 to 1,500 miles long, 400 to 700 miles wide—form a giant borderland between the mountains and truly arid deserts to the west and the lushly watered prairies to the east.

The Plains were the last part of the nation that whites permanently occupied. Most late-nineteenth-century pioneers wanted to cross the Plains and get farther west. The non-Plains parts of most Plains states were settled long before the Plains; western Montana was a thriving mining and timber area a generation before farmers and ranchers moved into central and eastern Montana. In the settlement of the Plains, waves of farmers and ranchers were tested and often uprooted by the 1880s blizzards, the 1890s drought and financial

North
Dakota

Montana

Rocky

Mountains

98th

Meridian

South
Dakota

Wyoming

Nebraska

Denver ●

Colorado

Kansas

New
Mexico

Oklahoma

●Lubbock

**The
Great
Plains**

Texas

San
Antonio ●

Peggy Robin

panic, the Great Depression (which hit much of the Plains by the early 1920s), the 1930s Dust Bowl, and the smaller 1950s and 1970s droughts. Even today, settlement is thin, tentative, insecure. Large chunks of the contemporary Plains amount to relics of the American frontier.

The Plains are spare and weather whipped. The wind has a speed of ten to twelve steady miles per hour, day and night. Its lowing is more constant than at many seashores. The long winter 60-mile-per-hour blizzards throw up as much sharp black grit as they throw down sharp white snow. Rainfall is more variable on the Plains than anywhere else in the country—an important fact in a region where the timing of two inches of rain can make or break a farmer's year. Many Plains newspapers report rainfall to the hundredth of an inch.

Major rivers often do not flow half the year. Trees are rare away from rivers, irrigation systems, a few national forests, and windbreaks and shelterbelts. The sense of flat empty wind-blown endlessness is a historic Plains preoccupation. Arbor Day, the annual community tree-planting day in the spring, originated the plains parts of Nebraska and Kansas in the 1870s.

Privacy is almost too easily obtained. The visitor learns to recognize the Plains person's characteristic 20-yard stare, and not to take it as rudeness. Teenagers frequently drive forty miles to the nearest school or movie, a hundred to a clothing store or dentist, and still have more than the ordinary adolescent restlessness. Rates of youth suicide, homicide, and accidental death are traditionally high. Motorists and police ignore speed limits on the lightly traveled roads.

There is an urban Plains, primarily in the south, and especially in Texas. The Plains part of Texas has nearly 2.2 million people, almost two-fifths of the region's population, mostly in cities such as Lubbock, Amarillo, and Abilene. Oklahoma and Colorado also have relatively urban, high-growth Plains populations, particularly near Oklahoma City and Denver. The three southern Plains states account for more than half the region's population. But the largest city in the Plains' northern half is Billings, Montana, population 70,000. The Dakotas, Montana, New Mexico, and Wyoming have the smallest Plains populations, ranging from North Dakota's 414,000 to Wyoming's 250,000.

Despite a few urban enclaves, the region remains profoundly rural. Most maps are dotted with towns that have been unoccupied for decades, like Keota, Colorado, or Carlile, Wyoming. Kansas alone has two thousand ghost towns. A stable small town will have one- or perhaps two-story houses on big lots, some lightly grassed or near-bare lawns, many vacant lots and wide dusty streets, and few sidewalks.

Life on the Plains has its compensations. Spring and fall are breathtaking after the rigors of winter and summer. The region offers the nation's finest sunsets, the largest flights of birds, the most spacious skies, the broadest amber waves of grain. The soils are excellent when watered, and air and water pollution nearly absent. The humidity is so low that falling rain may evaporate before it hits the ground, leaving huge watery stripes that hang halfway down from the sky.

Some Plains people feel cut off from and unappreciated by the rest of the country. They consider the Plains a colony, resent urban outsiders, and dislike the way surrounding Denver, Houston, and Minneapolis appear to combine with distant corporations and the federal government to exploit the Plains.

The few national political figures the Plains have produced—for instance, William Jennings Bryan, George Norris, Lyndon Johnson, James Watt—spent much of their early careers attacking Washington, D.C., and the East, and in later life still displayed the prideful, defensive populism distinctive to the Plains.

In many respects the Plains lack a coherent sense of self. No state is entirely in the Plains. No newspaper is the voice of the Plains in the way that, for example, the *Atlanta Constitution* has been the voice of the South. The census does not recognize the Plains as a region; instead it divides the ten Plains states among the Mountain West (Montana, Wyoming, Colorado, New Mexico), the Midwest (the Dakotas, Nebraska, Kansas), and the Southwest (Oklahoma, Texas).

Within Plains states, most political, economic, and intellectual power lies outside the Plains. Only two Plains states have their largest city in the Plains: Billings, Montana, and Casper, Wyoming. Half of Texas is in the Plains, but only seven of its twenty-four congressional seats are. Two-thirds of Kansas is Plains, but only one of its five seats. Only three Plains state capitals are in the Plains—Cheyenne, Wyoming; Bismarck, North Dakota, and Pierre, South Dakota. No Plains state has its flagship state university in the Plains.

The History of a Hinterland

The Plains have long been bypassed. All the major early American explorations went east-west across and often beyond the Plains, rather than north-south within them. The prime pioneer paths—the Oregon, Mormon, and Sante Fe trails—and the Pony Express also traversed the Plains. So did the early railroads; by 1890 five transcontinental lines reached the West Coast, but none connected the northern and southern Plains. Today seven east-west interstates cross the Plains, while a single north-south one, I-25, runs along part of the east edge of the Rockies. (Another small north-south interstate, I-15, goes from Montana's Canadian border to Helena, and then into the Rockies, away from the Plains.) The few tourists in the Plains' magnificent national parks—for instance, Theodore Roosevelt in North Dakota or Carlsbad Caverns in New Mexico—are mainly transcontinental travelers who spend less time and money than the more numerous visitors to national land treasures elsewhere.

With the end of the Civil War came the first large-scale white attempts to settle the Plains. James J. Hill, founder of the continent-spanning Great Northern Railway, sincerely foresaw "little green fields and little white houses and big red barns"—another New England, only more fertile. Between the 1860s and 1890s social and technological innovations encouraged rapid Plains settlement: the 1862 Homestead Act, construction of the railroads, introduction of light steel plows, barbed-wire fences, windmills, dry-land farming techniques, and the beginnings of modern irrigation.

By 1880 the Indians had been defeated, the buffalo had been slaughtered, and the Cattle Kingdom was well established in much of the Plains. Gold, silver, copper, and oil strikes occurred in parts of the region. Between 1880 and 1890 the population of Colorado multiplied by three, that of Kansas by four, that of Texas by six. The boom period after the Civil War marked one of the few times when America thought the Plains would be thickly settled. The early settlers of the 1870s had a few good years of rain, a few bumper harvests. The euphoria did not last; nature and the economy turned cyclically hostile. A sequence of bad blizzard years, beginning in 1885, almost wiped out the cattle industry. Nearly half the stock in Montana died in the first ten weeks of 1887 alone.

By the early 1890s a panic—the era's term for a depression—hit farming, ranching, and mining. Severe drought appeared. For the first time many large convoys of fully loaded wagon trains headed east, leaving some Plains counties in the western Dakotas, central Montana, and western Texas nearly deserted. The Plains had been revealed as the malicious margin of American agriculture.

Another boom-and-bust cycle began in 1899. Wet years returned. The nine rail lines that went cross-country by 1912 competed for traffic and gave settlers discount fares. Pioneers poured in; between 1900 and 1913 Montana's and North Dakota's population quintupled; the southern Plains grew at least as rapidly. The peak year for homesteading was 1912, rather than, as generally assumed, in the late nineteenth century, when the frontier was declared closed.

The boom was topped off by World War I's demand for commodities. The region's farmers and ranchers, realizing their precarious position, overplowed, overplanted, overgrazed, did far too much sodbusting, and ignored conservation or never knew about it. Retribution was rapid. Drought and locusts came to the Dakotas, Montana, and Wyoming in 1919. European farming recovered earlier than expected. The spread of the tractor, the truck, and the combine harvester reduced demands for farm labor, in some Plains counties by a factor of five.

For much of the Plains, the Great Depression began in 1921, eight years before it struck Wall Street. By 1925 Montana had suffered 214 bank failures—more banks than exist in the state today. The average value of all

Montana farm and ranch land dropped by half. Thus the Plains underwent a dozen years of depression before the onset of the Dust Bowl in 1934. The Dust Bowl was the ecological consequence of the too-assertive agriculture of the 1910s. It was nature's signal that the shortgrass and soil were gone.

In the late 1930s the Dust Bowl covered 150,000 Sahel-like square miles of southwestern Kansas, southeastern Colorado, northeastern New Mexico, and the Oklahoma and Texas panhandles—nearly a third of the Plains. Entire counties were again almost depopulated, particularly in Kansas and Colorado. The Dust Bowl kicked up dirt clouds five miles high and large enough to obstruct navigation of planes on the eastern seaboard and of ships three hundred miles out in the Atlantic. It tore the paint off Plains houses and asphyxiated small children. It sent the Okies to California, where they described themselves as "blown-out, tractored-out, and broke." It inspired John Steinbeck's *The Grapes of Wrath* and Dorothea Lange's photography, as well as more radical nativist movements.

The federal government responded effectively. In 1934 it abolished homesteading. In 1935 it established the Soil Conservation Service, which undertook measures such as windbreaks and shelterbelts. Beginning in 1937, the federal government bought up 7.3 million Plains acres of largely abandoned farm holdings (an area bigger than Maryland) and made most of them into national grasslands. After the Dust Bowl, recent Plains history seems anticlimactic. A measure of agricultural prosperity returned during World War II and afterward.

Throughout this period the federal government, building on earlier initiatives, found new ways to intervene. The crop-subsidy programs, experimentally introduced in the 1930s, greatly expanded in the forties and fifties. The dam and irrigation projects accelerated in 1944 with the $6-billion Pick-Sloan plan for the Missouri River, a 100-dam effort aimed primarily at the Plains portion of the watershed. Now many Plains farmers and ranchers could, like their competitors farther west, get federal water at below-market prices. In 1946 the Bureau of Land Management evolved from the 1934-vintage Grazing Service of the Interior Department and continued to offer below-market grazing rates to ranchers in the Plains, particularly in Montana, Wyoming, and New Mexico.

Compared to earlier eras, agriculture was relatively stable. Moreover, the energy boom of the 1970s quintupled prices for the southern Plains oil and natural gas and made it newly profitable to produce coal, oil, and natural gas in the northern Plains.

About two hundred energy boomtowns suddenly sprouted in the Dakotas, Montana, Wyoming, and Colorado; previously quiet places like Gillette, Wyoming, and Colstrip, Montana, became odd crosses between the old Wild West and the new Kuwait. At the same time, agricultural stability was also turning into a boom. Commodity prices were rising rapidly, and Plains farmers and ranchers, forgetting the 1930s, began to chop down windbreaks, to plant fence post to fence post, and to sodbust in the classic late nineteenth-century manner, but on a much larger scale. Conservation no longer seemed to matter. The energy boom was a wonderful bonus. Even the droughts seemed less severe. The land, as Plains people always said in good times, was becoming more "seasonable."

The Coming of the Crisis

The 1980s punctured that illusion. Today, as the 1988 drought illustrated, the pressures are as ominous as they have ever been. Farm, ranch, energy, and mineral economies are in deep depression. Many small towns that had steadily lost population throughout the twentieth century are now emptying and aging at all-time-high rates. Soil erosion is approaching Dust Bowl rates. Water shortages also loom, especially atop the Ogallala aquifer, a giant, nonrenewable source that irrigates more than 11 million Plains acres. Important long-term climatic and technological trends do not look favorable, and government seems unable to react constructively to these trends, much less anticipate them.

The agricultural crisis is more serious on the Plains than in the more publicized cornbelt of the Midwest. By the late 1980s the Plains had become an epicenter of agricultural disaster. The region's farming and ranching had always been less profitable than those of other regions, more vulnerable to water shortages, less able to withstand high costs, more debt oppressed. Most Plains farmers and ranchers have always operated under conditions that their counterparts elsewhere would have found intolerable, and now they are worse. In 1985 the Montana Agriculture Department estimated that almost half of the state's farmers and ranchers would be out of business by 1990. The 1988 drought probably accelerated the process.

The situation is comparable in the energy sector. Oil prices have fallen drastically since 1983. Many oil and natural gas companies have laid off most of their employees. The Plains energy boomtowns have long gone bust. The last federally subsidized synthetic-fuels plant, a coal gasification facility in Beulah, North Dakota, went into receivership in 1985. In the Permian Basin of Texas, seven banks failed between 1983 and 1986, and the Federal Deposit Insurance Corporation became Midland County's third largest employer. In western Oklahoma large comfortable houses sold in 1986 for $15,000.

Collapses reverberate. When local banks fail or are endangered, remaining ones lend more conservatively and charge higher interest. When an agricultural county's farmers and ranchers cannot make a living, neither can its car dealers, druggists, or restaurants. Local public services, never generous, fall off. Schools, roads, law enforcement, and welfare are always expensive in large, lightly populated areas. They are especially expensive because of the Plains tradition of many small local governments. In the late 1970s Oklahoma towns rode the oil boom to leadership in school reform; now a tenth of the state's teachers have lost their jobs, many others have had their salaries frozen, classroom sizes have grown, buses are not repaired, textbooks go unreplaced.

The quality of life declines. Service cutbacks fall hardest on Montana farm laborers, South Dakota Indians, Mexican-Americans along the Rio Grande, migrant workers, and clients of social work and public health agencies across the Plains. Agricultural market towns such as Newell, South Dakota, get smaller, older, poorer; already-modest downtowns become gap-toothed streets of increasingly marginal businesses. Fields are barren and untended, many farmhouses abandoned. Throughout the Plains, entire counties do not have doctors or banks, and more are about to lose them. Hard-pressed farmers have begun selling their water rights to distant cities. If another serious drought occurs, newly arid ex-farms could become the nuclei of a late twentieth-century Dust Bowl.

The long-term outlook for the Plains is frightening. Most climatologists believe the Plains rainfall over the last fifty years has been comparatively stable; when it becomes more variable, droughts will hit harder and more often. The long-standing Plains attempts to seed clouds or otherwise arti-ficially induce rain continue with no result. Water supplies are diminishing throughout the Plains, primarily because of agricultural overuse. Farmland has already been abandoned for lack of water in the Pecos River Valley of New Mexico and between Amarillo and Lubbock in Texas. In 1950 central Kansas had 250 wells that drew on the Ogallala aquifer; today it has more than 3,000. The Kansas portion of the aquifer was fifty-eight feet thick in 1950; today in many places its thickness may be less than six feet.

As parts of the aquifer approach exhaustion within a decade or so, water-hungry farmers, ranchers, energy companies, bankers, localities, and home-owners will be staring down tens of thousands of dry holes, looking for groundwater that is gone forever. Some farmers, firms, and localities are undertaking serious water- and soil-conservation measures, but it may already be too late: large portions of the Plains are eroding fast. Many Plains coun-ties—for example, Gaines in Texas and Crowley and Kiowa in Colorado—appear to be near Dust Bowl conditions. In Gaines County, David Sheridan, an investigator for the federal Council on Environmental Quality (CEQ), reported: "With the wind at your back, you can see a brownish haze hugging the land ahead. Soon it envelops you. The sky is cloudless, but you cannot see the sun. Visibility is diminished to about a quarter of a mile. . . . The sub-stance you see in the air is topsoil—Brownfield fine sand, most likely—blown off fields that are bare and dry because they have been plowed in preparation for planting cotton."

The CEQ has classified the desertification of most of western Texas and eastern New Mexico and parts of Colorado, Kansas, and Oklahoma as "severe." It is termed "moderate" in nearly all the rest of the Plains. The CEQ's lowest classification for desertified land is "slight"; none of the Plains qualifies for that classification.

When a Plains farmer or rancher gives up his land today, agribusiness and other large outside corporations are usually unwilling to buy it, even at bargain prices. Hopes for cashing in on energy resources have dissipated, and nothing has replaced them. In any plausible use, the bulk of Plains land is not competitive. The only people who want it are already on it, and most are increasingly unable to make a living.

Everything now conspires against the Plains. The national energy and mineral economies may eventually recover, but the larger national agricultural economy may never recover, and a recovery will benefit the Midwest and South long before it benefits the Plains. The region's ordeal will continue, intensify. Plains farmers and ranchers will probably not emigrate in large numbers to the West Coast as the 1930s Okies did; instead they will take town jobs, double up with relatives, go on welfare, rent out their land, or—in the frequent worst cases—be driven off altogether. An admirably upright, self-contained way of life that goes back several generations will disappear, often painfully. No likely changes in cultivation techniques, water technologies, agricultural subsidies, financing practices, export policies, or conservation devices will save it.

Plains Possibilities

"Grass no good upside down," said a Pawnee chief in northeastern Colorado as he watched the late nineteenth-century homesteaders rip through the short-grass with steel plows. He mourned land on which Indians had hunted buffalo for many millennia. After the plowing, that land grew wheat for a few years, then became part of the Dust Bowl. Three separate waves of farmers and ranchers, with increasingly heavy federal support, tried to make settlement stick on the Plains. The 1890s and 1930s generations were largely uprooted, as the 1980s one soon will be. Without federal support this part of America might never have been farmed or settled at all; with federal support it is the great failure of American agriculture. Yet the 1890s and 1930s are forgotten traumas, the 1980s an ignored one.

The experience on the Plains represents a spectacular, large-scale, long-term variant on "the tragedy of the commons," Garrett Hardin's ecological fable of how individual short-term economic rationality can lead to collective long-term environmental disaster. To the Indians and the early cattlemen, the entire Plains were a commons. The Homestead Act and other subsidies for settlers attempted to take the land out of the federal domain and put it permanently in individual or corporate hands. Present subsidies for crops, water, and grazing land are efforts to buttress the privatization. But the private interests, responding to markets and to federal subsidies, overgrazed and overplowed the land and overdrew the water. Thus they never produced a stable agriculture or found conservation devices that could reliably preserve it in the face of market forces. In some places they supplemented agriculture with energy and mineral development, which are also inherently unstable.

The population continually dropped, even in the long periods when the federal subsidies grew and the market incentives were favorable—for instance, the 1940s through the 1970s. Now that both markets and subsidies are weakening, the private interests are, as "the tragedy of the commons" predicts, rapidly degrading land and leaving it.

In retrospect, only the Indian hunter-gatherers knew how to live lightly on the land. The Indians treated the Plains as a coherent region, a place distinctive and worthwhile in itself. Whites almost never did. When whites began to see economic value in the Plains, they imposed arbitrary boundaries and attached all of the Plains to non-Plains states. The mentality is visible on any map: there are more straight state and county boundaries in the Plains than anywhere else in the country. Moreover, the federal government has rarely adopted policies that take into account Plains conditions or that are specific to the Plains, starting with 160-acre homesteading on the Plains after the Civil War. The general run of Plains farms and ranches took more than seventy years to grow out from under the Homestead minima and catch up to Plains reality. Of the federal government's many 1930s and 1940s measures, only the national grasslands and the Pick-Sloan plans for the Missouri River were directed primarily at the Plains; of its 1980s measures, none is. We have never grasped that federally subsidized privatization that settled most of the United States west of the Appalachians is not effective on the Plains. Thus we are, for the third time in a century, losing an environmental war on the Plains.

The Dust Bowl may recur, or it may not; the Plains will suffer anyway. Even after the extent of the suffering becomes clear, it will be hard for the nation to realize that five or six generations of agricultural and land-use policy, going back to the 1862 Homestead Act, may have done the Plains at least as much harm as good. But the region's pain will offer a chance to admit that Stephen Long and the other early American explorers had it right: the Great Plains are the Great American Desert, or part of it. The true architect of the Plains has always been the desert, its immense expansions and contractions, its pitiless resistance to cultivation.

Historian Walter Prescott Webb understood that. In 1958 he wrote in *Montana: The Magazine of Western History:* "The conventional view of the West is from the East, the direction from which the viewers approached it. The West should not be looked at from the outside, but from the inside, from the center. The West is concentric, a series of moisture circles extending outward from the arid, to the semiarid, to subhumid and finally to the humid land. . . . The Great Plains are the burnt right flank of the desert."

It is difficult to predict the future course of the Plains ordeal. The most likely possibility is a continuation of trends that go back to the 1920s: a long-term, painful draining. A few relatively urban areas that are also near large non-Plains cities may pull out of their decline. A few cities within the Plains—the Lubbocks and Cheyennes—may hold steady as self-contained enclaves that provide services. The Plains will remain the nation's prime source of wheat, but the many small towns that depend on extracting other low-priced natural resources will empty, wither, die. They cannot hold their young people. They cannot attract manufacturing because they are too far from major markets and offer a labor force that is unskilled or too small. Nor can they lure those seeking to move to an arcadian setting. The frequent harshness of landscape, climate, and economy has always meant that the region chooses its own; now there will be no one left to choose. The rural Plains will be virtually deserted.

Little stands in the way of this outcome. New, not yet known minerals or energy sources may be discovered. New crops may be developed, but most conceivable replacement crops for the Plains do not exist yet or are better produced elsewhere. The few exceptions—for instance, the Angora goats in central Texas that produce mohair—have limited markets.

NBR

At the National Bison Range in Montana

For some of the Plains, tourism and recreation could be plausible options. Yet tourism and recreation cannot offer much. Farmers cannot tap the market, and most ranchers are unwilling to pamper demanding city customers. At a public meeting in Casper on attracting tourists to Wyoming, one rancher said: "What it comes down to is your wife and daughters go to work cooking for tourists and making their beds, and your son is driving a bus around for them or whatever. I'm sure that's fine for some people, but I'd rather stay on the land and starve right along with the rest of the cowboys."

The Buffalo Commons

The most intriguing alternative would be to restore large parts of the Plains to its prewhite condition, to make it again the commons the settlers found in the nineteenth century. This approach would for the first time treat the Plains as a distinct region and recognize its unsuitability for agriculture. Bret Wallach, a University of Oklahoma geographer and MacArthur fellow, has suggested that the Forest Service enter into voluntary contracts with Plains farmers and ranchers, paying them the full value of what they could cultivate during each of the next fifteen years, but require them not to cultivate. Instead, the farmers and ranchers would reestablish native shortgrasses. Afterward, the agency would buy out their holdings, except for a 40-acre homestead.

Under Wallach's proposal farmers and ranchers would be able to pay off their debts, keep their homes, salvage their pride, and plan their future and provide for it. The Forest Service would use its new acreage to expand its successful national grasslands—whose 4 million acres do not loom large on a Plains scale—and create bigger national Plains parks with landforms, animals, and vegetation not now preserved in the national parks.

Similar proposals to deprivatize the Plains—to deliberately enlarge the Plains frontier—have appeared in subregional settings. In the southern Plains, Charles Little, former editor of *American Land Forum,* has suggested that expansions of the national grasslands, of the grazing districts operated by the Department of Interior's Bureau of Land Management, and of the antisod-busting national conservation reserve could retire enough agricultural land to slow the depletion of the Ogallala aquifer. In the northern Plains, Robert Scott, of the Institute of the Rockies, has urged that fifteen thousand square miles of eastern Montana—about a tenth of the state—be transformed into an East African-style game preserve called the Big Open. With state and federal help, fences would come down, domestic animals would be removed, and game animals would be stocked. According to Scott, the land could support 75,000 bison, 150,000 deer, 40,000 elk, and 40,000 antelope. A ranch of ten thousand acres (nearly sixteen square miles), by now normal for the area, would net at least $48,000 per year from hunting licenses alone. About one thousand new jobs—for outfitters, taxidermists, and workers in gas stations, restaurants, motels—would develop. Scott's approach, unlike the others, lets ranchers and farmers keep their land, but treats it as free range.

These proposals would provoke great resistance from most farmers and ranchers. Wallach, writing in Landscape in 1985, says his program gives them the choice of selling most of their land or going bankrupt on all of it. That poses "a bitter choice, but it is also a better one than they will find in the marketplace to which an urban Congress will, sooner or later, lead them."

In 1987 the mayor of Jordan, Montana, a town of 485 at the center of Scott's proposed Big Open, told an Institute of the Rockies conference in Missoula that if the idea became serious, "you may have a revolution on your hands." A Helena-area rancher suggested that Scott "first play this scenario in the Hell Creek Bar in Jordan."

We believe that despite any conceivable efforts much of the rural Plains will suffer near-total desertion over the next generation. It will come slowly to most places, quickly to some; parts of Montana, New Mexico, South Dakota, and Texas, especially those away from the interstates, strike us as likely candidates for rapid depopulation. After the desertion has run its course, the federal government will step in to buy back the Plains, to deprivatize. Wallach, Little, and Scott, seeing that the nation is losing the environmental war on the Plains, hope for a planned, orderly, relatively small-scale retreat; we foresee a rout. In our estimation, government will have to respond in the deprivatizing manner they envision, but on a much larger scale than they seem to anticipate. The likely issue is not how to deprivatize during withdrawal, but after withdrawal turns into flight and abandonment. The goal of our proposal is to keep most of the Plains from turning into a wasteland, a place whites surrendered, an American Empty Quarter.

If the federal government has to intervene late rather than early—after the desertion instead of before it—much of its buy-back task will, however regrettably, be easier. There will be fewer farmers and ranchers, and their resistance will be weaker, making it simpler for government to reassemble the commons. Parts of the Plains will survive with traditional or alternative economic activities; there government would make no deprivatization attempts. But we suspect there will not be many such places.

Deprivatization will have two thrusts, one for people, the other for land. On the people side, the government will negotiate buy-backs from landowners and should also take responsibility for easing the transition of people forced off the Plains. These economic refugees will feel aggrieved and impoverished, penalized for staying too long in a place they loved, and treated as fools for pursuing occupations the nation supposedly respected but evidently did not. On the land side, the government will take the newly emptied Plains and tear down the fences, replant the shortgrass, and restock the animals, including many buffalo. It will be at least twenty to thirty years before the vegetation and wildlife reassert themselves in semiarid Plains settings, where land changes so slowly that century-old wagon-trail ruts are still visible.

There may be competition for the land. In South Dakota several Sioux tribes are bringing suit for eleven thousand square miles, including much of the Black Hills. The government might settle these and other claims by giving the tribes chunks of the new commons or money to buy them. The possible settlements suggest that the federal government's task on the Plains for the twenty-first century will be to recreate the nineteenth century: to reestablish the Buffalo Commons.

In many parts of the commons, the distinctions between present national parks, grasslands, grazing lands, wildlife refuges, forests, and Indian lands will largely dissolve. The small cities of the Plains will be urban outposts scattered across a frontier much bigger than today's cement islands in the shortgrass sea of the commons. It will be the world's largest historic preservation project, the ultimate national park. Most of the Great Plains will become what all of the United States once was. On both the land and people sides, the creation of the Buffalo Commons will represent a substantial administrative undertaking. The federal government will finally have to create an agency with a Plains mandate. We will need a regional agency like the Tennessee Valley Authority or the Appalachian Regional Commission, but one with much more power.

The deserted Plains will not see an after-the-storm social emptiness, nor will it be totally deprivatized. New private activities (sometimes rediscoveries of old ones) will appear. We foresee safaris across Kansas, Indian ingatherings of the lost tribes of Texas, giant abandoned North Dakota power plants that become environmentalist shrines, jump-off spots in Wyoming like the Fort Laramie of Francis Parkman's day, recreational mass horseback riding through Nebraska—a sort of Pony Express chic.

Less happily, we can also imagine refugee riots in Montana, tribal dictatorships in South Dakota, criminal colonies in New Mexico, and hijacking on many roads and railroad lines. It will be the fulfillment of Washington Irving's 1836 frontier-violence prophecy in *Astoria*, that on the Plains would "spring up new and mongrel races, like new formations in geology, the amalgamation of the debris and abrasions of former races, civilized and savage; the remains of broken and almost extinguished tribes . . . of adventurers and desperadoes of every class and country yearly ejected from the bosom of society into the wilderness."

Walter Prescott Webb published his masterwork, *The Great Plains*, in 1931, a few years before the Dust Bowl. He told how the nineteenth- and early twentieth-century pioneers sought to adapt to a new region that was level, arid, treeless. Elsewhere their culture "stood on three legs—land, water and timber." In the Plains "not one but two of these legs were withdrawn—water and timber—and civilization was left on one leg—land. It is small wonder that it toppled over in temporary failure." In our time, after the two most recent defeats on the Plains, it may emerge that the failure is permanent. The Buffalo Commons will be the response.

CHAPTER THIRTEEN

"Wyoming" Is Dead— Long Live "Wyoming"

Tom Wolf

IT IS NOT my purpose to discourage the effort, by Gretel Ehrlich or anyone else, to tell the truth about Wyoming. I just want to hold her to a higher standard. I want the whole truth. The official "Wyoming" Ehrlich makes visible will not do. She may mean to save the cowboy from himself, but I don't think her idealizations square with the realities of industrial-style ranching.

When there has been a death, a murder perhaps, it is customary to request an examination of the corpse. With Wyoming's economy busted flat, right now may be a good time to kick back and consider the larger question of "Wyoming," which is both a state and a state of mind, something we half-perceive and half-create. The writer Gretel Ehrlich considers the larger question of "Wyoming" in her book *The Solace of Open Spaces*. Having suffered a great personal loss, which she details in this book, Ehrlich ritualizes her resurrection, depicting herself born again into a new world she calls "Wyoming."

Ehrlich originally came to a geographic place called Wyoming to chronicle the death of the West, to shoot a film on old sheepmen, the last of a dying breed. She had left her former life to escape the slaughter of the cities, to seek a new world dedicated to life, not death; social order, not anarchy. Oddly enough, she discovered "Wyoming." Now Ehrlich has become something of a cult figure, a visionary, a diviner, a healer: someone who travels the literary circuit, speaking for "Wyoming," for people she calls "Westerners," who seem to be mute, busy, inarticulate, or just never at home when the phone rings.

She finds a natural setting removed from man and his works, reductive in its few elements—seasons, sky, and land—utterly basic to the great questions of serious literature. The setting raises her from the dead, beckoning her and her grateful readers into a new cosmogony, a seemingly infinite recession toward remote or unseen horizons, a spatial mystery of shallow and deep, horizontal and vertical, first and last, and without end. There is one familiar literary reference point on Ehrlich's horizon, one way she chooses to define her place among other nature writers. There on the horizon of her "Wyoming" is the figure of the cowboy.

Gretel Ehrlich is hands down the best writer Wyoming has ever seen. Yet the very quality of her achievement and the promise of her talent raise troubling questions about the relationship between her "Wyoming" and the ones others know. She writes that American culture has lost its memory, and to her, Wyoming is the antidote for America's collective amnesia. To many of her readers, real as well as would-be Wyomingites, her work voices the values we would like to believe exist in Wyoming.

Ehrlich is not the only writer to attempt to portray Wyoming as a state of mind. There is a competing version called "The Wyoming Hick Syndrome." It goes this way: Wyoming is obviously a harsh place to live, and we natives are a match for it. Outsiders are right to look down on us for living here, but we can't admit that. Instead, we close ranks, rejecting new people and new ideas in violent ways bound to confirm their low opinion of us. Yes, newcomers might make Wyoming a better place to live, but then it wouldn't be Wyoming, which is a lousy place to live. Admitting newcomers who won't accept the official rancher's version of things would amount to admitting that there is something wrong with Wyoming, something wrong with the way we treat each other and the land. That admission is inconceivable. So we continue to avenge ourselves on this terrible place and on anyone who suggests otherwise.

Official Wyoming loves to seduce outsiders into accepting its cowboy mythology. People will tell you with pride that Wyoming is hard on women and horses. How plain do you need it said? Ehrlich's "Wyoming" is not the "Wyoming" of the Hick Syndrome. So is the "real Wyoming" just a figure of speech?

Something is wrong here, where so much is so right. Ehrlich's need for the cowboy by her side may be her book's fatal flaw, a failed attempt to find warmth in the dead hand of cowboy mythology that, having crushed Wyoming's windpipe, still clutches at the throat of the corpse it calls "Wyoming." The crux of the paradox of Ehrlich's writing is that while admitting nature and women to visibility, she also depicts the cowboy as hero, even though the cowboy is obviously hostile to both nature and women, at least in his officially approved, USDA-certified incarnation.

"Real" Wyomingites, the kind the Wyoming stockgrowers like, love Gretel Ehrlich because she idealizes rather than critizes Wyoming culture. She has little to say about rape or rapaciousness, and so her writing does not go as far as it might toward giving us the strength to see life in Wyoming clearly. To speak bluntly, official Wyoming has co-opted her work.

Any reader of *The Solace of Open Spaces* will recognize the essential trick of a socially conservative form of literature, the old pastoral, where the writer makes simple people express strong feelings in appealing language. "By golly," says the dues-paying Sierra Clubber reading Ehrlich's book on the subway in Manhattan, "those ranchers can't be so bad after all. Ranching as a way of life breeds such noble thoughts in such simple people! Wish I could be like the Marlboro Man!" Thus dies Wyoming, in order that "Wyoming" might live.

Ehrlich's use of the pastoral ruse is particularly well done and particularly disturbing. A reader typically feels like saddling up the Pinto or Bronco and riding right to Shell, Wyoming, where one expects to find the author roaming the range (*lope* is her favorite verb) with her Owen Wister–vintage cowboys, those wisely simple, simply wise souls, their lips all puckered up with immutability, not quite knowing (without her help) how to express the tenderness they feel, their hearts sprained (I am paraphrasing her now), torrential beauty, pouring down all around them, nay, fit to tickle any woman's silver palate. The cowboy as hors d'oeuvre, as (the ultimate compliment) androgynous.

I hope the paraphrase makes the point. I hope so, but there is more. When Ehrlich goes to New York to see her agent, her editor, her publisher, and the folks down in marketing, she tells us how she moons over the pictures of the Marlboro Men in the subways, "a reminder of the ranchers and cowboys I've ridden with the last eight years." She claims to bring her strong, silent subjects' "tenderness into the house," because they "lack the vocabulary to express the complexity of what they feel."

Enough. Or rather too much. The death of Wyoming is too high a price to pay for a literary trick, however beautifully expressed. Ehrlich accepts a rapacious, brutally exploitative extractive industry in terms of its own self-serving myth. Wyoming's caste system is based on the social pretensions and political realities of cowboy mythology, as is made chillingly clear to anyone who attempts to question them. It is one thing to pull on your Tony Lamas in the morning; it is another to feel a cowboy boot crash into your face.

Perhaps there are other possibilities. Perhaps we need not let the endlessly celebrated, endlessly lamented death of "ranching as a way of life" deceive us into missing the real death. It is the healthy, natural ecosystems in Wyoming that are dying. They are being killed by the cowboy mythology and cynically exploited by a class system that pretends to concentrate all value in a cow and a

Mike McClure

man on horseback, rather than in the messy complexity of a healthy range complete with predators and large ungulates other than cattle.

Consider Gretel Ehrlich's revision of "the Westerner": "The iconic myth surrounding him is built on American notions of heroism: the index of a man's value as measured in physical courage. Such ideas have perverted manliness into a self-absorbed race for cheap thrills." No one could disagree with this sentiment in the late twentieth century, but can you swallow the rest of her argument? "The Westerner's courage is selfless, a form of compassion. . . . He's androgynous at the core." Speaking of this heroic Wyoming cowboy, Ehrlich says, "Language, so compressed, becomes metaphorical. . . . What's behind this laconic style is shyness. There is no vocabulary for the subject of feelings." Aw shucks, ma'am.

I wish I had had such compliments on the tip of my tongue when a cowboy from the Wyoming Stockgrowers Association sweetly lisped whiskey in my ear in the Stockman's Bar in Pinedale, Wyoming. "Son," he whispered, "when I catch you environmentalists in Sublette County, I'll skullfuck you myself."

The topics for literature expand and contract over time. Much is lost. Death comes for everyone, for everything: for the cowboy, for me, for Wyoming. I dream of a newly imagined Wyoming, where the female and nature achieve literary enfranchisement as a truly androgynous corrective to Ehrlich's all-too-traditionally-male cowboy. I dream of an art that sees us humans as not separate from, but part of, nature. So, too, in her best moments, does Gretel Ehrlich: "The truest art I would strive for in any work would be to give the page the same qualities as earth: Weather would land on it harshly; light would elucidate the most difficult truths; wind would sweep away obtuse padding. Finally, the lessons of impermanence taught me this: Loss constitutes an odd kind of fullness; despair empties out into an unquenchable appetite for life." Beautifully said. Let the dance begin. But it will have to be a dance on the grave of the cowboy, of "Wyoming."

CHAPTER FOURTEEN

South Dakota Farmers Reject a Free Lunch

Peter Carrels

ALTHOUGH THE drought of 1988 blistered South Dakota's crops and eroded topsoil, a farmer who helped kill a plan in the 1970s to build a billion-dollar irrigation project remains opposed to that project. "It's a bad drought, all right. But I'd fight the Oahe Irrigation Project today, just like I fought it ten years ago," says John Sieh, now a retired farmer from Groton, South Dakota, but back then a leader of United Family Farmers.

The Oahe Irrigation Project was one in the long line of major diversions planned by the Bureau of Reclamation to water and colonize the West. Unlike nearly all other large-scale bureau irrigation projects, however, Oahe would have irrigated lands east of the one-hundredth meridian, in an already productive area. It was a sign that the bureau was running out of places to play in the West. Instead of arguing that new land would be opened to farming, proponents had to use a weaker argument: that the project would stabilize existing farms. This argument stood unchallenged from 1944, when the Pick-Sloan Plan promised a million acres of irrigation to South Dakota, to 1976, when the farmers in the area won a major victory. Although Oahe was not true desert reclamation, that fact alone didn't beat it. Oahe was beaten because the area was already under cultivation, and the farmers knew a fair amount about both farming and irrigation.

Three men who fought the Oahe Irrigation Project; from left: John Sieh, George Piper, Curt Hohn

Like all major reclamation projects, Oahe goes way back. It gained initial congressional authorization in 1944 as part of the Pick-Sloan Plan (and the Flood Control Act). But it didn't come to life until the early 1960s, when the bureau began building the local political foundation that always precedes the pouring of concrete. Although Oahe was mainly a creature of the bureau and of state-level and national-level leaders, an on-the-ground sponsoring entity was a necessity.

That entity was a conservancy subdistrict covering 15½ counties, and two irrigation districts. Those who lived within a potential irrigation area but who were uninterested in irrigation did not have to join a district. Those land-owners, however, lost the right to vote in irrigation district elections, which minimized potential opposition to the irrigation project.

The original physical plan the bureau designed and the districts endorsed called for 490,000 acres of irrigation. The project was to have one large pocket of irrigated land near the Missouri River and another straddling the James River, about 160 miles to the northeast. However, by 1965 the bureau had scaled back to 190,000 acres of irrigation, all in the James River area. The water was to come out of the Missouri River's giant Oahe Reservoir and was to be pumped into large canals. The water would then flow by gravity toward the Lake Plain region, a farming area between Aberdeen and Huron, split by the

James River. The project was heralded as one that would help South Dakota while repaying a debt the nation owed the state.

Since their completion, Oahe and the other five Pick-Sloan reservoirs in the Dakotas and Montana had served the needs of the lower Missouri River states by generating electricity, controlling floods, and providing water for navigation on the Missouri below Sioux City, Iowa. But that service to the lower Missouri River states had taken a heavy toll on the upper basin states. Montana and the Dakotas had lost valuable bottomland so that the reservoirs could protect and aid the lower basin states. That was a sore point with the upper basin states. Now South Dakota was to be compensated by the Oahe Irrigation Project for the damage the Pick-Sloan Plan had done to it.

In the beginning there was little opposition to Oahe. Citizens accepted the bureau's argument that the project would fuel new prosperity in the state. *Oahe*, a Sioux word meaning friend, meant protection against drought, hefty construction payrolls and contracts, lots of center-pivot irrigator sales, and

Montgomery Archives, Northern State College

Only 3 miles of the proposed 214-mile Oahe ditch was completed before construction was halted in 1977

more business for farm chemical sellers and bankers. It was economic development of the gift-horse type: a present to the people of South Dakota from the
federal government.

One reason for the lack of opposition was lack of information. Like most
bureau projects, the details were to be withheld until the last minute. So for
years in South Dakota, there was fanfare around a project whose shape was
unknown. That didn't change until 1971, when a work plan was released. But
it wasn't until 1973, when the draft environmental impact statement (EIS) was
made public, that environmentalists and farmers were jolted awake.

George Piper was among the first to begin to grasp the significance of the
plans. Piper, a reserved, thoughtful man, had left his parents' farm near
Carpenter, South Dakota, after high school, and had come home with a Ph.D.
in zoology from the University of Missouri about the time the draft EIS was
released. The first thing he learned was that the farm he had returned to could
soon be partially submerged. The EIS told him that a large portion of the Piper
farm, homesteaded by Piper's grandfather in the 1880s, was to be flooded by a
project reservoir. Disturbed, he began to dig, and the more he learned, the
more concerned he became. As his findings became known, he was joined by
neighbors with similar concerns.

Soon there was an organization—the United Family Farmers (UFF). Working out of an abandoned one-room school on Piper's property, the small group
began contacting other landowners, telling them that their land was to be
flooded, or bisected by a large canal, or bought up to provide new habitat for
wildlife. Membership grew steadily as project details became better known. It
was classic grassroots organizing.

The UFF's counterpart was the Oahe Conservancy Subdistrict, created in
1960 to serve as liaison between the local residents and the bureau. Legally, its
role was to sign a contract with the bureau, getting the farmers to pledge to
repay that small part of the project not paid for by federal funds, and to
maintain and operate the project once it was complete. The subdistrict also
had taxing powers to finance its activities. But the main function of the
subdistrict was political: to sell the project to the community, and to cloak a
federal undertaking in a local garment. Meetings of the 11-member board of
the subdistrict had been placid events, characterized by uncritical praise for
Oahe. One board member said that Oahe would "act upon the economy of
South Dakota in much the same manner that a blood transfusion serves to
restore vigor and vitality to all parts of a severely wounded person."

The tone of the meetings changed radically when UFF members began to
attend and ask critical questions about soil irrigability, the project's cost-
benefit ratio, the probable channelization, or straightening, of a popular river,
and alleged abuses by the bureau during land condemnation. Between 1971
and 1974 UFF transformed the glorious Oahe project into an issue so hotly
disputed it split neighbors, communities, and even families. Many farmers

Members of United Family Farmers erected this sign near Huron, South Dakota, during the fight over the Oahe project

came to see the bureau not as Santa Claus, but as a self-serving bureaucracy intent on building a project that would harm family farms.

State leaders, including the subdistrict board, dismissed the allegations, and the media painted the group as populist radicals. The pro-Oahe front was solid, with one television journalist even losing his job because he tried to cover UFF positions. But UFF grew. More than two thousand members contributed money, and droves of them traveled to Washington, D.C., to lobby and testify against the project. What the group lacked in support from politicians and media it made up for with grassroots persistence and generosity.

With three years of organizing behind them, UFF leaders decided to go to the voters. The problem was to find an election. Efforts to gain a public vote on the project had been rejected by South Dakota state leaders. So UFF turned its attention to the subdistrict board. Board elections had been humdrum, one-candidate events, and in 1974 the eleven board members were all solid Oahe backers. Of the eleven, five were up for election. This time, instead of an uncontested election, the five pro-Oahe incumbents found themselves challenged by five opponents fielded by UFF.

Until then U.S. Senator George McGovern, a powerful Oahe supporter, had largely ignored UFF. But McGovern was running for reelection to the U.S. Senate at the same time as the very hot Oahe election. McGovern decided to be publicly neutral. In fact, he indicated that he would view the Oahe election as a referendum of sorts on the project. McGovern won, and so did four of the UFF candidates. Then the senator backed away from his promise and pressed for accelerated project funding. Dejected UFFers could only look to 1976, when six more board seats and control of the subdistrict would be up for grabs.

Although 1976 brought the election, it also brought two serious obstacles for the six UFF candidates: South Dakota was reeling from its worst drought since the 1930s, and George McGovern was no longer pretending to be neutral. Instead, he was championing the project and tacitly endorsing the pro-project candidates. He encouraged formation of a new group, Friends of Oahe, funded mostly by bankers, construction interests, and Main Street types. To spark interest in pro-Oahe candidates, he also sponsored a grandiose water development conference several days before the election. Featured speaker at the conference was G.G. Stamm, then commissioner of the bureau. An angry UFF activist wrote to McGovern: "Why did you schedule this rain dance two days before the subdistrict elections? Why would you be so interested in influencing our elections now? . . . Why have you stood in the way of congressional review of the Bureau of Reclamation's plans for Oahe? We need a genuine water conference in the area affected by the discussion. We don't need an expensive public relations show."

UFF candidates were also taking a beating in the state's media. Newspapers in the area editorialized against them, and the Friends of Oahe funneled big money into the campaign. UFF was even accused of being a front group for Texans hoping to divert water from the Missouri River. The UFF had its own skillfully managed campaign. At the helm was Curt Hohn, a former McGovern staffer who had been an Oahe supporter until he met George Piper in 1974. A trip to North Dakota to view the Garrison Project, which was North Dakota's version of Oahe, converted him to an Oahe opponent.

On election night hundreds of UFF members gathered, first to watch the returns, and then to celebrate the victories of five of the six UFF candidates. In the midst of a severe drought, farmers in the area had decided that they were better off without the irrigation project. And they had decided by impressive margins: four of the five winners swept more than 60 percent of the vote. The UFF's sole loser went down by less than 0.5 percent of the vote.

Worried, the bureau and other project supporters waited to see what the UFF-controlled board would do. Action came quickly. John Sieh, who had been elected in 1974 to serve rural Brown County, was chosen chairman at the new board's first meeting. Sieh was a strong-willed former Farmers Union organizer who had returned to his family's farm near the James River. He announced that the new board would sponsor seven public hearings to review the project.

At the hearings, farmer after farmer came forward to criticize the bureau and the project. Their objections were of the kind you'd expect from farmers. They dealt with soil types, costs, waterlogging of the soil, and the amount of land to be sacrificed to the project. Why, they asked, should 120,000 acres of farmland be lost to canals, reservoirs, and wildlife mitigation in order to provide only 190,000 acres of irrigation? They also complained that bureau soil irrigability tests were inaccurate, and they pointed to areas where bureau classifications contradicted existing conditions. Irrigation, they said, was more than just putting water on the land. It was just as important to properly remove that water from the land, and here, witnesses said, the bureau had fallen down. They said that the space between return-flow drains in irrigated fields had been increased in order to save money. The reduced drainage, they said, threatened soils with salinization and waterlogging.

Some landowners objected to what they described as bullying tactics used by bureau officials handling land condemnations. Others talked about how the canals and reservoirs would disrupt their farms and their lives. The opponents included environmentalists, who protested channelization of the James River. The disruption of existing farming patterns and the damage to the environment would not come cheap. It was to cost $5,000 for each acre put under irrigation. And an analysis by Johns Hopkins University indicated that the return on this investment would be only 54 cents for every dollar spent.

Shortly after the hearings, with seven volumes of testimony in hand, the Oahe Conservancy Subdistrict asked the Carter administration and Congress to suspend funding for Oahe. In Washington word got around quickly about a water project whose beneficiaries were coming to Washington to complain about it. One farmer from the Spink County Irrigation District told a Senate Appropriations subcommittee: "I never thought I'd see the day when I would have to come to Washington to ask Congress not to give me something, but here I am."

Although it was now obvious that most farmers in the Oahe subdistrict did not want the project, George McGovern and Governor Richard Kneip, also a Democrat, tried to strip the Oahe board of its power and set Oahe back on the road to construction. A legislative task force had been organized by Governor Kneip to investigate how to keep the project alive, and Kneip wrote to the Department of Interior to ask that the task force be recognized as speaking for South Dakota on Oahe. Piper accused McGovern, Kneip, and other Oahe supporters of trying to undermine the elected Oahe board. "We played by the rules of the game. We won. And now they're trying to change the rules."

The election of 1976 had brought to the White House former Georgia Governor Jimmy Carter, who included Oahe on a "hit list" of eighteen water projects. Although elsewhere in the West the bold move hurt Carter, it brought applause from UFF members and most of the subdistrict board. But even with a like-minded person in the White House and firm control of the subdistrict board, Oahe was still a potential threat. Moreover, the farmers who had helped beat back Oahe weren't against federal help. Like the rest of South Dakota, they believed that the state needed economic help and that South Dakota was owed something for the loss of Missouri River bottomland. So the board began touting an alternative to Oahe called the WEB Pipeline. Many small communities and farms in rural South Dakota lacked good drinking water, and WEB would provide drinking water to those living in north-central South Dakota, including the area that was to have been served by Oahe. The water was to come from the Missouri River.

Local support for WEB was strong, but political leaders feared that accepting the pipeline would kill their beloved Oahe. Among those leaders was Senator McGovern. Piper recalls, "Everything we (UFF) faced that tried to destroy our movement, all the efforts to put us in a bad light, could be traced to McGovern's office." Many Oahe opponents had been McGovern supporters, but the 1976 subdistrict election had turned them against him, and when it came time in 1980 for McGovern to stand for reelection, they were ready for him. More than just revenge was involved. Irrigation projects have a phoenix-like ability to rise from the ashes of past defeats. UFF reasoned that until Congress deauthorized Oahe, there was always a chance of its resurrection. And they also reasoned that deauthorization would be much easier with McGovern out of the Senate.

The dissatisfaction with McGovern was apparent in the Democratic primary, when a little-known challenger garnered 40 percent of the vote, carrying seven counties and coming close in some traditional McGovern strongholds. McGovern looked especially vulnerable in UFF country. And the 1980 general election was, of course, disastrous for the Democrats, with Ronald Reagan's conservative tide sweeping the nation. But McGovern's loss to Republican James Abdnor was particularly humbling. No incumbent U.S. senator or representative was defeated as resoundingly as McGovern that year. The one-time presidential candidate, and the man credited with building the Democratic party in South Dakota, managed only 39 percent of the vote. McGovern's strident position on Oahe was at least partially responsible for his showing.

With McGovern out of the way and with farmers in the area continuing to stand firm against Oahe, South Dakota leaders realized they had no choice. In 1982 Congress deauthorized Oahe and authorized the WEB Pipeline. WEB is now more than half complete. When finished, the $110-million project will be the largest rural water system in the country. Thirty thousand people will be served by the pipeline, including twenty-seven hundred farms and ranches and dozens of small towns. People who contemplated leaving the farm because water for household use, for drinking, and for livestock was poor or hard to get can now remain.

The lessons of the Oahe fight are becoming clearer as time passes, and the differences between once combative factions are narrowed. By rejecting the Oahe Irrigation Project, farmers in eastern South Dakota reaffirmed their faith that the soil and climate could sustain family farms. "There are a lot of happy farm families around. That says something about our way of life here," said George Piper recently, from the farm he fought to save.

In Piper's view the need has never been for billion-dollar irrigation projects or even for price supports. He says government should deemphasize crop production and instead stress crop marketing. "The education of farmers in our land-grant universities has been focused on production and not marketing," he says. "There is a lack of commitment from government to protect family farms. We don't want huge subsidies. We need other services. For example, government assistance to help farmers understand marketing their crops instead of government help to maximize production would be useful." Piper, who does not participate in any government farm program, also says, "If the farmer could market his production for what it costs to produce it plus a little profit, it would help the farmer through periods of drought."

The Oahe struggle also holds larger lessons for South Dakota. If nothing else, it illustrates the weakness of top-down economic planning. Perhaps Oahe might have been salvaged, and been made useful, had there been genuine consultation with the people living on the land. Instead, bureaucrats and politicians planned and promoted the Oahe project, and then attempted to slip it by or shove it past those who were its intended beneficiaries. As a result, it failed.

Are things in South Dakota different today? At a conference in Sioux Falls last spring, nearly forty organizations representing a cross section of South Dakota's population, expressed a common feeling: the small circle of special interests making economic development decisions must be broadened to include working people, farmers, environmentalists, Indians, and others. "We deserve a seat at the table where economic development policy is made," said Bob Kingsley, a union leader, speaking for wage earners. Kingsley criticized state leaders for encouraging new companies to pay low wages. He described a government program where most of those waiting in line for free food were fully employed, but miserably paid, South Dakotans. "This, my friends," Kingsley explained to the crowd, "is the evidence of economic development gone awry." Ten years ago, a farmer testified to Congress that he and his neighbors had not been consulted about Oahe. He was making a statement that still merits the attention of policy makers and planners.

CHAPTER FIFTEEN

Bust Trounces a Once-Tough Town

Stephen Voynick

In 1981 all visitors inquiring what Leadville, Colorado, did for a living got the same answer: "We're a mining town." And the tone of the reply said Leadville was damned proud of it. It had good reason for pride. Under an earlier name, Oro City, it was the richest placer gold strike of the Pikes Peak rush. Then came the big silver discoveries of 1877. As four hundred mines produced 11 million ounces of silver annually, Leadville exploded into a city of more than thirty thousand, which included the likes of H.A.W. Tabor, Meyer Guggenheim, and the "Unsinkable" Molly Brown.

By World War I, which Leadville contributed to with record production of lead and zinc, it had experienced more booms and busts than most towns see in a lifetime. Then the Climax Molybdenum Company quickly grew into a huge mine and mill that supplied virtually all of the world's molybdenum. During both World War II and the Korean conflict, Leadville's miners earned another stack of production awards. When the old base metal mines closed in the late 1950s, Climax, now a bona fide industrial giant, more than took up the slack. In 1981 alone Climax mined $250 million worth of molybdenum, tin, tungsten, and pyrite, paid 85 percent of Lake County's property tax base, provided thirty-two hundred employees with an $80 million annual payroll, and sent hundreds of pension checks to Leadville residents. The corporation's impact on Leadville cannot be overstated. Climax provided confidence and self-sufficiency, as well as direction and purpose. Even those who operated bars, gas stations, and beauty salons depended on Climax for their livelihoods.

Mining was Leadville's past, present, and future. High school kids didn't have to leave the county to choose from a variety of high-paying careers in production or professional fields. Leadville didn't need new businesses, resorts, or anything else. If tourists visited, fine, but Leadville didn't go out of its way to lure them. That secure world changed forever on January 18, 1982—the day Climax laid off six hundred workers, the first step toward closing the entire mine. Unemployment has since gone from 5 percent to 32.4 percent, the property tax base has been halved, and the county population has declined by one-third, to only six thousand. Many businesses, including J. C. Penney and Skaggs Drugs, shut their doors. By June, *Newsweek* described Leadville in an article titled "Rocky Mountain Low."

Along with its paychecks, Leadville lost its confidence, direction, and purpose. Some say it's still a mining town, but that things are "a little slow." But you'll also hear it's a tourist town, even a bedroom community. Others call Leadville an "economically developing" community, while still others call it just another busted-flat mountain town. Truth lies in each description, for there is little agreement on what kind of town Leadville has become, and even less on where it should go. A sign of its identity crisis came in March 1983 when it hired a professional economic developer and unveiled "Operation Bootstrap." The once jaunty, irreverent, tough mining town had joined many other Western communities in the pursuit of economic revitalization and diversification. The results have been disappointing, and Leadville has still not even reached economic rock bottom. Rather than diversifying and growing, Leadville has survived by adapting to a much lower economic level.

Dick Rodgers is president of the Commercial Bank of Leadville, where accounts have fallen from ten thousand in 1980 to four thousand today. "Economic renewal has collided head-on with Leadville's entrenched mining mentality," Rodgers complains. "We hoped Bootstrap would convince merchants that their traditional trade with customers who make twelve dollars an hour was history, that survival meant adjusting their operations to lower-income customers by changing hours, merchandise, store appearance, even personal lifestyles. But few would change. And economies don't turn around overnight, you've got to spend money to get a future return. Anyone in a mining culture becomes hardware oriented. When they spend money, they expect immediate material gratification. Leadville wasn't interested in the soft costs necessary for future economic development."

According to Rodgers, the mining culture refused to give up its dream. "People here refused to accept reality. They believed Climax would reopen and everything would be the way it was. We have many pensioned Climax people here—they're financially secure, content, and not interested in changing anything. A lot of those old miners will have to fade away before Leadville can recover economically." Their nostalgia for the past was reinforced by the fact that, although Leadville's mining economy bent, it never completely broke. With the 50 remaining Climax jobs and another 150 at ASARCO's Black Cloud lead-zinc mine, mining remains Lake County's biggest private employer.

"Leadville will always be a mining town," says Carl Miller, Lake County commissioner and former Climax miner. "Five years ago Leadville saw tourism as a quick fix. Some still want tourism at any cost now. The motel and shop owners are most vocal, simply because they can gain direct, financial benefits from tourism. But I can't take care of a few people. As a county commissioner, I have to work toward putting the entire county back on solid economic footing. And mining is still the best way to do it. Tourism may make a damned good second industry, but it will never replace mining."

"Western mining has been depressed for a decade," continues Miller, who is often criticized for his conservative stance on economic development. "But it's recovering with greater efficiency, higher metal prices, and new, high-tech methods that will even make reprocessing of old mine wastes possible. Right

Mine-drilling contest in Leadville

Steve Voynick

Steve Voynick

The Delaware Hotel in Leadville, built in 1885, is now restored

now, we have four small mines working, a pyrite recovery mill, and other small projects gearing up. In 1983 we had 200 mine jobs. Today we have 320 and counting. And that's economic development."

Miller says that although tourism has probably doubled, tourism jobs have not followed suit. "And tourism jobs are low paying, seasonal, and attract temporary-type workers. Mining offers year-round jobs with good pay."

Disillusionment with five years of economic development is apparent, but that negative assessment is not entirely accurate. A lot in Leadville is new, including a nationally televised, 100-mile trail race; the month-long Loyola University Jazz Festival; expanded summer programs at the local campus of Colorado Mountain College; establishment of the National Mining Hall of Fame and Museum; the $350,000 Victorian restoration of the 1885 Delaware Hotel; a million-dollar face-lift on the main street; a million-dollar upgrading of county-owned Ski Cooper facilities; the Oro City summer historical festival; reopening of the Climax rail line as a tourist excursion; and the Environmental Protection Agency work on local mine drainage pollution problems. These efforts have brought visitors, an improved image, and outside exposure. But they haven't brought an economic bonanza to even begin replacing those

Row of Victorian homes in Leadville, most of which are for sale

lost Climax paychecks, and they haven't replaced the lost direction and purpose.

Dr. Rick Christmas, assistant dean at Colorado Mountain College's Timberline Campus, helped establish the Oro City festival. "In 1983 we spent $10,000 and drew two thousand visitors. This year we'll have an annual budget of $25,000, a gate of seven thousand visitors, and we've already put well over

$100,000 back into the Leadville economy. Oro City is just one example of the potential that's begging to be developed." But mining itself is history, he points out. "The college has even had to cancel the mine training program. A limited mining recovery might help sustain Leadville, but it will never be enough. We must diversify now for future growth and development."

While the mining and tourism forces do battle, Leadville has been voting with its feet and has undergone sweeping socioeconomic changes. In 1980 the entire Lake County work force was employed in the county. Today, of the 3,700-person county work force, 700 are unemployed, and only 1,300 work in the county. The remaining 1,700 commute to fill tourism-related jobs in places like Beaver Creek, Vail, Copper Mountain, and Breckenridge.

"We're still a mining town in attitude," says Larry Tanglen, editor of the weekly *Leadville Herald Democrat*. "But economically we've already made a quiet transition from mining to a tourism-type, service-based economy. Unfortunately, the tourism jobs aren't in this county. And many Leadville stores that once served the community with things like clothes and shoes have switched to selling tourist trinkets and gifts." Tanglen says Leadville doesn't realize that economic development is a highly competitive game played by half the towns in the West. "We can't afford to wait for mining any more than we can afford to wait for Quail Mountain [a proposed and controversial new ski area]. Every day we wait means more tourists and businesses lost to other towns. Leadville's trouble is that it's going in too many directions at once, with little communication between different groups. Leadville is in a true identity crisis."

Although the effort at economic development has been disappointing, a lesson may have been learned: how much Leadville was a creature of Climax. Now that the mine's cloak of security, direction, and purpose is gone, Leadville is finding itself to be a disjointed community of individuals pursuing different goals. Mike Cerise of Buckhorn Sporting Goods believes Leadville still has some growing up to do. "Climax was so big, so overwhelming, that no one had to think. Climax did that for you. Leadville was like a little kid in the woods. As long as Daddy was there to point out the trail, everything was fine. But Daddy's gone now, and the kid doesn't know which way to go."

CHAPTER SIXTEEN

Stroke and Counterstroke

Raymond Wheeler

The Collapse of the Energy Economy

CHAPTER THREE described how the Sagebrush Rebels overwhelmed the Bureau of Land Management and privatized the Colorado Plateau in all but name. This chapter relates how energy conservation and the Reagan administration yanked the economic underpinnings out from under the Sagebrush Rebellion and how Utah environmentalists metamorphosed from lambs into lions.

On December 18, 1980, the *Moab Times-Independent* carried an article that was all but lost, like a toy boat, in a flood of Yuletide consumer-mania. In a meeting the previous week, the Grand County commissioners had rejected a proposal for a budget increase for the county's economic development committee. Between the Reagan Revolution and the Energy Crisis, this was to be the year of the Big Bang. This was D-Day for Moab's economic future. Why should Grand County have to spend money on economic development?

Why indeed? asked Sam Taylor in an editorial aside. For a man at the cutting edge of a gold rush, Taylor was oddly pessimistic. The story opened with remarks by Thayne Robson, an economic forecaster at the Utah Bureau of Economic and Business Research. Robson had recently cast "dark clouds" over forecasts of booming growth. Citing the recession, high interest rates, and the precarious future of massive construction projects, including the MX missile "racetrack" system and the $8-billion Intermountain Power Project, Robson warned that economic growth in Utah "had almost ceased."

"In light of Dr. Robson's predictions," Taylor observed dryly, "it is comforting to know that the Grand County commissioners did not entirely kill the county's industrial promotion budget for the coming year." Taylor continued, saying that if the community were to lose the Atlas Minerals Plant, the results could be devastating. "Things in general are not good in the mining industry," he said.

It took two years for Moab to learn whether Sam Taylor was a prophet or a fool. For the moment he looked like a fool. After all, just five years earlier Thayne Robson had been forecasting a booming energy economy for the West. "There is an increasing recognition," Robson wrote in 1975, "that the development of Utah's energy and mineral resources . . . will bring in rapid and sustained growth (4 percent to 7 percent per year) for the next decade, and possibly for the balance of this century."

In October 1987 I found Thayne Robson ruminating quietly in his study on the University of Utah campus. Books and journals jammed the walls, forming a mountain on Robson's desk and an even higher mountain on an enormous table filling the center of the room. I had expected an interview bristling with numbers. Instead I found a man for whom numbers, it seemed, were no longer the answer. In twenty years of forecasting, Thayne Robson has seen it all. He has watched a handful of Arab nations turn the world's economy upside down. He has seen an "energy crisis" that has somehow transformed itself into an oil glut. He has watched a Middle East war lower energy prices and increase the flow of oil from the Middle East. And during the past eight years, he has watched a conservative administration pile up a massive federal budget deficit. What, then, of the future?

As he turns a lambent crystal ball over and over in his mind's eye, Robson's gaze becomes fixed; his voice drops into a monotone; he speaks for ten, fifteen minutes without pausing for breath. Will there be another energy boom in the West? Well, that depends on the Middle East. True, the Middle East is volatile. But on the other hand, that hasn't stopped the flow of oil from the Middle East.

Will the uranium market revive? Well, that depends on our national import policy. And that depends on who gets elected in 1988. Some say we'll have a Republican administration. Others think we won't.

What will happen, long term, when the world runs out of oil? Well, some people believe we'll have another energy crisis. But on the other hand, there are all kinds of exciting new energy production and conservation technologies.

Something happened out here in the West in 1980, Robson continued,

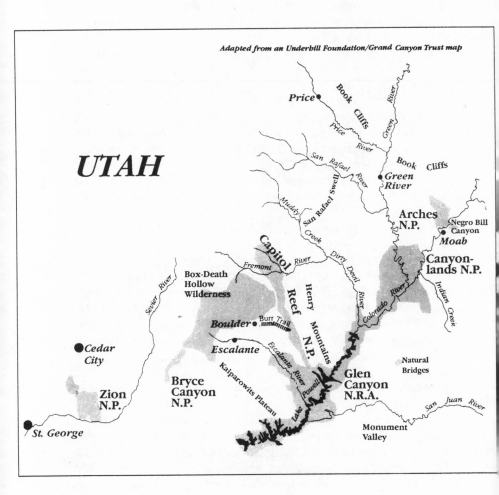

UTAH

Price

Book Cliffs

Price River

Green River

San Rafael River

Book Cliffs

Green River

Muddy Creek

San Rafael Swell

Arches N.P.

Negro Bill Canyon

Moab

Capitol

Fremont River

Dirty Devil River

Canyon-lands N.P.

Sevier River

Box-Death Hollow Wilderness

Reef

Henry Mountains

Colorado River

Indian Creek

Boulder

Burr Trail

N.P.

Cedar City

Escalante

Escalante River

Natural Bridges

Glen Canyon N.R.A.

Zion N.P.

Bryce Canyon N.P.

Kaiparowits Plateau

Lake Powell

San Juan River

St. George

Monument Valley

something as strange as Alice's fall through the rabbit hole into Wonderland. In the midst of an energy "crisis," there arose a phenomenon so unorthodox that it shattered econometric projections like a hammer on crystal. It was a dramatic conservation of energy resources. "Instead of the demand for energy growing from 5 percent to 7 percent per year, it got back to negative growth in petroleum for a few years, and electric power to 1 or 2 percent a year. So we ended up with surpluses . . . and the energy boom became an energy bust. All of those bright forecasts of the mid-1970s were predicated on sustained growth in the demand for energy in the United States and abroad," he says.

The first bust came in 1976, when Southern California Edison backed out of the Kaiparowits Power Plant project. Though Edison blamed rising costs and opposition from environmentalists, the real reason was a lack of demand: between 1971 and 1975 the growth rate for electrical power in southern California had plummeted by nearly 50 percent. The demise of Kaiparowits, explains Rod Millar, an analyst in the Utah Energy Office, happened just when some of the early returns on conservation efforts started showing results. "I think some people in the industry woke up and realized, 'Hey, we're making a mistake.' "

It took three more years for Utah's uranium industry to "wake up," but when it did, the consequences for southern Utah's economy were devastating. In late 1979 the market for uranium suddenly took a sensational dive. Southern Utah's political leaders unanimously blame "hysteria" resulting from the April 1979 Three-Mile Island nuclear power plant accident for the plunge in the price of uranium. But there are other explanations.

"By 1978 everybody was beginning to see a couple of amazing things happening," says Rod Millar. "One, the demand for energy went way, way down, and growth rates of 10 percent per year were no longer realistic at all, particularly with electricity. Instead, they were projecting 2 or 3 percent growth rates for the 1980s. If you're going to have a 2 or 3 percent growth rate, and you've been planning in your power plant construction program for a 10 percent growth rate, you've got a problem. You've got plants out there that you can't possibly sell electricity for. By 1980 over a hundred nuclear power plants had been canceled that were ordered just a few years earlier."

The energy-industrial complex had gambled on insatiable demand and lost. Between 1979 and 1985, world demand for oil actually declined by 12 percent, or 6 million barrels per day. "Conservation worked," says Millar, shaking his head at the memory of it. "The critics of the conservation movement were totally refuted."

By 1983 it was clear who would pick up the tab for the nation's gambling debt: the residents of small towns like Moab, Utah, which had bet their futures on a mining economy. "This town's dire economic situation can be directly linked to the uranium 'boomlet' in the late seventies," explains Bob Dudek, editor of Moab's counterculture newspaper, the *Stinking Desert*

Gazette. "Many people geared up to get more prosperous, expanded their businesses, bought investment properties at high prices, went into debt counting on high wages, and generally bet the farm on the coming influx in population. It lasted about a year, and the damage that resulted haunts us to this day," Dudek says.

Along with energy conservation came two more blows in 1980: uranium exploration companies discovered phenomenal deposits in Canada, and Ronald Reagan was elected president. Because domestic uranium is of a far lower grade, and therefore far more costly than that of Canada and Australia, the domestic uranium industry was now wholly dependent upon import restrictions. But where Jimmy Carter had been obsessed by the need to stimulate the rural, energy-based economy of the West, Ronald Reagan was obsessed by laissez-faire economics and international free trade. So when uranium producers sued the federal government to force it to limit uranium imports to 25 percent of domestic consumption—arguing that section 161B of the Atomic Energy Act required the administration to sustain a "viable domestic uranium industry"—the Reagan administration responded with legislation to establish a free-trade pact with Canada and repeal section 161B.

Craig Bigler recalls the effect of that national struggle on Moab. He is an economist who has worked in the Utah State Planning Office and the Rural Development Service of the U.S. Department of Agriculture. After retiring in 1985, he settled in Moab. "When I got here," Bigler recalls, "a lot of people were still convinced that the declining uranium industry was just an aberration brought on us through some kind of conspiracy of the federal government—the agencies, the bureaucrats—and the environmentalists. But people finally began to realize that the culprit is the Reagan administration. And if you really like to get to the root of things, the culprit is the Carter administration, for creating the boom in the first place," Bigler says.

Carter's "moral equivalent of war"—the drive for national energy independence—affected more than southeastern Utah. Oil-shale projects were booming in western Colorado; electric power plants were under construction in Montana and elsewhere; small towns were booming in Wyoming's overthrust belt; uranium was being mined in Wyoming, New Mexico, and Colorado; a coal gasification plant was being built in North Dakota; and new coal mines were being opened in every Western state. The energy boom played itself out in different ways in different parts of the region, but it was all part of the same dynamic. "The price of uranium skyrocketed in 1977, 1978," explains Bigler. "The energy companies just went bananas—the bids they put up for the oil-shale properties, and the prices they were paying to get uranium mines dug and plants built, and wages, and so forth. It was like, 'My God, this is permanent. It is going to be this way.' "

If it was Carter's campaign for energy self-sufficiency that created the golden goose, it was Ronald Reagan who chopped off its head. "The Reagan adminis-

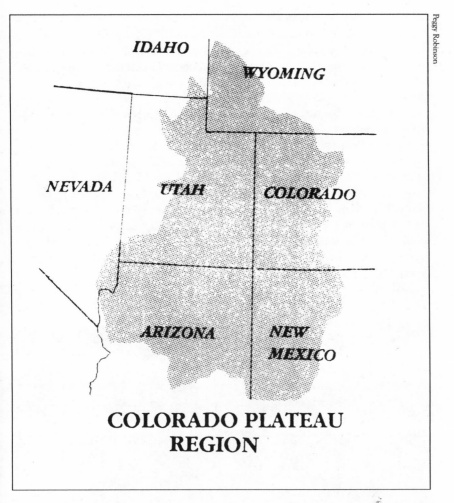

Peggy Robinson

**COLORADO PLATEAU
REGION**

tration didn't merely dismantle Carter's energy policy," says Bigler, staring off into the starlit sky above the 700-foot wall of blood red sandstone behind his home. "They tore it to shreds. Being free traders in their hearts and souls, they opened the market. And you know what happens when you open the market. The industry that's really overpriced just falls apart."

For thirty-five years the federal government had been subsidizing the energy economy of the West: building hydroelectric dams, building roads, selling off water and coal and petroleum and uranium resources at fire-sale rates. Moab's spectacular uranium boom of the fifties, for example, was wholly a creation of massive federal subsidies. Federal subsidies had been a way of life as long as anyone could remember. In 1976, even as the Sagebrush Rebels were castigat-

ing the federal government for meddling in local affairs, a nonprofit organization called the Utah Foundation did a study of federal expenditures in Utah.
The results were revealing. For every dollar of tax revenue, the federal government was spending $1.25 in Utah. Federal outlays in Grand County for fiscal
1976 totaled $16 million, or nearly half of the wage and salary income of all
Grand County residents. That was a whopping $2,462 of federal expenditures
for every person in the county—a per capita rate 46 percent higher than the
national average.

Bigler, now a free-lance journalist, says, "Back in 1973, the man who
created the Economic Development Administration in the Department of
Commerce came to Utah to make a study of rural economic development
programs—simply because the programs in Utah were better at getting federal
funds than those in any of the surrounding states. "The fact is, all rural
communities in southern Utah have been very successful in getting those
kinds of federal subsidies. . . . If you read the history, it's one government
program saving the community after another, always. Building roads, building
dams, building irrigation systems . . . that sort of thing has been going on for a
long, long time."

Raymond Wheeler

Craig Bigler

In 1980 the residents of Grand County had marched off to the polls to vote Ronald Reagan into office by three to one. Reagan had won their support by promising to slash federal spending. In their rush to the polls, Grand County voters had forgotten one important fact. If Reagan followed through on his promise, they would be the first victims.

The Battle for the Colorado Plateau

If the election of Ronald Reagan proved disastrous to the Sagebrush Rebels, the defeat of the Bureau of Land Management wilderness inventory was even worse. To understand why, one must examine the history of environmental warfare on the Colorado Plateau.

The Colorado Plateau is a 130,000-square-mile oval of land straddling Utah, Colorado, New Mexico, and Arizona—the "four corners" states whose borders intersect at its navel. Originally named the "Colorado Plateaus" by explorer John Wesley Powell, the "plateau" is in fact a basin—the erosional masterpiece of the Colorado River and its tributaries. Shaped by simultaneous erosion and uplift, its landscape is formidable, an impenetrable maze of canyons studded with soaring laccolithic mountain ranges, cliff-banded mesas, high forested plateaus, and domes and "reefs" of folded, tilted sedimentary rock. From anywhere on the rim of this huge basin, one has the sensation of peering into a single, vast room. Its high desert climate and savage topography have molded history to its shape. The trails of the Southwest tell the story: in their westerly march, explorers veered wildly in the vicinity of canyon country. The Spanish Trail, for example, wandered two hundred miles north between Santa Fe and Las Vegas.

By deflecting the pioneer advance, the wild core of the Colorado Plateau shaped an enduring anomaly. Unexplored, it remained unsettled. Unsettled, it remained wild. Wild, it remained public domain. It harbors today one of the largest concentrations of publicly owned wilderness in the lower forty-eight states. The plateau is one of the most charismatic landscapes on earth: a world of dazzling sunshine, crystalline air, infinite vistas, profound silence, and landforms so powerful, so mysterious, so diverse, ingenious, colorful, intricate, and bizarre that they constitute, in toto, a separate reality.

This huge basin is a world apart, one of entirely fresh possibilities. Stand upon any one of its power points—the lake-spotted, waterfall-siphoned rim of the Aquarius Plateau; the spaceship-dome summits of the Henry Mountains; the knife-edge of the San Rafael Reef; the exquisite solitary rock needles of Monument Valley; the flight deck called Cape Final—and one feels its strange power in one's soul. Where else can one scan one thousand miles of entrenched canyons without sighting a trace of human habitation? Where else can one find the intact remains of a lost civilization scattered carelessly across 150,000 square miles of desert and canyon wilderness? Where else are there 10 million acres with a smaller population than one thousand years ago?

The wild core of the Colorado Plateau is one of the last places where both environmentalists and developers can still dream impossible dreams. That is why, for fifty years, the plateau has been a battlefield. The war began in 1935 with two events: the completion of Hoover Dam and the campaign within the U.S. Department of Interior to designate a 4.5-million-acre Escalante National Monument.

The construction of Hoover Dam was a watershed in more ways than one. The project's magnitude inspired the formation of an industrial cartel—the so-called Six Companies—Bechtel, Kaiser, Morrison-Knudsen, McDonald Kahn, J. F. Shea Corporation, and Utah Construction Company (now Utah International). The firms earned more from Hoover Dam than the $10 million in profit. They also gained a vision. They saw that just as the hydroelectric potential of the Colorado River had been captured for export by Hoover Dam, so could the other vital resources of the interior West—Colorado River water, coal, uranium, tar sands, oil shale, and clean air—be exported. In the past these resources had not been developed because of the cost of transportation across the plateau's vast, rugged landscape. But by combining their capital and political clout, as with Hoover Dam, the Six Companies had proved stupendous construction projects were both possible and profitable.

Thus was born the Grand Plan described by Robert Gottleib and Peter Wiley in their book, *Empires in the Sun*. The strategy of the Grand Plan was elementary. The Colorado Plateau would become a natural resource colony and garbage dump for the sunbelt towns around it. By combining their political influence, the leading industrial powers of the Southwest would persuade the federal government to throw open the interior of the Colorado Plateau to massive, federally subsidized development: dams, aqueducts, oil-shale projects, coal mines, power plants, transmission lines, and an infrastructure of new highways, pipelines, and railroads.

Coal mined on the plateau would be burned, in situ, in huge new coal-fired power plants, whose polluting emissions could be expelled across the vast wastelands at the heart of the plateau. A string of huge dams on the Colorado and Green rivers would supply Los Angeles, Phoenix, Denver, and Salt Lake City with the water they would need to sustain growth. Additional electricity could be generated by a string of nuclear power plants on the West Coast, which would consume uranium mined and milled on the plateau, only to return it—for permanent storage—as nuclear waste.

Even as Western energy, construction, and utilities companies formulated their Grand Plan, a second constituency was rising. In 1935 the National Park Service announced a plan to designate several huge new national monuments in southern Utah. By 1936 that plan, enthusiastically endorsed by Secretary of the Interior Harold Ickes, had become a proposal to create a 4.5-million-acre Escalante National Monument, stretching from Moab west to the town of Escalante and south to the Arizona border. In November 1936 Wilderness Society founder Robert Marshall published a map of America's largest remaining roadless areas. On it the single largest block in the lower forty-eight—at 8.9 million acres—was the canyon country at the heart of the Colorado Plateau. Marshall identified 19 million acres of wildlands on the plateau. Thanks to Ickes's proposal and Bob Marshall's map, a national constituency for the Colorado Plateau had been born.

The Escalante monument proposal was quashed by vigorous opposition from Utah's governor and congressional delegation, but national interest in protecting the canyon country grew. That growth became visible in 1956, when the Western water lobby introduced legislation to construct a dam in Echo Park on the Green River inside Colorado's Dinosaur National Monument. The reaction was fierce. Environmental groups all over the nation joined forces, pooling resources to churn out brochures, books, magazine articles, and letters opposing the dam. The Echo Park Dam battle was the first of a series of spectacular confrontations and trade-offs between developers and environmentalists.

To ward off the Echo Park Dam, environmentalists supported construction of a dam in Glen Canyon. In 1966 environmentalists waged a second campaign to block the damming of Grand Canyon, only to watch the proposal transformed, by Interior Secretary Stewart Udall, into strip mining on Black Mesa and the construction of the Navajo coal-fired power plant at Page, Arizona.

But by 1980 the national constituency for the Colorado Plateau had proved itself one of the most powerful political forces affecting the West. In rapid succession it had succeeded in stalling, relocating, or killing five major development projects: the Kaiparowits coal mine and power plant in 1976; the proposed Intermountain Power Project plant near Capitol Reef National Park in 1977; the proposed Trans-Escalante highway in 1979; the proposed Warner Valley power plant near Zion National Park; and the proposed Alton coal strip mine near Bryce National Park in 1980. With each confrontation the membership and financial backing of the national environmental groups soared. In 1966 and 1967, during the controversy over dams in the Grand Canyon, the membership of the Sierra Club doubled. During the reign of Interior Secretary James Watt, it doubled again.

When the Forest Service and BLM launched their nationwide wilderness inventories in 1979, developers and conservationists understood that the future of the Colorado Plateau was at stake. Virtually every major potential development site—the Kaiparowits Plateau, the original Intermountain Power Project site near Capitol Reef National Park, the Escalante canyons along the Trans-Escalante highway route, the Utah Tar Sands Triangle straddling the Dirty Devil River canyons, the proposed nuclear waste dump site near Canyonlands National Park, the Henry Mountains coal fields, the oil and gas deposits of the Book Cliffs, the potash deposits adjacent to Labyrinth Canyon—all lay in the heart of enormous roadless areas that easily qualified for designation as wilderness.

By November 1980, when both agencies had completed their wilderness inventories, the legacy of the Sagebrush Rebellion was clear. All across the Colorado Plateau—virtually everywhere wilderness coincided with mineral resources, commercial timber, or major development sites—the Forest Service and BLM had omitted vast blocks of pristine wilderness from its wilderness inventory. In the Book Cliffs, the BLM had omitted 227,000 acres of wildlands harboring oil, natural gas, and coal. In the San Rafael Swell, BLM had omitted 350,000 acres of wildlands surrounding the proposed Intermountain Power Plant site. North of Canyonlands National Park, BLM had omitted 80,000 acres of wildlands to accommodate exploration and production of potash.

Sixty-five thousand acres of spectacular slot canyons surrounding Natural Bridges National Monument had been cut from BLM's wilderness inventory to facilitate uranium exploration. Eighty-seven thousand acres of wilderness bordering Canyonlands National Park had been omitted to facilitate tar sands production and the siting of a nuclear waste repository. Two hundred thousand acres had been whacked from wilderness study areas in the Henry Mountains to allow strip mining of coal in the Mancos Shale badlands. And some 387,000 acres of pristine wildlands on the Kaiparowits Plateau had been cut to allow the future development of Kaiparowits coal. For the Colorado Plateau, the wilderness inventories of 1979–1980 had been precisely the reverse of what Congress had intended. Congress had asked for a thorough inventory of the nation's last unprotected wildlands. Instead it got commercial and industrial zoning.

But the Sagebrush Rebels' campaign had an unforeseen side effect. While it worked well on politicians and bureaucrats, its effect on Utah's grassroots environmental movement was equal and opposite. Between 1981 and 1984 a coalition of local and national environmental groups filed appeals challenging BLM's wilderness inventory in Utah. The appeals were the largest and most successful in the history of the Interior Board of Land Appeals. In all they added 625,000 acres in fifteen wilderness study areas. The very first wilderness study area restored was Negro Bill Canyon.

The administrative appeals were the tip of an iceberg. In 1984 a new environmental group arose in Utah. Based in southern Utah and managed by a former BLM wilderness coordinator, the Southern Utah Wilderness Alliance (SUWA) was dedicated to correcting the BLM wilderness inventory. If the Sagebrush Rebellion was a backlash against FLPMA (the Federal Lands Policy Management Act), the Southern Utah Wilderness Alliance was a backlash against the Sagebrush Rebellion. Fueled by bitter memories of the Bulldozer

Wars and a membership of committed Colorado Plateau aficionados, SUWA's growth was the kind southeastern Utah had expected from energy development. Within three years the organization had thirteen hundred members, five full-time employees, a "metro" office in Salt Lake City, and a budget of more than $100,000 a year.

The emergence of SUWA triggered a battle for control of the environmental movement in Utah. Prior to 1985 the Utah Wilderness Association had dominated Utah environmental politics. Its general policy was to live with rather than confront Utah's prodevelopment politics. By comparison, SUWA and other Utah and national groups were becoming more and more aggressive. The differences came to a head in 1984 when a dozen local and national environmental groups held a series of meetings to hammer out a consensus BLM wilderness proposal for Utah. The meetings quickly evolved into a contest of wills between moderate and activist factions. The moderates, led by the Utah Wilderness Association, argued that environmentalists should quietly drop controversial areas such as Negro Bill Canyon. The activists, led by SUWA and the Utah chapter of the Sierra Club, argued that it was foolish to make concessions simply to avoid controversy.

After five meetings, the attempt at consensus broke down. When the dust cleared, the Utah Wilderness Association stood virtually alone with its proposal for 3.8 million acres of BLM wildlands. And a coalition of sixteen local and national groups supported a 5.1-million-acre proposal. By 1987 the consortium, calling itself the Utah Wilderness Coalition, had grown to twenty-two groups. In the past Utah and national conservation groups had been divided by suspicion. Now they were working together. By pooling their resources they could tap a large number of local and national supporters. In the spring of 1986 the new coalition tested its strength.

In February BLM had announced its preliminary wilderness recommendation for Utah. Out of 22 million acres of roadless land, the agency could find only 1.9 million acres worth protecting as wilderness. The Utah Wilderness Coalition launched a massive campaign for public comment critical of the BLM recommendation. In five months BLM received comments from more than two thousand individuals supporting the coalition's proposal. And for the first time ever, in public hearings held across southern Utah, wilderness supporters outnumbered opponents.

When this news reached national environmental leaders, there was a predictable response. By November 1987 three national conservation organizations had established new field offices in Utah—the Sierra Club, The Wilderness Society, and The Nature Conservancy. Both the Sierra Club and The Wilderness Society had made it clear that the battle for wilderness on the Colorado Plateau would be among their foremost national priorities. The political landscape of Utah was bristling with environmental lobbyists—no fewer than seven separate offices manned by a dozen paid staff.

The Sagebrush Rebels had defeated the wilderness inventory, but they were finding it more difficult to defeat public opinion. Each year the American public, including an overwhelming majority of Utahns, grew more oriented to environmental protection. That shift—the greening of America and of the West—has been illustrated by a number of political events. The first was the resignation of Interior Secretary James Watt. Watt personified the political power of the Sagebrush Rebels, and his departure was a death rattle of the Sagebrush Rebellion.

Closer to home, another event threatened the Sagebrush Rebels. In November 1986 outspoken environmental advocate Wayne Owens won election to Utah's second congressional district seat, representing the Wasatch front. For a decade the second district election had been a cliff-hanger. Owens had won the seat in 1972, only to lose a Senate race to Orrin Hatch in 1974. In each subsequent election year, the battle for the second district seat had been a confrontation between liberal, environmentally oriented Democrats and conservative, development-oriented Republicans.

Owens had made his 1986 campaign a test of the "Green Vote"—the constituency for environmental protection. Throughout the campaign he hammered at the need for a change in the Utah delegation—consistently rated among the lowest in the nation by the League of Conservation Voters. He was rewarded with vigorous support from a coalition of conservation groups led by the Utah chapter of the Sierra Club, and then with a solid 10 percent margin of victory. In local elections seven of eight candidates backed by the Utah environmental coalition won election to the state legislature.

The election results were confirmed by a series of public opinion polls. In 1983 a statewide opinion poll revealed that 69 percent of the respondents favored wilderness designation for at least 900,000 acres of BLM land in the state. Forty-nine percent wanted substantially more BLM wilderness than the agency had recommended; 36 percent wanted less. A 1986 poll by Utah State University found that 83 percent agreed that "environmentally sensitive areas need official designation as wilderness," 75 percent agreed that "wilderness designation enhances recreation opportunity," and 78 percent agreed that wilderness enhances the image of Utah as a tourism state.

By 1987 it was clear that the Sagebrush Rebellion had changed the balance of power between environmental moderates and activists. In July 1987 the moderate Utah Wilderness Association arranged a meeting with Wayne Owens to promote BLM wilderness legislation for Utah.

Mindful of disagreement between the Utah Wilderness Association and other conservation groups, Owens invited representatives of the Utah Wilderness Coalition to join the discussion. As the meeting began, a dozen people representing Utah Wilderness Coalition member groups walked in and hammered the moderate proposal to death. They told an astonished Wayne Owens that they were not interested in a weak wilderness bill. They had accepted, back in 1984, a wilderness bill for national forest lands in Utah that had resulted in a small amount of wilderness and a large amount of land being released to logging. Never again, they told Owens, would they support a "release bill" masquerading as a wilderness bill.

In the view of the coalition, the local and national constituency for wilderness had only begun to grow. Conservationists felt "strong enough to wait," Wilderness Society representative Darrell Knuffke said, "until we are strong enough to win." Utah environmentalists had metamorphosed from lambs into lions. The Sagebrush Rebellion had hardened their hearts. If the federal land management agencies would not enforce federal law, then Utah's environmentalists would do it in the media, in the voting booth, and in federal court.

A major test of that resolve came in January 1987, when Garfield County secured funding to "upgrade" the remote Burr Trail, a narrow dirt road surrounded by 750,000 acres of proposed wilderness. It was a familiar scenario. The upgrading proposal was the first stage in a master plan for widening, paving, and ultimately transforming the 66-mile-long Burr Trail into a major east-west transportation corridor across the remote wildlands of the Escalante country.

Once again, Utah county commissioners were lobbying for federal subsidies to finance development at the heart of the Colorado Plateau. Estimates by the Federal Highway Administration pegged the total cost of the paving project at $37 million—$9,000 for every person in Garfield County. The reaction of the environmentalists was prompt: they went to court in an extended attempt to stop the project.

The Utah Wilderness Coalition had been forged in response to the Sagebrush Rebellion. Now this latest effort by those who fomented the Sagebrush Rebellion—to build a major highway through the Colorado Plateau—was being fought by the environmentalist organization the rebellion had provoked into being. By combining resources, the new coalition could afford a prolonged legal battle over the Burr Trail and similar proposed actions.

The struggle over the Burr Trail project is much more than a battle to protect the fragile canyons through which the road passes. "It's about power," explains Clive Kincaid, former executive director of the Southern Utah Wilderness Alliance. "And it's about the future of the Colorado Plateau. Will it be developed with an eye to what's exceptional about it, or will it be developed haphazardly? Who's going to have the authority to provide that guiding hand?"

Part Three

THE IMPACT
OF
ENVIRONMENTALISM

CHAPTER SEVENTEEN

Coming into a New Land

Ed Marston

OVER THE last twenty years or so, quietly and without any organizing help, a new kind of people moved into the rural West to make new lives. They came with a variety of skills and for a variety of reasons. They were both pushed out of the nation's urban areas and pulled to the new land and new lives represented by the rural West. They were of all types, and few of them realized they were part of something that could be called a movement. They came in search of a difficult mix: the social and physical freedom the rural West represented and to build a new, collective way of life. For the most part, they came to rest in the rural West's larger cities and in the resort towns: the Bozemans, Grand Junctions, Boises, Aspens, and Santa Fes. But a significant number moved into traditional small towns.

In many of the places they chose to settle, they were a new phenomenon. The West has always been populated by migrants from other parts of the country, but in the past most newcomers have come from mining backgrounds or from other rural areas. The Rocky Mountain valleys, for example, have always beckoned to those who dwelled on the arid plains to the east. But these relatively well-educated seekers of both lifestyle and community, many of them children of the 1960s, came from urban areas and were neither miners, farmers, nor merchants. Moreover, they didn't come to get rich, as did the forty-niners and the more recent construction boomers. If anything, these children of often well-to-do parents came to get poor. Or rather, they came in search of things that had little to do with material possessions.

Whatever their personal motives, the newcomers were to become a key element in the recent successes of environmentalism in the rural West. They were the on-the-ground troops, some would call them the fifth column, that forged the environmental victories of the past two decades. Their impact was a result of their being where people with urban values and environmental leanings had never before lived. Almost against their will, they found themselves functioning initially as a sort of early-warning system in fights over logging, coal leasing, the deletion of wilderness study areas, and the birth of efforts to build dams. Later, as their numbers and their awareness of the pressures on the surrounding public lands increased, they coalesced into groups and became more than just sounders of alarms.

Suddenly, then, the damned environmentalists were no longer people with addresses only in San Francisco, New York, and Denver. Appeals of Forest Service and BLM actions, letters to the editor, speakers at public hearings on public land development projects, and letterheads of environmental groups came with names and addresses from within the affected locales. Forest Service and BLM officials were being engaged in conversations by local environmentalists in their offices, while shopping on Main Street or at open-school nights. It was a new phenomenon, and it had results out of proportion to the numbers involved.

In Frederick Pohl's and C. M. Kornbluth's science-fiction novel *The Space Merchants,* an oppressed group called the consies—short for conservationists, and a play on commies—attempts to slow the environmental devastation of the earth. Environmentalists who think their movement has done poorly over the past few decades should read that novel and see what the future looked like back then to two futurist novelists.

Environmentalists' achievements have been especially impressive in the rural West. Their efforts on offense have led to vast expanses of legislated wilderness, the growing movement to protect rivers, the use of the Clean Air Act to maintain the clarity of the air flowing through parks and wilderness, and the protection of numerous endangered species. On defense, environmentalists have made a bulldoglike effort to stop or reduce the logging of forested lands, the exploration for oil and gas, and the mining of sensitive public lands.

It is a measure of the dispersed strength of the movement that there is no one spectacular battle, as there was over the Grand Canyon or Dinosaur National Monument in the 1950s. Instead, there are continual skirmishes fought on every unit of public land in the rural West. They start on the ground, in district or area offices of the Forest Service or BLM, and by a process of natural selection the strong cases and those that gain local and national

support go to the Congress or through the appeals and judicial system to the
ninth or tenth circuit courts of appeals. Those efforts act as a deadweight on
natural resource development—a viselike hold on the exploration legs of oil
and mineral companies. The corporate behemoths keep moving, of course, but
they must drag one or both legs. It is a war of attrition, fought in hundreds of
valleys and drainages, and no one knows the extent of that war or how it is
influencing the West's development.

At the other end of the scale, as far from the grass roots as you get, are the
efforts that passed the array of laws that make possible environmentalists' on-
the-ground success: the National Environmental Policy Act, the Endangered
Species Act, the Clean Air Act, the Wilderness Act, the various land management acts.

Somewhere in between are the court cases, many out of the ninth circuit
court of appeals, that have made the management of the public lands less
arbitrary. Many of these cases had their roots in local conservation outrage
over some activity undertaken by the Forest Service or Bureau of Land Management. But the ultimate disposition of the case, and its value in setting
policy for the region, depended on the deeper pockets and the legal expertise of
a national group.

These are the tangible results of two decades of extensive on-the-ground
action by environmentalists in the rural West. But there are also intangible

Ed/Betsy Marston

results that may prove more important. For starters, it appears that the Forest Service has tipped. It may take a decade or two for that tipping to become clear, but the agency has reversed its proextraction, pro–tree farm direction. It has begun, in an uneven way, to pull back from the brink, despite a cadre of Reagan-era administrators who tried for eight years to push the agency to its death.

The Forest Service may have been saved by the example of a sister land management agency, the U.S. Bureau of Reclamation, which is falling to its death, this time shoved there with a large assist from environmentalists. It is difficult to tell, in a land whose waterways are largely dammed, that the West's most powerful group—the water establishment—has been defeated. But it has been, and that defeat is symbolized nationally by the shrinking budget and internal confusion of the bureau.

There is another major intangible: unlike any private or government entity in the West, environmentalists have an agenda for the land and the streams and rivers. It is embodied in the let-burn policy for fires, in reintroduction of wolves and grizzlies, in the creation of more wilderness, in the beginnings of wild-river protection, and in the effort to transcend state boundaries and to focus on the land by talking of Colorado Plateaus and Yellowstone ecosystems.

Another intangible accomplishment is the achievement of so many far-reaching environmentalist goals and the establishment of a strong agenda without generating a significant backlash. Even in the rural West, hostility to environmentalists—local and national—is low. The lack of a backlash doesn't mean environmentalists are wonderful people. Rather, it means that the extractive culture in the West and the pave-it-over culture of the larger America have been unable to establish themselves as more legitimate than environmentalism. America in the 1980s has turned away from compassion toward people but has retained a softness for the land and its denizens.

The above reads like a brochure for the Sierra Club. It is accurate, so far as it goes, but it glosses over complications and deeper truths. Much of what is attributed here to environmentalism was helped along mightily by the global economy and the ending of certain economic cycles. The Bureau of Reclamation ran out of dam sites and irrigable land. In many of its forests, the Forest Service ran out of trees it could cut economically. Urban populations grew and became less convinced that the production of commodities was tied to their well-being and became more concerned about nature. Finally, the consequences and long-term costs of dam building, logging, grazing, mining, and milling have become ever more clear and have received ever more publicity.

There is something else that detracts from the meaning of the environmentalist triumph: much of it was forged in Washington, D.C., rather than on the ground. A powerful force, like the oil companies, may put faith in top-down influence. But environmentalists must know that dependence on Washington and on a large, but largely distant and uninformed, constituency is stopgap at best. Those who believe in a livable future for the rural West look to the grass roots to create that future. The closest word for this strategy is bioregional. But bioregional has a highfalutin sound—it implies a drawing of boundaries by experts in flora, fauna, geology. It sounds as if man and his works are excluded, or only tolerated. A broader term is needed: something that means "an attachment to the West"—to its air, its sky, its several kinds of magnificent landscapes, its communities, and, perhaps most important because it determines so much else, to its ways of earning a living. The replacement for bioregional—I don't have one in mind—should also incorporate the differentness of the West from the rest of America. This does not mean a civil war, or a quest for separation. It simply means cultural and economic self-determination.

In what direction will this evolution, partly provoked by newcomers fleeing the other America and partly due to larger economic forces affecting the region and the nation, take the West? To answer that, we must see where we started. Part of America's rural renaissance, as described by Dennis Brownridge in Chapter Two, was an uncoordinated, spontaneous flow of urban people into small communities in the West. There were some back-to-the-land attempts, but the bulk of rural migration focused on small towns rather than on ranches and farms, The West, it is important to remember, is very urban. Houses don't dot the countryside—towns dot the countryside. The newcomers didn't swap a typewriter or drill press or teller's cage for a tractor; they simply changed the scale of their lives from big city or suburb to small town and from $10 to $15 per hour to $4 to $7 per hour.

The flow of urbanites to the rural West can be compared to the Mormon migration to Utah's Great Salt Lake. The Mormons arrived, after an incredibly arduous trip, at Zion in late July 1847. A day after they arrived, they were at work plowing, planting, and diverting water out of streams onto the land. Today's urbanite didn't come west to escape religious persecution and found a nation, as the Mormons did. But they did come for the land, and, uncoordinated and individual though their migration was, many shared an ideology. It is safe to say that the day after today's migrants arrived in the West, they were out on the land hiking, skiing, fishing, hunting. It is also safe to say that the land they were out on was public land.

The newcomers were brought west by the public land; but it was an uncritical attraction—the land was beautiful, the air was clear, the possibilities endless. It was only after they moved into the region that the land came into focus, and they saw the problems and the conflicts. That realization, in turn, separated newcomers into bands. Some, probably most, remained nonpolitical and uninvolved. They avoided issues. They found the streams that had access and fish, or the land that hadn't been logged or hadn't had its access closed.

Others reacted oppositely and were drawn by the problems. Rather than shift their attention from a threatened or damaged area, they shifted to that area. Their fear was that if this threatened stream or valley went, the next one would go soon after. These people coalesced into groups such as the chapters of the Idaho Conservation League, the Northern Plains Resource Council, the Western Colorado Congress, the various state wildlife federations, the Wyoming Outdoor Council, the Montana Wilderness Association.

Those who became active environmentalists in the small towns found themselves in opposition to the local establishment and to their neighbors. Those neighbors, friendly when met at the post office or supermarket, turned angry, and sometimes mean, at public meetings. It was usually at public hearings on development projects that newcomers first saw what a strain they were putting on their new hometown or how their presence jarred. In the heat of public discussions about a new mine or power plant or logging mill, the feelings emerged.

Local people wondered why well-educated young people would accept a low-wage life in a rural area when their own children felt compelled to move away in order to pursue the money available outside the West's rural valleys. They wondered why these urban young people, these hippies who had been raised in a comparative lap of luxury, were now opposing progress and the creation of well-paying jobs. Local people were especially bitter because the young newcomers were writing letters, filing appeals, and creating organizations to oppose the creation of jobs that might bring the area's *real* children home.

That was the polite part. The impolite part had to do with remarks about the newcomers' sources of income—food stamps and trust funds were equally objectionable—about their tendency to grow and consume marijuana, about their sexual habits, and about all the other matters of lifestyle that small-town residents are bound to note, imagine, and criticize about outsiders who move in among them. The surprising thing wasn't that there was friction but that there was no worse than friction and that the existing community, despite its differences from the newcomers, was far more open and accepting than might have been expected. In formal settings clashes could be strong and angry. In everyday life, there was acceptance, or at least enough tolerance to prevent unbearable hostility.

Newcomers and local people might not play bridge together, or ride snow machines together, or—especially—intermarry. But there was enough formal and informal interaction to keep the place stuck together. The need for that interaction was clearest to those few who tried to make it on the land. There was one young urbanite-turned-farmer who took his cues from his nearest neighbor. He planted when the neighbor planted, irrigated when the neighbor irrigated, and harvested when the neighbor harvested. One August, when most of the other hay in the area had been cut, the neighbor still hadn't started cutting his. Finally, the newcomer ran into the neighbor at the post office and asked, "When are you going to start your second cutting."

"I'm already ten days late," came the reply. "I'm waiting on a part for my tractor."

But the newcomers brought skills too, although they were not always welcome. Usually frustrated on public land issues at the local level, and recognizing that they were outnumbered, they started using their corridor-smarts of bureaucratic procedures that any urbanite has: they wrote letters, filed appeals, set up telephone-calling trees, lobbied bureaucrats. Fifty percent of the land in the West is owned and managed by public entities, and every inch of it, in theory, is subject to bureaucratic procedures.

Obviously, the users of the public lands were not helpless. The traditional good-old-boy methods were firmly in place. Ranchers, loggers, and others who used the public lands had a rapport with land managers that the newcomers could not achieve. Moreover, the local people were very well connected politically. The head of a national environmental group, let alone a local group, couldn't get a BLM manager transferred; almost any morning cafe gathering of ranchers could.

The result was predictable. Local environmental groups always tried to get decisions moved up to higher, more "objective" levels. They ran to the appeals procedure or the courts; the local people ran to their county commissioners or legislative representative or senator. Local people used the hometown weekly; environmentalists sought to bring in the larger newspapers or even national press, which would recognize them as legitimate objectors rather than as hippie newcomers or a vocal minority. This was the basic strategy employed in a wide variety of fights: access to public land, coal mining leases, oil and gas exploration permits, ski area permits, establishment of wilderness areas, protection of grizzlies, building of dams, spraying of herbicides and pesticides.

A different kind of struggle was going on within the communities on issues that had nothing to do with the land. But they were underlain by the same divisions. Craftspeople in a community would want to have the main street blocked off for a crafts fair. Had the request come from any other organization, it would have been honored. In this case, however, the town council finds five reasons to refuse the permit. Stores sprout "No shoes, no shirts, no service" signs; a more forthright one advertises "Hippies stay out!"

A roadside hot springs, long ignored, becomes a gathering place for newcomers and is bulldozed or signed off-limits by the county. A place long opposed to controls suddenly decides to bend its own dislike of rules to outlaw tepees or yurts or outhouses. An infant public radio station, started of course by newcomers, goes looking for funds among local merchants and gets turned down. A newcomer, resident in the community for only five years, can't get a teaching job; the district prefers someone with a more conventional background.

Within nearly every rural Western community there was this newly arrived, squirmy body of newcomers—incredulous both at how much was *right* within the community and on the public land around it, and at how much needed improving.

Perhaps the most interesting clashes came over planning and zoning. Rhetorically, the long-time residents were against planning and zoning. "A man has a right to do what he wants with his land." The newcomers were for planning: "We've got to protect this wonderful place." The unspoken, perhaps unthought, argument was different. At least until the early 1970s, most small communities hadn't needed planning or zoning, which was rigidly controlled by a lack of money and by strong social interaction. A newcomer with a house on the highway discovered the social controls when he began to prune some beautiful old cottonwoods on his land. Everyone, he said, seemed to have a right to stop and question him closely about what he was going to do to the trees.

Newcomers moved to the small Western towns because they were attractive communities made up of low-priced modest homes, dirt streets in many places, large trees. There was unregulated "mixed use"—typically a beauty shop or gunsmith or taxidermist in a residential area. Occasionally, there was a backyard mechanic—every 1,000-square-foot home seemed to have attached to it a 1,000-square-foot heated workshop. But there was so little traffic that the few extra cars generated by a small business was no problem. That's the way things were and the way things had been for a long time. Despite the lack of controls, the towns looked good to those newly arrived from planned and zoned suburbs.

The need for planning, or the imagined need for planning, arrived with the energy and mineral boom, but it was hastened by the newcomers' need to protect the "nice" houses some of them wanted to build, by their need to create an economy that met their needs, by the need to protect the town against the next wave of newcomers.

The way was being prepared for this next wave by the first wave of newcomers, who were changing the small towns by their social and political efforts, and by their unconscious or conscious promotion of the area to distant family and friends. (People who wouldn't have thought of living in a small Western town in the early 1970s find them quite acceptable places in the late 1980s because they have been transformed by an earlier generation of newcomers.)

These conflicts over development and regulation raged into the early 1980s, and then were cut short by the bust. As schools, churches, subdivisions and trailer parks, and Main Streets emptied, fights over development, education, and planning took a backseat. In addition, the social and economic position of the newcomers changed. Overnight, skills that the newcomers had used to oppose development that the larger community wanted were suddenly in demand, as tourism, retirement, and other nonrural economic activities became potential saviors.

Just as quickly, the presence of extractive industries receded, and then essentially vanished. It was as if everyone—executives, miners, county commissioners and mayors, and the cadres of developers and boosters—suddenly realized that extraction's day was done. Equally surprising is how shallow were the roots of the extractive industries. The mines and exploration drills may have gone deep into the ground, but companies did little in the communities. Looking back, it is clear that they were not in business for the long term. They built their mines and mills, managed them from afar, put little or nothing into the communities in the way of education or spin-off businesses, and when they left, they left as if they never intended to return.

They were true colonial occupiers in the sense that they had put down only mechanical and financial roots. They had never committed to the region from the top down. That made it easier to pull out of a community, but it also meant that the occupied community had no loyalty to the company. Pittsburgh may have loyalty to U.S. Steel; Lander, Wyoming, which once hosted a U.S. Steel iron ore mine, has no such attachment. The extractive industries' hearts are not where their workers and their ore bodies are; their hearts are where their front offices are. So long as the rural West's only options have been extraction, coal and oil and timber companies could treat local towns like dirt. But now that the West may have choices, the situation is changing.

Take, for example, what happened in Crested Butte, Colorado. It was originally a silver and then a coal-mining town. When the mines closed and the companies left, vacationers bought up the miners' homes for pennies on the dollar. A laid-back summer tourist economy and then a ski industry grew up in and around the town's wooden frame houses and unpaved streets. Twenty years later, when the mining industry sought to come back in the form of a proposal from the AMAX mining company, for a large molybdenum mine, it got a hot welcome. A transformed Crested Butte, including its city government, chamber of commerce, and representative to the board of county commissioners, wanted no part of a mining economy, however much AMAX and the Forest Service talked of returning the town to its roots.

The mining industry had abandoned Crested Butte, forcing the miners to sell out and move. It had let nonmining interests pick up the homes and community infrastructure for spare change. Then when the industry tried to return, newcomers used the town as a base from which to fight the proposal. The struggle, which took place in the late 1970s and early 1980s, was rich in ironies.

The Forest Service, for example, was accustomed to wrapping itself in the flag of local economic need and playing on the desire of the local community for the extractive jobs. That worked especially well against environmentalists who lived elsewhere. In this case the agency was confronted with a community that was joining distant environmental groups in opposing the development. The agency, of course, did AMAX's bidding as best it could, but it had to do it shorn of the usual rhetoric. The delaying tactics of the locals and the crash of the molybdenum market killed the 800-person mine. Crested Butte avoided the crash that would have come had work on the mine begun, and AMAX lost only the $120 million it had put into planning and land acquisition. Both were lucky.

In general, the extractive industries didn't build a social environment that could last. They took no long-term responsibility for the communities that grew up alongside their operations. If they practiced philanthropy, supported the arts, and built better schools and colleges, they usually did so in their headquarters cities rather than at the rural roots of their wealth.

There may be a lesson here for the environmental movement—insofar as one can talk about this loose grouping as a movement. This movement is focused on the land, and over the past several years that focus has made it triumphant. But unless the environmental movement figures out how to live in the West among Westerners and as Westerners, it runs the risk of losing the present advantage in the next inevitable economic upheaval, just as the extractive industries have lost their grip on the region. The environmental agenda of more wilderness, more wild rivers, less logging, less drilling, and less mining is well enough, so far as it goes. But a vision that sees only land and wildlife has the same weakness as a vision that sees only ore bodies and old-growth forests. A vision that does not recognize the small communities and rural human activities that accompany the land and wildlife has an enormous blindspot.

Until recently, environmentalist attempts to involve themselves in the lives of small, traditional Western communities would have been like Americans making plans for the French countryside. That may no longer be true, for things have changed drastically in the rural West. First, it has had a very large economic rug yanked out from under it. Second, there are newcomers—people who have been in the region only fifteen or twenty years but who do have some sense of the place—who may make it possible to discuss such plans, to seek a cohabitation of cultures and economic strategies.

I have a theory about the rural West and a fear for its future. The theory is that what I think of as the "real" residents of the region have been on the run from the organized wage economy for several centuries. When Scottish economist Adam Smith's economy began to dominate Europe, they fled that continent to settle in America's wild places—Appalachia and the Ozarks. When the time clock reached those areas, they came to the rural West, where they could continue to live as free people.

The "environmentalists" who most clearly recognize this are Earth First! adherents and writer Edward Abbey. Although Earth First! may rail at organized environmentalism and its professionalism, its real target is middle-class environmentalists—people who want to have good jobs, and to use the public lands for recreation. These people bring a middle-class, parklike vision to the

West that sets Abbey's and Earth First!'s teeth on edge. Abbey and Earth First! spokesman Dave Foreman are anything but middle-class park seekers. They are in flight from that kind of America, attracted to the relic anarchy and violence of this nineteenth-century region. People who think ecotage is a tactic miss the point: ecotage is the end, not the means.

That the Southwest is beautiful is almost incidental to its appeal. They gather in the Southwest because it is gritty, scruffy, dusty, unpaved, rough. When Earth First! and Abbey say "environmentalist," they mean something very nearly opposite to what the Sierra Club means when it says "environmentalist." In the Summer 1988 *Mother Earth News Special*, for example, Abbey writes: "Nor is it by chance that my two friends and I live in this region; we live here because we could not survive anywhere else. What most take for granted as simply the way things are, *urbanism*, Loeffler and De Puy and I regard as a stifling impoverishment of human possibility. So we cling to this blessed island of the American Southwest, refugees from the nightmare of contemporary times."

My fear is that Abbey and his forces will win the struggle for the West. Abetted by an economic collapse, the West could tip into a sort of Appalachian dark night. My other fear is that the Sierra Club and its forces will win and transform the rural West into another suburb of America. If I could, I would stop the clock. Perhaps things were once better in the rural West, but they are now as good as any time in memory, where the word "good" is averaged over the condition of land, wildlife, and small communities.

Danger lies on all sides, however. From one, the region is threatened by an ever-growing tourism and lifestyle industry, which might leave the West its landscape and air but would remove the way of life that makes it unique. On the other side is the threat of a resurgent extractive industry, whose damage to the land, air, and wildlife is obvious, but which has the virtue of supporting, through contemptuous neglect, an admirable way of life. Hope lies, I think, not in a search for a middle ground but in locating a fulcrum upon which to balance these opposing forces so that neither becomes dominant.

CHAPTER EIGHTEEN

Southern Utah: The Trauma of Shifting Economies and Ideologies

Raymond Wheeler

WHO WILL control the destiny of the Colorado Plateau? Clive Kincaid, former executive director of the Southern Utah Wilderness Alliance, says the struggle over the Burr Trail reconstruction is more than a fight to protect the land: "It's about power. And it's about the future of the Colorado Plateau. Will it be developed with an eye to what's exceptional about it, or will it be developed haphazardly? Who's going to have the authority to provide that guiding hand?"

The answer to that question is locked in the riddles of the past and the present. One clear lesson of the past is that the environmental and economic future of the Colorado Plateau are one and the same. As we manage the environment, so, too, will the economy be affected. As we manage the economy, so, too, will the environment be affected. In a sense the Colorado Plateau—because it is publicly owned, because it is undeveloped, and because its future is uncharted—will be a litmus test for our society as a whole. And what of the future? Is the future driven entirely by expectations we bring to it out of the past? If we believe our society capable of preserving the beauty and silence of the Colorado Plateau, will it happen? And if we instead believe that massive development is inevitable, will not that, too, be a self-fulfilling prophecy?

What, then, do we believe? In the spring of 1987, I set out to ask, if not answer, that question. In four months I traveled across the heart of the Colorado Plateau from Moab to Escalante and on, working south and west to Kanab, Saint George, and the north rim of Grand Canyon. Along the way I talked to miners, ranchers, land managers, county commissioners, and environmentalists.

At each step of the journey, I asked, "What will become of the mining economy?" Two recent economic development studies have reached the same conclusion. "The boom is over," predicted a study of Monticello's economic prospects, "and most of our analysis shows little hope for its return."

Sitting in the Poplar Place, Moab's counterculture emporium, making my own study, I heard this: "The uranium industry, for my lifetime, anyway, has had its heyday. With breeder reactors . . . the day will come when we'll have very cheap energy from fission, because it doesn't have the nasty by-products of nuclear waste. That's definitely what's coming down."

What was extraordinary was not the idea but that the man opposite me was Joe Kingsley, president of the Moab Chamber of Commerce. "You have to be pragmatic," Kingsley continued cheerfully.

"Yes, I suppose you do."

"I'd be the first one to say, 'Great, let's open Atlas Minerals.' It's a big eyesore at the north end of town. If we have to have it, let it work. And I'm in real estate. Hell, I want to sell houses. But I'm also a realist. It won't happen. So why spend the energy?"

Wow, I thought to myself, weaving out of the Poplar Place later that evening with a bellyful of vegetarian pizza and 3.2 beer. Beer notwithstanding, I was high on reality.

The next morning I strolled up the street to the offices of the *Times-Independent* to consult with Moab's publisher, editor, reporter, typesetter, and resident oracle, Sam Taylor.

"I don't discount uranium in Moab's future economic life, but I don't expect it to ever be a dominant factor in the life of the community again," Taylor announced.

What?

"I think that we're realistic enough to know that there aren't that many big reserves of ore left in southeastern Utah."

Uh . . . surely potash?

"The same could be said for our potash industry. Unfortunately, farmers now would rather go bankrupt than buy fertilizer. So we're not going to see much rebound in the commercial fertilizer industry."

But surely coal mining would boom again soon?

"I don't think we'll see any coal strip mines to speak of, and I certainly don't think we're going to see any large coal-burning power plants."

Tar sands? Oil shale?

Boulder, Utah

"Probably not in my lifetime. Possibly not at all."

Three weeks later I experienced the ultimate reality check. For a solid week I had been preparing interview questions for that Darth Vader of southern Utah's Eco-wars—San Juan County Commissioner Calvin Black. By all accounts Cal Black was one of the baddest bad boys in southern Utah. I took the precaution of parking my car five blocks from Black's office. The last thing an environmental reporter needs on a fact-finding tour of southern Utah is to give the chairman of the San Juan County Commission his license plate number. As the hour approached, I dialed Black from a phone booth near his office.

"Hello. It's Ray Wheeler. The reporter for *High Country News.*"

"Yeah. Where are you?"

"A phone booth outside the Best Western Motel."

"Well, hell, you're right outside my window. I can probably see you." A round head appeared at a window.

Inside the office I found a genial, fierce, and garrulous man. Together for five hours we explored the fabulous political terrain of southeastern Utah, boosting one another over obstacles, wading together across streams, hacking through brush, scrambling across talus slopes. Surely here I would find an optimistic prognosis for the future of the mining industry. Cal Black had made a fortune on uranium. He had always been the ultimate booster of a mining economy and the king of the Sagebrush Rebels. But the latest mining bust had taken something out of Black. During the next two decades, Black told me, "based on the international trade situation and the environmental factors, mining and milling will not come back significantly, if at all. The demand for uranium for fuel in this country will still grow a little bit, because there are still some nuclear power plants under construction, but I don't look for any new nuclear power plants in this country in the next decade or so."

Well, what about coal? Surely, the Kaiparowits . . .

"There's a world supply of coal that's cheaper to mine and easier to get. In mining and natural resource production, we can't compete with the rest of the world, and the reason we can't is our standard of living, our rate of pay, and the environmental costs—justified and unjustified."

Indeed, the smart money in southeastern Utah had gotten out of the mining and milling business years ago. Black himself has liquidated the uranium holdings that made him rich. And he has moved to purchase motels, gas stations, restaurants, and other service-type businesses in downtown Blanding. For men who believe the mining economy is the sole hope for southern Utah's economic future, the Sagebrush Rebels have been investing a great deal of their energies lately in an entirely different trade—tourism.

"We have been spending a lot of effort trying to diversify through tourist-oriented, outdoor recreation," Jimmie Walker, Grand County Commission chairman told me. "We only have a nine-hole golf course, and it's becoming more and more apparent all the time, that with the direction we're trying to go, we need more than nine holes."

Direction? What direction?

"Moab and southeastern Utah, we think, have got a very good potential of being a hub for outdoor recreation," Walker said.

"I would like to see the maximum potential of recreation and tourist development," Cal Black told me.

When analyzing the behavior of southern Utah county commissioners, it is instructive to examine the economic bottom line. In 1986 Utah's travel industry generated nearly $2 billion in revenues—well over twice the total value of all the oil, coal, and uranium produced in Utah during the same year. While the mineral industry generated $285 million in wages from seventy-eight hundred jobs, the travel industry provided twice as much wage income and six times as many jobs.

While the revenue gap between the two industries has obviously been exaggerated by the recent mining bust, the steady decline of the mining and agricultural industries—and the steady rise of the service and government industries—has been a trend for at least a half century. In 1929 mining and agriculture accounted for nearly one-third of Utah's total personal income earnings, while government and services amounted to just 18 percent. By 1985 government and services had more than doubled in importance, providing 40 percent of Utah's earnings income, while mining and agriculture together contributed less than 4 percent of personal income and less than 1 percent of employment. Between 1975 and 1985, Utah's travel industry grew at a rate 27 percent faster than the rest of the economy. Between 1981 and 1986, Utah's income from tourism more than doubled.

It is instructive to compare southwestern and southeastern Utah. While southeastern Utah's economy has been driven since the 1950s by the boom-bust cycle of the mining industry, the economy of southwestern Utah has been almost wholly dependent upon tourism, retirement, and recreation. In 1981, at the peak of the last boom, mining provided less than 3 percent of employment in southwestern Utah, while it provided more than 30 percent of the jobs in southeastern Utah.

The tourist attractions of the two regions are about equal. Southeastern Utah harbors three national parks and half of Glen Canyon National Recreation Area. Southwestern Utah harbors two national parks, a national monument, and the other half of Glen Canyon National Recreation Area. So one might expect that southeastern Utah's economy—bolstered as it supposedly is by the extra income from mining and milling—would be double or triple that of southwestern Utah, which must depend entirely on tourism and its notoriously low-paying jobs. But it is not. Southwestern Utah has been economically healthy and growing during the 1980s; southeastern Utah has been in its own version of the Great Depression.

Indeed, all of southern Utah casts a covetous eye toward Saint George, the county seat of Washington County and one of the fastest growing municipalities in the state. "Saint George, I think, is where we would like to be in a number of years down the road, and I think possibly could be," says Moab's Sam Taylor. The secret of Washington County's success: tourism, retirement, and recreation.

If Washington County is the envy of all southern Utah, and if tourism is the secret of Washington County's success, one would expect a great deal of enthusiasm for tourism throughout southern Utah. But for southern Utah's power brokers—its county commissioners—tourism remains a dirty word. "The people that say, 'What we need is tourism' and have stopped everything else, are devastating southern Utah. You cannot survive on tourism alone," says Cal Black.

Judging from the respective unemployment rates in Washington and Grand counties, one is hard-pressed to believe that survival is precisely the issue. Indeed, jobs are far more abundant where tourism dominates mining. The question is not whether tourism can provide jobs, but whether tourism can

provide *high-paying* jobs. "When you lose natural resources, you lose manufacturing, you lose . . . high-pay jobs," explains Calvin Black. "Tourism is low-
pay jobs."

"At one time," explains Jimmie Walker, kids went from high school to the
mines, and within six months were earning $30,000 to $50,000 a year. Today,
Walker continues, almost all of those miners are out of work. The trouble is
"those particular individuals didn't go through the learning experience of
someone who goes to college and this sort of thing, start out at $15,000 a year
and then go to $20,000, $30,000, and $40,000 like everyone else." That is
why the mining bust was so "devastating" to southern Utah. "The toughest
thing that they've got to do is to learn that they're not going to be making
$30,000 or $40,000 or $50,000," says Walker. "And now they're making
anywhere from minimum wage up to $5 an hour."

Mining and milling jobs pay far better, on average, than tourism and service
jobs. In 1986 per capita income in Utah was 3.6 times greater for the mining
sector than for the services sector. And for southern Utah residents, the
mining industry provides yet another and even more compelling attraction—
the opportunity to get rich by staking and then leasing or selling mining
claims on public land.

"The American dream is to strike it rich—that's the dream that settled the
West," says Jimmie Walker.

"To varying degrees, these people believe that mankind was created, put on
this earth, to conquer it," says Craig Bigler, a retired economic planner. "They
subscribe very much to the puritanical notion that a sure sign that you're saved
is wealth. And, therefore, the only thing that's really important—to you as an
individual, to society, to God—is that you create wealth."

That insight answers some questions about southern Utah. If the Sagebrush
Rebels have been benefiting from government subsidies and profiting from the
buying and selling of mining claims on federally owned land, why in the world
would they attack the federal government? "A lot of people get real psychic
income from the hope, the belief, that someday they'll strike it rich," says
Bigler. "That's why they hate government so much. The only thing between
them and riches is government."

"All wealth comes from the land," says Calvin Black. "Who controls the
land, controls wealth."

The desire for "riches" is equally responsible for the attitudes of the Sagebrush Rebels toward the land itself. While the national parks are the principal
tourist attraction for southern Utah, southern Utah's county commissioners
have repeatedly campaigned for massive industrial development projects
within or immediately adjacent to the national parks. If tourism is southern
Utah's number-one industry, why industrialize the parks?

"There is no need to preserve, to conserve anything—because God doesn't want it to be preserved," explains Craig Bigler, recalling the attitudes he observed while growing up in a small Mormon community in southern Idaho. "God wants us to exploit the earth. That's what we're here for. If people really want there to be a wilderness area, they'll figure out a way to make a profit at it. And if you can't make money at it, then it shouldn't be."

That certainly is the attitude of the Sagebrush Rebels—the county commissioners and businessmen who own most of southern Utah and run it like a feudal estate. But is the worship of "riches" important to the majority of southern Utah residents? Is it indigenous to the culture, inherent in the religion, a sacred, inviolable tradition? Most certainly not, says the venerated Mormon scholar Hugh Nibley, professor emeritus of ancient scripture at Brigham Young University, and a leading authority on Mormon scripture and doctrine. "If there ever was a conservationist—a rabid conservationist—it was Brigham Young," says Nibley. Young, who led the Mormons west to Utah and who masterminded their colonization of the interior West, deeply revered nature and continually exhorted his followers to enjoy and protect it.

"The earth," Brigham Young wrote, "is very good in and of itself. It has abided the celestial law, consequently we should not despise it, nor desire to leave it, but rather . . . strive to obey the same laws that the earth abides. . . ." Brigham Young had a "passion for recycling," says Nibley, and "his abhorrence of waste was almost paranoid." Young preached against hunting for sport, warned sternly against overgrazing, and exhorted his followers to "preserve the wild country. Keep it wild, and enjoy it as such."

Above all, says Nibley, Brigham Young fought against materialism—particularly the virulent strain transmitted by the forty-niners who surged through Utah on their way to the California goldfields. "A man says . . . 'I will have the credit of making the first iron in the territory.' By the beauty and glory of this kind of proceeding is the blackest of darkness and commonness and deformity," Brigham railed. He was talking about a proposal to open an iron mine near Cedar City.

"Brigham Young knew the real issue," says Nibley. "He was fighting a losing battle, and he knew it. The issue—and he made no secret of it—was simply covetousness, that was all. It was a matter of money." In the battle between materialism and what we might call the Mormon pioneer tradition of good stewardship of the land, Brigham Young's death was a pivotal event. "You can almost date it," says Nibley; "1886, around there, a group of businessmen got together—they were just waiting, with a stopwatch, for Brigham Young to die so they could move in and take over."

Nibley has a keen understanding of the "complete switcheroo" that took place in the decades following Brigham Young's death. His own grandfather, Charles W. Nibley, was one of those businessmen most responsible for it. In partnership with David Eccles, whose Utah Construction Company was to become one of the Six Companies that have dominated the Intermountain

DREAMS ON THE ROCKS

In the settling and unsettling of the West there has not been a single American dream, but several fantasies moving along different tracks. When my Mormon ancestors fled bullets and cholera to straggle into the Great Basin and squat on lands claimed by the Ute and Shoshone, their dream had a lot to do with getting away from an intolerable situation back in the States.

It was a collective dream and spawned collective effort, even a Mormon form of socialism known as the United Order, which could have been cited by Marx had he known of it. Their exodus for reasons of conscience had economic consequences: they had to learn to make a living in the arid lands, which they did through irrigation and a cooperative ethic.

The early years were thin and desperate. If the Gold Rush of 1849 had not brought to their settlement in the Salt Lake Valley a market for eggs, beef, smithing, and fresh stock, they might have dispersed to California or Oregon, as many wished to do, and as the Ute and Shoshone probably still wish today that they had done.

Even though Brigham Young and other leaders were often the chief beneficiaries of Mormon enterprise, the effort at settlement had a humane aim, which was to provide a decent living to the community as a whole. Their system of tithe and storage, with distribution at least partly corresponding to need, had biblical precedent. It was also the way in which the Pueblos of the arid lands to the south had managed to sustain complex societies in tough and varying conditions.

The guiding spirit was of religious separatism, self-sufficiency, and humane enterprise. That it has degenerated into a mercantile theocracy is lamentable. Another dream on the rocks.

C. L. Rawlins

West, Charles Nibley cut down thousands of acres of forest on unsurveyed public land in Oregon without bothering to pay for it.

"He would explain to me," recalls Nibley, "when I was in my teens, how you should manage this sort of thing—how easy it was to buy off the government agents, and how easy it was to have all of your men homestead five hundred acres or so and then deed the land to you, and then you just go and cut it down." Later in life, recalls Nibley, his grandfather "felt guilty as hell."

But if Utahns have become ever more materialistic since Brigham Young's death, says Nibley, they are violating—not revering—Mormon doctrine. "Half the hymns in our hymnbook are on the beauties of nature. In Sunday school we usually pray and thank the Lord for the beauties of nature all around us, which we then proceed to burn and defile." The Mormon prophet Joseph Smith retired to the woods to receive the vision that led him to discover the Book of Mormon. "I tremble to think," observes Nibley dryly, "what would have happened if those woods had had any real commercial value."

Utah conservation leader Clive Kincaid might venture an opinion on the subject. In 1983 Kincaid filed a protest of a timber sale in the Dixie National Forest near the town of Escalante, Utah. The sale was the final phase of a 5-year timber harvest program that had mowed down 100 million board feet of old-growth ponderosa pine, carving some 250 miles of new roads across 25,000 acres of pristine wilderness on the south slope of Boulder Mountain. When the managers of the Kaibab Forest Products sawmill in Escalante learned of the protest, they stuffed employee paycheck envelopes with a notice declaring the protest would put the mill out of business. Several days later, Kincaid recalls, residents of Escalante assembled to perform a timeworn southern Utah ritual.

"They took this effigy with our names on it and dragged it up and down Main Street for a couple of hours. Everybody had an opportunity to drag us behind their pickup. They would go up to one end of the town and then back, and they'd yell and scream, and then somebody would tie it onto the next pickup. Then they threw a rope up over a lamp post, and hoisted it, and left it hanging for three days." Assisting with the hanging in effigy was Escalante's deputy sheriff, Boyd Woolsey.

In four years of environmental activism in southern Utah, Kincaid has received so many death threats he can no longer remember them all. Was it Woolsey or Escalante Mayor Norm Christiansen who announced that whoever put a bullet hole in Kincaid would be doing the community a favor? In the fall of 1984 in a confrontation in front of the Burr Trail Cafe, a road construction worker shoved a pistol in Kincaid's face. On another occasion a Moab rancher told Kincaid, "Those boys over in Escalante are pansy-asses. If it had been me over there, you'd have been dead a long time ago."

In spite of evidence, the Sagebrush Rebels have long maintained that tourism contributes little to the economy. "Garfield and Kane and Wayne counties are right in the center of the oldest national parks in the state of Utah," says Cal Black. "They're known nationally and internationally. They have millions of visitors. And those three counties have among the lowest historic per capita income in the state of Utah and the highest average unemployment. That's what tourism, alone, does."

Elsewhere in Utah, however, there are small, isolated towns that, though wholly dependent on tourism for their income, are exploding with growth. Springdale, at the entrance to Zion National Park, is just such a town. On a warm spring morning, one can hear the whine of saws and the thunder of hammers emanating from the old Mormon temple—now being converted into a restaurant/giftshop complex by the town's entrepreneurs. "If there were no

Brad Nelson

The effigy of environmentalists that was hanged in Escalante, Utah, 1984

tourists, there would be no Springdale," says Michael Parry, owner of the Bit and Spur Restaurant and a native of Saint George. "Most of the old families around here either have a motel, a restaurant, or a giftshop, and that's what they've done for a couple of generations."

It is puzzling that tourism has turned Springdale and Saint George into boomtowns, but not towns like Moab and Price. Why should tourism thrive in one town and fail miserably in another? Theoretical answers to that question are as abundant in southern Utah as corn in Kansas. Springdale, it is said, thrives on tourism because it is directly adjacent to a national park. But Saint George, which also thrives on tourism, is more than sixty miles from the nearest national park, while Moab, one of the most economically depressed

towns in Utah, lies adjacent to not one but two national parks. It is said that
Saint George is thriving because it is located on an interstate and has golf
courses and tennis courts to attract visitors. But Springdale is twenty-five miles
from the nearest interstate—almost exactly the same distance that separates
Moab from Interstate 70. And Springdale has no golf.

If there is a pattern, it is that the communities which are least successful at
reaping income from tourism are those with a history of virulent antagonism
toward outsiders. With few exceptions those communities are the ones that
have been dominated by mining and timber interests and the legacy of the
Sagebrush Rebellion. In May 1986 Cal Black's protégé, Blanding Mayor Jim
Shumway, leaned into a microphone at a BLM wilderness hearing in Moab and
issued a public-service announcement: "We know that you want our lands. You
will not get them. . . . We are tired of the wilderness terrorists. . . . Those
seeking the solitude of our beautiful lands shall now be expected to furnish
themselves with armed guards while enjoying the serenity of our county." It is
little wonder that many tourists feel a shade uneasy in certain southern Utah
communities. If tourists feel uneasy, it is likely that businessmen do too.

Certainly filmmaker Robert Redford must have felt uneasy in April 1976,
when he learned that the townspeople of Kanab, Utah, had burned him in
effigy. The problem, it seemed, was that Redford had made the error of voicing
his opposition to the proposed Kaiparowits coal mine and power plant project,
which would have disturbed more than six thousand acres of land, carved
hundreds of miles of new roads, and pumped pollutants daily into the clear air
over the Escalante Canyon country and Capitol Reef National Park.

For nearly fifty years the movie industry has poured vast sums of money into
Kanab's economy. Kanab was "Hollywood East"—the scenery behind more
than two hundred westerns and scores of television productions and commer-
cials. In the thirties, while the rest of the country was agonizing through the
Depression, the town of Kanab was prosperous because of Hollywood's lar-
gesse. But after Kanab torched Robert Redford, the town's lucrative ties to
Hollywood began drying up.

"Redford liked Kanab a lot," says Melvin Heaton, a Kanab-area rancher
who has worked with Hollywood filmmakers all of his life. "Now he won't come
back." Instead, Redford, a resident of Utah, has taken movies such as *The
Electric Horseman* precisely where so many other businessmen and tourists have
chosen to take themselves and their business—to the Saint George area.
"Hanging Robert Redford was a mistake," says Heaton angrily. "It's cost me a
lot of money. I've cussed them a lot."

Heaton is referring, of course, to those ubiquitous mischief makers, the
Sagebrush Rebels—southern Utah's old-boy network of county commissioners, some BLM district managers, local businessmen, real estate and
mining claim speculators, and the local representatives of the energy multina-

tionals. And there is a great deal of evidence that Melvin Heaton is not the only southern Utah native who has "cussed them a lot."

Winston Hurst is an archaeologist at the White Mesa Institute and a Blanding native whose family helped to settle the town. As a teenager, Hurst roamed San Juan County's dirt roads "with a jeep and a dog." Like most kids, he had a favorite secret place—the top of an 800-foot-high sandstone fin called Comb Ridge, a place from which, Hurst says, "You could see the whole county."

In 1969, home from college and newly married, Hurst took his wife out to Comb Ridge to show her the view. But it had radically changed. Slicing a gash in the ridge and snaking across the valley below was a new paved highway. The highway, largely financed with San Juan County tax dollars, was the sole access route to Hall's Crossing Marina on Lake Powell—then owned by San Juan County Commissioner Calvin Black. "That made me really deeply angry," recalls Hurst. "The anger comes from the frustration that you can't even make an argument. I mean, what is the argument against it? What am I going to say—'That's where I used to go with my dog?'"

In five months of interviews in southern Utah, almost everyone I spoke to repeatedly extolled the beauty of the land. Often the accolades came from the most committed of Sagebrush Rebels.

"The desert, or the hills, or whatever, always was fascinating to me," Jimmie Walker told me. "If a person really believes in God . . . it's awful hard for him to just destroy, tear up God's world. Nonrenewable resources, once they're removed, what is the land good for? Farming? Maybe. Ranching? Maybe. Beauty to look at? Absolutely. So why in the hell would we want to mine, or do anything, to destroy the beauty? That's our long-range asset."

"I just simply love it down here," said Sam Taylor. "I like the aesthetics. I live here because I like the red rocks and the dry desert climate. I like the availability of the high alpine country we've got here in the La Sal Mountains."

On a Sierra Club hike across the heart of battered Mancos Mesa, I met Alfred Frost, a 67-year-old Monticello pinto-bean farmer who had taken up backpacking at age 60. Frost had mastered a technique of bending forward, grabbing his fully loaded backpack, and flipping it straight up over his head onto his back, all in one spectacular fluid motion. After struggling to the top of a 500-foot canyon wall, the 20- and 30-year-old yuppies on the trip would heave off their packs and collapse, only to find Frost waiting calmly for them, sucking contemplatively on a blade of grass. Frost radiated health, optimism, joy. And while he had no particular love for environmentalists, his love for the land—for wilderness—was exuberant.

As we watched evening flow down into the bed of North Gulch, Frost reminisced about a hearing on the proposed siting of the nation's first nuclear waste dump near Canyonlands Park. Frost had been asked to speak out against

Notch Peak, Utah

the proposal by a friend who could not for fear of losing her job. As the hearing began, the county commissioners each stood and gave a pro-dump speech. When they were finished talking, they simply walked out the door. "They wasn't about to listen to us," Frost recalled with a laugh.

How many Alfred Frosts, how many Winston Hursts, how many Melvin Heatons live in those small towns scattered around the perimeter of the canyon country? What would happen if their political leaders actually listened to them for a change?

The Southern Utah Wilderness Alliance has earned a reputation, because of its aggressiveness, for being the "junkyard dog" of Utah conservation groups. That has earned the organization a great deal of dislike in southern Utah. But it has also aroused a strange new phenomenon. "People in Boulder, for the first time, in the last six months—because of the intensity of hatred, I suppose, the open animosity toward me—have started coming out of the woodwork," says Clive Kincaid of the Southern Utah Wilderness Alliance. After seven months of intense psychological warfare over the Burr Trail lawsuit, Kincaid began to notice a change among some of his neighbors. "SUWA supporters that I was always sort of protecting by trying not to associate with them very much have suddenly, on their own, begun fighting back. It's kind of nice to see people who were previously cowed and hear them say, 'You know what, I met so and so last week . . . and I told them to go to hell. I told them I was an environmentalist, and I didn't want to see that road paved.' "

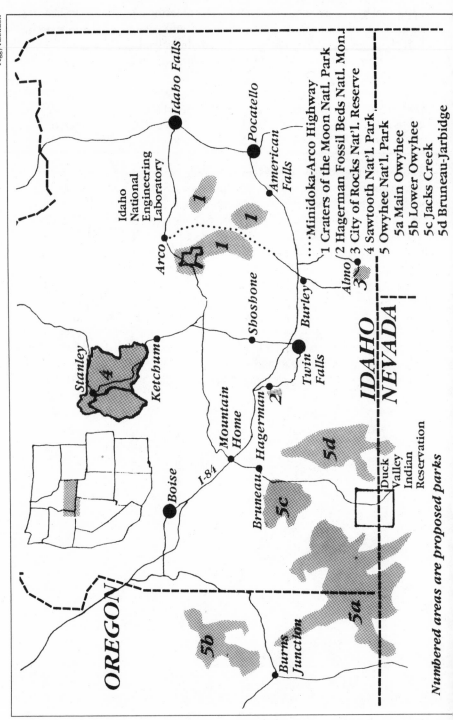

Peggy Robinson

·········· Minidoka-Arco Highway
1 Craters of the Moon Nat'l. Park
2 Hagerman Fossil Beds Nat'l Mon.
3 City of Rocks Nat'l. Reserve
4 Sawtooth Nat'l. Park
5 Owyhee Nat'l. Park
  5a Main Owyhee
  5b Lower Owyhee
  5c Jacks Creek
  5d Bruneau-Jarbidge

Numbered areas are proposed parks

CHAPTER NINETEEN

Now Idaho Wants
National Parks

Pat Ford

IN THEORY, wild, beautiful, and lightly populated Idaho should be bursting with national parks. In fact, its ranching, logging, and mining roots have kept it totally free of parks. But the times are changing, and small communities all over Idaho today are clamoring for national parks and the visitors they attract. Fifteen years ago Paul Fritz had a vision for south-central Idaho's future—a string of national parks and monuments displaying, within a long day's drive, a time-lapse series of the earth, animal, and human history of this place where the Northwest, the Northern Rockies, and the Great Basin contend.

Fritz is a salesman. First, as head of the National Park Service's Idaho office, he worked the chambers of commerce, city halls, and newspapers in the farm towns dotting south-central Idaho. His passion was for the landscapes and what they held—lava flows and craters, fossils, wildlands, salmon and bighorn sheep, the ruins of stage stations, and the ruts of wagon wheels. But he knew enough to lead with another argument—the travelers whom parks would attract and the dollars they would spend. Despite the lure, few were interested.

Today Fritz's old office is long closed, and he is retired. But for the businessmen in those same towns—some new, some the men he couldn't persuade in the 1970s—his vision has come alive. Now when he traces on a homemade display the routes visitors would take among his prospective parks, mayors and merchants need little further urging. There is a new look to the enduring tangle where Idaho public lands, pocketbooks, and politics meet. Idaho, which has no national parks and not long ago was almost proud of it, is awash today in proposed parks and monuments. The places and chances vary, but dominant in all but one is "building Idaho's recreation economy." The natural, scientific, and historical values are substantial, but they are passengers in a dollar-driven vehicle.

An Unearthly Moonscape

Thank the American space program for the concept of a Craters National Park. In the 1960s Dr. Fred Bullard became interested in the vast volcanic laboratory on the Snake River Plain. (Get an Idaho road map; west of Pocatello is a huge white empty space—no towns, no roads, no rivers. That's the place.) Bullard was a world-eminent vulcanologist, and among his former students was NASA's chief geologist. Bullard suggested that NASA use the Idaho lava flows to acquaint astronauts with lunar landscapes. A group of astronauts spent three days there in 1969.

Paul Fritz was then superintendent of Craters of the Moon National Monu- ment—fifty-three thousand acres of volcanic debris on the northern edge of the enormous flows Bullard had investigated. It was created in 1924 and remains Idaho's only contribution to the National Park system. Little of the monument proper had ever seen a human footprint—the jagged, fissured, waterless lava is not something you just stroll into—and Fritz knew even less about what lay south. "The astronauts' visit made me realize what was out there beyond the monument," Fritz recalls. "Bullard said the entire story of vulcanism was right there, with only an active volcano missing."

For instance, there is the Great Rift—the longest (sixty-five miles) and deepest (up to eight hundred feet) rift system in North America. Seven times in the last fifteen thousand years, most recently two thousand years ago, lava poured from the vents, fissures, and cracks of the rift to create the huge Craters of the Moon lava field. The eruptions left behind craters, cinder and spatter cones, lava tubes, caves, monoliths, and about 450 kipukas—islands of vege- tation surrounded by lava—ranging from less than one to twenty-two hundred acres.

A few miles south of the Craters of the Moon flow are two others on the rift—the Kings Bowl and Wapi flows. Both were created quickly, perhaps in just a few months, some 2,000 years ago. Kings Bowl contains the 155-foot- deep Crystal Ice Cave, the only rift ice cave in the world open to the public. The Wapi flow has a kipuka containing huge juniper trees up to 850 years old.

Thus spurred, Fritz developed a proposed expansion containing most of the rift's length (only one-fifth of it is inside the monument). He also included 7,550-foot Big Southern Butte, a dormant volcano that is the most prominent landmark in the area. His proposal included three hundred thousand acres in three units. Fritz wooed mayors and Main Street in the small towns nearby— Arco, Carey, Burley, Rupert, Shoshone, and Aberdeen. But there was little interest, even when he stressed the income from tourism. In the early 1970s rural Idaho's idea of economic growth didn't include travel or tourism; times were good, with agriculture the engine (ranching and farming surround the lavas). Fritz shelved his idea and, as we shall see, moved on to others.

Fifteen years have changed those Main Streets. Farming and farm towns emerged from the recession shriveled and shaky and have stayed that way. When Burley or Rupert look for economic health today, they see it in recreation-based towns like nearby Ketchum/Sun Valley, or at INEL, the nuclear research and defense facility northeast across the lavas. In 1985 a group of local businessmen formed the Minidoka-Arco Highway Committee to push for paving a primitive 60-mile dirt road that cuts through the lavas between Rupert and Arco. "We wanted to tie our part of the state together more," says former Idaho Governor John Evans, now a banker in Burley. Arco farmers saw it as opening a potential new market for their surplus production. Burley and Rupert boosters saw it as a way for their businesses to reach the INEL market.

In early 1987 a few of the same people revived the national park idea. Fritz, retired in Boise, dusted off his proposal and drove over in May to meet with them. His proposal envisioned that dirt road as the park's major through road. The two ideas became one. In the next few months park expansion was endorsed by every nearby chamber of commerce and the Idaho Farm Bureau. The highway committee became Craters of the Moon Development, Incorporated, with Governor Evans as point man. The Idaho legislature passed a resolution endorsing the idea. "Economics was their main impetus," Fritz concedes, "but they are getting interested in the geology and scientific values as they work on it." The group arranged a field trip in the fall for the staffs of Idaho's congressional delegation. Democratic Representative Richard Stallings was convinced; he endorsed expansion and wrote the Park Service requesting a formal study of the area. "That's the first step," Fritz says. "Once the Park Service has studied the area's potential, and reported to Congress, Congress can act."

Enter politics. Park Service Director William Mott's March 1988 reply to Stallings was cool and noncommittal. Stallings is the only Democrat in Idaho's delegation, and Mott works for a Republican president. Idaho Republican Senators Jim McClure and Steve Symms have not endorsed expansion, in part because doing so now would help Stallings get reelected this fall. Local boosters, many of them Republicans, are frustrated. "We feel like this project is being held hostage to petty politics," the head of Burley's Development Commission told a reporter recently. "We need a united delegation backing this." But in a late August meeting with park supporters—by now including nearly every chamber of commerce in southern Idaho—McClure refused to come on board.

The economic motivation of backers is the other difficulty. Stallings's letter to Mott said a park "could help stimulate the economy of many Idaho communities." Fritz winced when he saw that phrase: "It hands Mott an excuse to do nothing. You have to lead with the natural and scientific values. And they are there. The U.S. National Park Service should certainly be protecting and interpreting the most complete record of vulcanism in our country."

One would have to guess that there will be a Craters of the Moon National Park soon. Beneath the politics, Park Service professionals want to proceed. McClure would seem to have little reason to withhold support after the election. There is some grazing within a few parts of Fritz's proposed boundary, but otherwise it's about the most conflict-free piece of ground imaginable. The existing monument, despite its relative remoteness, does draw visitors— 202,800 last year.

A Change of Heart

Senator Jim McClure recalls two hearings he chaired in south-central Idaho, one in 1974 at Burley and one in 1976 at Hagerman. Both were on Park Service proposals to create national monuments, at the City of Rocks and Hagerman Fossil Beds. Testimony was light at both, and McClure said the message was that "local people didn't want either one." So nothing was done.

McClure's recollection came in August last year, when he was back in the same two towns for hearings on the same two areas. This time local support was overwhelming and enthusiastic for a Hagerman Fossil Beds National Monument and a City of Rocks National Reserve. By the end of 1987 McClure's legislation to create both had passed the Senate, and both bills are certain to pass the House once a dispute over water rights language is resolved. What had changed, once again, were the relative prospects of agriculture and tourism.

The City of Rocks lies thirty miles south of Burley, near the tiny town of Almo not far from the Utah-Idaho border. It is named for a 1,500-acre assemblage of weird rock monoliths, humps, and portals that wind and especially water slowly exposed and then sculpted from 2.5-billion-year-old granites—some of the oldest rocks in North America.

"We were so spellbound with the beauty and strangeness of it all, that no thought of Indians entered our heads." So reads a typical reaction to City of Rocks from one of the emigrants who passed through in the mid-1800s. The area was a junction for several major routes west—the California Trail, Hudspeth's Cutoff, the Salt Lake Cutoff. Wagon ruts, ruins of stage stops, and emigrant graffiti (painted with axle grease) remain from that historic traffic. The larger surrounding area also possesses unique natural values thanks to the merging there of the Columbia and Great basins.

In 1973 Paul Fritz directed a Park Service study of thirty thousand acres; it recommended a national monument to protect and interpret these geological, historical, and natural values. "We had support from the Republican congressman at the time, and most of the local ranchers seemed favorable," he says today. "But then the Park Service said they planned to buy out the ranchers over twenty-five years. That turned them, and the politicians, against us."

Fifteen years later, with no help from the Park Service, most of the ranchers are gone. Some of their old lands are now owned by Burley businessmen who want to develop campgrounds rather than graze cows. And, with no one on site to protect the area (it is a mix of private and BLM land), off-road vehicle use and defacement of the emigrant markings is eroding the values that draw visitors. At the urging of Burley and Almo businessmen, Senator McClure revisited the issue in 1987 and found unanimous local support for protection.

McClure's legislation creates a 14,000-acre "National Reserve," to be cooperatively managed by the Park Service and Idaho's Parks Department. The state gets lead management, with federal oversight. It is modeled on a reserve recently established in the New Jersey Pinelands. The bill is well short of the old national monument proposal. And conservationists argue that including an adjacent Forest Service roadless area, Cache Peak, as a wilderness addition would attract further visitors. But for now they are generally supporting McClure's approach. "The priority," Fritz says, "is to get someone on site to clean up, regulate ORVs [off-road vehicles], stop vandalism, and build greater local awareness of what's there. This bill can do that."

Roughly 3.5 million years ago saber-toothed tigers, sloths, mastodons, camels, and early horses roamed the tropical savannahs and warm lakeshores of what is now southern Idaho. Then 30,000 years ago the cataclysmic Bonneville Flood carved the Snake River canyon and exposed a few miles of long-buried strata from those Pliocene days. Fifty years ago Elmer Cook, a Hagerman rancher, found some fossil bones in the canyon bluffs and contacted the Geological Survey.

Today the Hagerman Fossil Beds are recognized as the world's most complete known site of Pliocene mammal remains. More than 130 full skulls of *Equus Idahoensis*, an early zebra-size horse, have been taken from the bluffs, as well as bones of early cats, sloths, mastodons, camels, beavers, turtles, and more. Most excavation has been at the so-called main quarry, leaving years of further work in promising areas nearby.

In the early 1970s a huge irrigation project, Bell Rapids, began watering twenty thousand acres of desert land above these bluffs. It was the climax of

Idaho's postwar agriculture boom. The project was given a right-of-way through the fossil beds for a pipeline up to the new farms. That stimulated a few local residents, with some help from Paul Fritz, to get Idaho's congressional delegation to request a Park Service study of the site. Fritz led the study, which recommended the creation of a national monument. At McClure's 1976 hearing in Hagerman, only six people testified, four of them in opposition. "Farmers were doing well then," recalls Hagerman Mayor Merle Owsley. "People weren't that interested in the fossils." Two more Bell Rapids pipelines were built later, and the Bureau of Land Management continued its low-rent management of the beds.

In March 1988 a 600-foot bluff collapsed at the site, burying a pumping station and pipeline, and no doubt a lot of fossils. The slide dramatized the way seepage from the irrigation was gradually undermining the soft soils of the beds. It galvanized scientists working at the site, locals, and, of course, Paul Fritz, to organize a meeting.

Tourism was the other impetus. Burt Holmes, owner of a nearby hotel and chairman of tourism for the Hagerman Chamber of Commerce, pointed out the two hundred thousand annual visitors to Utah's Dinosaur National Monument and said the Hagerman Beds, if protected and publicized, could attract twice as many. "In these times of inflation and uncertain futures for our farmers," Mayor Owsley said, "this could create an extraordinary boost to the local economy." The Hagerman Fossil National Monument Council was formed. On the day McClure held his City of Rocks hearing, he visited Hagerman, and one-tenth of the town, sixty-five people, turned out to ask his help. A later hearing showed strong local support for a monument, and McClure's resulting legislation quickly passed the Senate.

The council is not sure McClure's bill goes far enough. It includes only the fossil beds themselves, forty-four hundred acres, and most want the boundary pushed a bit back from the bluffs, so that irrigation seepage right next to the beds can be stopped. They also want a few acres across the Snake River on the Hagerman side added to the monument so visitor facilities don't have to be in the beds themselves and will be closer to existing businesses. Fritz envisions a tramway to take tourists across the river to the beds.

There is a bigger problem with both the Hagerman and City of Rocks bills. Both contain McClure language denying any federally reserved water rights for either area. The issue is not practical but political, part of a broader campaign by western Republicans to erase or weaken potential federal water reservations on public lands. Representative Bruce Vento, a Minnesota Democrat, chairman of the House Subcommittee on Public Lands, in which both bills now sit, opposes McClure's language and thus is delaying action. Idaho Representative Stallings supports the language, but so far can't budge Vento. Neither bill will pass until a broader congressional compromise on federal water rights emerges. That frustrates local supporters, who have recommended deleting the water

Del Owens

Sawtooth Range in Idaho

language and moving forward. They want to start capitalizing on unique natural values, which ten years of farm troubles and empty storefronts have made them see with new eyes.

Sawtooth Country

Idaho does not often get prominent notice in the *Los Angeles Times*. But there, on March 17, 1988, was the lead editorial: "On behalf of an Idaho Park." After summarizing the long history of national park proposals for Idaho's spectacular Sawtooth country, the *LA Times* told its huge readership: "But the rugged wilderness of the Sawtooth is so compelling that the idea just will not go away. Rep. Larry E. Craig, a Republican from Boise, has assembled an advisory board to study the idea and its potential benefits." The *LA Times* ended by urging Idaho's members of Congress to come together and agree on a proposal.

California's fishermen and conservationists, and their counterparts in the *LA Times*'s national audience, must have been stirred. Perhaps a few hundred thousand of them have visited Sawtooth country and know firsthand how compelling, how worthy a park it would be. They must have assumed Idaho conservationists solidly backed the idea, and that if a Republican congressman is behind its revival, it has some political legs in Idaho itself. But not so. Larry Craig's Sawtooth park initiative is problematic at best. It does, however, have the same professed origin as Stallings's efforts on Craters of the Moon. With Yellowstone and Grand Teton parks "bursting at the seams," Craig said when announcing his study, "the potential economic benefits to Idaho are obvious."

Sawtooth country cannot be forgotten or mistaken. The Salmon River winds for twenty-five miles through its broad valley below dark foothill forests sweeping up to the vaulting rock faces and serrate spires of the Sawtooth Mountains. Glacier-made beauty is on display from dozens of places on and off the highway. Long lakes lie in folds of the foothills, and dozens more are in the high cirque basins. East of the river are the White Cloud Peaks, with their vistas, lakes, basins, and bighorns. At their heart is a hidden natural fortress, Idaho's grandest, if not quite tallest, mountain, Castle Peak.

In 1916 Stephen Mather, first director of the National Park Service, proposed a park in Sawtooth country—which was managed, then and now, by the Forest Service. Interior Secretary Harold Ickes did the same in 1935. In the mid-1960s the Park Service undertook a formal study and concluded that the area fully qualified to be a national park. Idaho opinion was always mixed, with local ranchers (who owned most of the valley floor) and miners most strongly opposed. It took a threat to force action. In 1969 the American Smelting and Refining Company, ASARCO, proposed an open-pit molybdenum mine at the base of Castle Peak. Conservationists and sports enthusiasts formed the Greater Sawtooth Preservation Council and endorsed a 1.3-million-acre Sawtooth National Park. Cecil Andrus rode his opposition to the mine to Idaho's governorship in 1970.

When Idaho Senator Frank Church initiated congressional action the next year, a national park was within reach. Andrus favored it, Church leaned toward it. The Idaho Falls, Pocatello, and Stanley chambers of commerce endorsed a park (Stanley is the only town, one hundred or so folks, in the Sawtooth Valley). But opponents, including Idaho's Republican congressmen, rallied, and the Forest Service proposed a national recreation area, under its continued management, as an alternative. Church chose the alternative, and the Sawtooth National Recreation Act passed Congress in 1972. "The cows whipped the people," is how Greater Sawtooth Council leader Ernie Day puts it today.

The act created a 750,000-acre Sawtooth National Recreation Area (NRA), including a 250,000-acre wilderness in the Sawtooths themselves. It mandates recreation-first management, allowing logging, grazing, and mining "insofar as their utilization will not substantially impair the purposes for which the area is established."

Park advocates were thrown a bone—a broader park study of lands in and near the Sawtooth NRA. Paul Fritz was put in charge (he had been a planner on the mid-1960s study), and in 1975 his team published a detailed, bold proposal: a three-unit national park in the Sawtooth, White Cloud, Boulder, and Pioneer mountains (the latter two ranges rise above Ketchum and Sun Valley, south and east of the White Clouds), connected by national recreation areas in the Sawtooth Valley and Copper Basin. The study never left the shelf. Andrus at first called the Sawtooth NRA a step toward a park, but by the time of his 1974 reelection campaign, he had changed his mind.

In 1977, soon after Jimmy Carter named him Secretary of the Interior, Andrus closed the Park Service's Idaho office. Paul Fritz transferred to Alaska. Most park advocates concluded that its time had passed, and their energies turned to fighting for more wilderness in and around the Sawtooth NRA. Through the late 1970s and into the 1980s, the recession battered Idaho's extractive economies and its towns. Meanwhile, the Sawtooth NRA and the adjacent Sun Valley ski resort area grew into Idaho's most mature example of a recreation-based year-round economy. Camping, fishing, hunting, river running, hiking, horsepacking, and cross-country skiing all grew steadily and gradually, but not beyond control. The Sawtooth NRA's restrictions on private land development in the Sawtooth Valley—for instance, no subdivisions—rankled at first, but slowly won acceptance as recreation grew. "Around here," says Ketchum Mayor Larry Young, "it's not environment versus jobs. It's environment is jobs."

Enter Larry Craig, a third-term Republican from Idaho's first Congressional District. His district is northern Idaho and part of southwestern Idaho; it does not include Sawtooth country. In late 1986 Craig said he would investigate creation of a national park in Sawtooth country, to "increase access," attract more tourists, and build the area's recreation economy. It came out of the blue. Representative Stallings, who represents the area, was taken by surprise. Cecil Andrus, just returned to the governor's chair after ten years, dismissed it as a bid for statewide recognition so Craig could run for the Senate in 1990 if Jim McClure retired. McClure himself, who had led the solid Republican antipark sentiment seventeen years earlier, said there was neither support nor reason to reopen the issue. Other Republican leaders were silent, nonplussed.

Conservationists were suspicious. Craig's record and rhetoric is solidly anti-conservation. "You won't find him proposing a park in his own district," says Ketchum sportsman Tim Crawford. "His timber and ranching cronies would scream." They fastened on his phrase "increase access." A few months earlier Craig had suggested building a paved road across the River of No Return Wilderness, just north of the Sawtooth NRA. The park proposal seemed a Trojan horse for roadbuilding.

Local ranchers were puzzled. Most dislike the Sawtooth NRA, which is trying to reduce (many ranchers say "eliminate") grazing in the area. But Craig's proposal seemed worse, since grazing is generally not allowed in national parks. The diminishing ranks of local miners reacted similarly. But the most vocal, and telling, opposition came from the very people Craig

tailored his message to—owners, managers, and workers in the local recreation economy. Their reasons took more people than Larry Craig by surprise.

"Everyone's trying to market Idaho, market our beauty to get more people
here. I've got a big problem with the whole idea—'more is better' is not my
business philosophy." So says Jack See, whose family owns and operates
Redfish Lake Lodge, the Sawtooth NRA's oldest recreation business. His
response is typical of the lodges, stores, and suppliers operating in and near the
Sawtooth NRA—small, locally owned, healthy, and about as busy as they can
manage.

His sentiments are also typical. "More or less everyone in the community is
against a park. Most of us are here because we want to live here, not to make
money. Obviously we want to do well enough to support our families and
stay—and we are. The recreation economy is healthy." The few businesses that
favor a park are largely absentee or corporate owned. The 1988 summer season
shows what See is talking about. It was the busiest ever for the Sawtooth
NRA—more visitors and money spent than ever before. On Labor Day
weekend, every room and campground space was occupied. Motels in Ketchum and Sun Valley were full.

The locals have another worry. "When businesses here get bought by out-of-
state companies, the dollar thing gets stronger," See argues. "It's not good. I'm
worried about a park bringing in big concessionaires and companies, squeezing
the local owners out." This local sentiment was quickly registered; the Stanley,
Ketchum, and Sun Valley city councils all opposed a park. Craig back-
pedaled—"a park is just one option; I want to look at them all"—and tried to
salvage what he could. In late 1987 he named an advisory board, with local
officials and ranchers, and nonlocal recreation businesses and conservationists, to study the Sawtooth NRA. (Its report was due in the fall of 1988.)

Though a Sawtooth National Park is not in the present political cards, Larry
Craig has gotten the Forest Service's attention. The Sawtooth NRA budget is
suddenly a little bigger, and its managers are talking about "showcase recreation management." Few expect this to last once the Forest Service feels the
dust has settled. Whether the dust settles depends less on Larry Craig than on
the local communities.

The key issue facing Sawtooth country is not Sawtooth NRA versus park
but the one raised by Jack See and his neighbors: how to bring a recreation
economy to maturity, preserving both the land and the community. Craig
began with the goal of attracting more people to spend more money. There is
agreement now that managing the impact of the thousands who already come
is far more pressing.

This is the first big step in Idaho's facing the "loved-to-death" problems. The
symptoms are familiar: deteriorating campgrounds and trails, garbage, beat-
out riparian areas, sharp conflicts among users (ORVs versus hikers, ranchers

versus fishermen, bears versus people), poor user education, and community conflicts rooted in the changes wrought by all this use.

Jack See says: "Idaho is new to tourism, newer than it thinks. What we really need is to step back and think through what we're doing. The Sawtooth NRA hasn't given near enough attention or money to managing recreation use. The tourism promoters haven't paid attention to whether we can handle more and more people, and what it will mean to those of us who live here. We have to stop and think a little." Can a recreation economy grow up, grow into an enduring balance with its land base and foster a community that serves not only tourists but its own best aspirations? That tough question will confront people and towns throughout Idaho in the next quarter century. It confronts Sawtooth country now.

A Desert Park

Idaho's final park proposal stands apart from the others. It has no history or prominent backers. Economic calculation has little to do with it. It is largely one man's vision, born of frustration, for the huge high desert reaches of the Owyhee Plateau.

In the southwest corner of an Idaho map, an empty expanse even bigger than the lava flows extends well into Oregon and Nevada. It is called Owyhee country—vast, high, dry plateaus rolling on endlessly before pitching into the deep sudden canyons of the Jarbidge, Bruneau, and Owyhee rivers. It is a remote and little-known place. Idaho's Owyhee County, for instance, has eight thousand people on 5 million acres. The few towns are tiny, the ranches scattered, water scant. One of America's poorest Indian reservations, Duck Valley, straddles the Idaho-Nevada border, out of sight and mind.

Though the area's northern edges are closer to Boise than the Sawtooths, you could assemble in a theater every Boisean who has explored beyond its rivers or few roads, and count on your fingers those who could claim to know it well. Two non-Boiseans who know it well, from much different angles, are Dave Tindall and Randy Morris. The Tindall ranch, a cow-calf operation near the Bruneau River, has been in the family 104 years: "It's a life we like. It's been handed down, we understand it, we don't live high, but we make a living. Except for Envirosafe [a commercial hazardous waste dump] ranching's about all there is in Owyhee County." Tindall depends on public land grazing: his cows are on Bureau of Land Management ground year-round in Idaho, and Forest Service land in Nevada for five months.

Randy Morris—tall, blond, friendly—is a dentist in Mountain Home, an air-base town forty miles up Interstate 84 from Boise. For the past decade, while other conservationists looked to the forests for their recreation and cause, he has gone into the desert, where he has found wilderness and wild rivers, history and prehistory, sweep and solitude. You get the sense he likes to walk alone in inhospitable country, a handy trait given his passion "to end the domination by livestock grazing of the Owyhee Plateau."

The different ways these two men see the Owyhee desert put them on opposite sides of a proposal to take 2.5 million acres of Owyhee Plateau and canyonlands away from the BLM and give it to the National Park Service. On his hikes, Morris has found sagebrush-steppe and salt-desert scrub communities that are today as they were one thousand years ago. These are remnant islands surrounded by what he calls overgrazed cow pasture disguised as public land. He has run the desert rivers in their brief season and seen on the way "awesome erosion from overgrazed plateaus during spring runoff." He has found nineteenth-century ranch structures wonderfully preserved and then returned several years later to find them dismantled by vandals. "If it were managed for wildlife," he says, "this country could be an American Serengeti. About two hundred thousand animal unit months are allocated to livestock in the key areas. That could translate into millions of animal unit months for elk and antelope. As it is, there are few of either because the cows get nearly all the forage."

Dave Tindall sounds tired; it's 8:30 P.M., and he just got in. "The thing we disagree with a lot of these people on is that we've been ranching 104 years on this place, and if we're doing such damage to the land, how come we're still here?" Overgrazing and wildlife? "Livestock numbers are way down from the past. We've got pictures from when my dad was first out here. There was no control on grazing then, and there was no grass. Now we've got control, better management, and a lot more grass to offer both cows and wildlife. Fish and Game says the wildlife is increasing. And most of us out here are willing to listen and learn how to get better, if the people who don't live here will also listen to us."

Merits aside, there's no doubt whose corner the BLM has been in since 1981—the year Morris and a like-minded handful formed the Committee for Idaho's High Desert to defend roadless areas, wildlife, and recreation on public desert lands. All their work—analyzing inch-thick plans, testimony, letters, appeals, publicity—has had the same impact on the BLM. None.

Morris ticks off a list from the last few years. Wilderness study areas destroyed, language slipped into the Owyhee River plan subordinating all recreation use to grazing, a 34-fold increase in vegetative removal slipped into the Jarbidge area plan before anyone knew. And—the clincher—the Egin-Hamer road. In 1986, based on a negative staff report and overwhelming public opposition, a BLM district manager in Idaho Falls denied a rancher's request to build a road through the winter range of Idaho's largest elk herd. The ranchers went to see Interior Secretary Don Hodel, the manager was removed, and the road built. "We got the message," Morris says. "Multiple use is a joke on BLM lands in Idaho. We won't see any kind of balance in the Owyhee country as long as they're in charge."

In February 1988 the high desert committee unveiled a "conceptual" proposal for a Park Service–managed mosaic: wild and scenic rivers for the Bruneau, Jarbidge, and Owyhee; national park or monument in the canyonlands; and national reserves or refuges, with hunting allowed, on the plateaus. There are four units: the main Owyhee, about 1.3 million acres, including most of the upper Owyhee River and its forks; the lower Owyhee, entirely in Oregon; and, in Idaho, the Jacks Creek and Bruneau-Jarbidge units. Each has unique values. Jacks Creek, for instance, has those surviving pristine remnants of land never touched by livestock. But common to all are the rivers and their deep rugged canyons, extraordinary archaeological remains (like fish racks and woven sagebrush mats still intact in a few caves), vast clear vistas, half the world's California bighorn sheep, and the elk and antelope potential.

The proposal is deliberately elastic, especially on the key issue of grazing. "We want specifics to emerge from thorough local discussion, including ranchers and local businesses," says high desert committee chairwoman Janet O'Crowley, who is far more flexible on grazing's future role than Morris is. The committee would like to enlist local support for a formal Park Service study of the potential; as at Craters, that study is the indispensable first step.

Dave Tindall doesn't sound enlistable. "The cattle people are pretty firm that we'd like to keep the multiple-use structure," and right now he clearly speaks for most of Owyhee County. Without local support, no Idaho congressman is going to request a park study. Larry Craig, whose district includes Owyhee County, has stayed silent.

After a rush of immediate publicity in Idaho and Oregon (thanks to Larry Craig and Richard Stallings, park proposals were a newsy item) and a quick endorsement from the Idaho Innkeepers Association, public attention to the high desert committee proposal faded. Morris admits it will be a long haul, but points out some small steps forward. When O'Crowley took a slide show on the concept to a dozen civic club meetings in southeastern Oregon, she found hostile ranchers but also some interested businessmen. Her next circuit, perhaps in the fall of 1988, will be through Owyhee County.

And the publicity is attracting more people to the public lands of the Owyhee Plateau. The committee helped organize a well-attended series of summer and fall hikes this year, and its newly published desert hiking guide by committee member Sheldon Bluestein is selling steadily. "We're sowing seeds," Janet O'Crowley says. "We think they'll sprout, even if we can't say when."

Note: In late 1988 Congress added the City of Rocks National Historical Reserve and the Hagerman Fossil Beds National Monument to the National Park system. They are the first such additions in Idaho since 1924.

CHAPTER TWENTY

Making Economics Less Dismal

Bert Lindler

Economics AND economists are traditional enemies of the environment. Behind a facade of neutrality and analysis, traditional economists have pushed for the extraction of natural resources and for the conversion of small communities and businesses into large ones. Now comes a Princeton-educated University of Montana economist to challenge traditional growth-at-all-costs economics. For the past twenty years Tom Power has been trying to get from economics the right answers about the things that matter most to him: livable communities and the natural environment. "The things that are important to me are a combination of community and nature," said Power, who has been chairman of the economics department at the University of Montana for the past decade. "Those are two things that are clearly central to people's well-being and central to commercial economic activity."

Yet economists have left such concerns to others. "They're excluded from economic analysis," Power said. "Nature in traditional economic analysis is a raw material input, and community is just the institutional background that goes undiscussed. It was clear to me that there was something wrong."

Like many other Westerners, Power is a refugee from urban America. He was a city boy in Milwaukee, Wisconsin, before studying physics at Pennsylvania's

190

Lehigh University. To mesh his social concerns with the mathematics in his undergraduate training, Power turned to economics for his doctoral studies at Princeton. "It was a matter of simply working with economics to get it to be a useful tool for the concerns I had," said Power of his struggles to get the right answers from economics. "It seemed to always give the wrong answer on any issue. I think it has ideological biases built into it. It took quite a bit of struggle to both escape those biases and find those ways of putting economic tools to work for the things that are important to me."

In 1968, before his dissertation was complete, Power left Princeton to take a teaching position in Missoula, Montana. "I came here quite consciously because I wanted to live in the mountains," he said. "I wanted to live in a political or social environment where I could get directly, politically involved, other than just carrying a picket sign and protesting after the fact."

When Power came to Montana, he wore his hair short. Long hair wasn't worth the hassle, especially when his energies were consumed in opposing the Vietnam War. During the 1970s he let his hair grow into a ponytail, which, combined with his wire-rim glasses, gave him a bookish, Beatles look. He appeared, complete with ponytail, before utility regulatory commissions across the West on behalf of low-income and consumer groups. In addition, he analyzed the economics of strip mining coal in eastern Montana from an environmental rather than an industrial bias.

Power's ponytail grew for nearly a decade, becoming something of a trademark. "I had started wearing it tied up in a bun," he said. "Some days I'd get up and look in the mirror and see my grandmother." His dean called him "a living anachronism." To Power, this was proof that he was a conservative. But in the spring following Ronald Reagan's election, Power cut off the ponytail, adopting a traditional hair style and dress befitting an economics professor in the 1980s. But he saved the ponytail and sometimes wears it at parties.

Whatever his dress or hair style, Power has always worked for livable communities and a healthy environment. And he has never figured that was uneconomic, despite the cries of business interests for tax relief, weakened environmental laws, and unfettered growth. "I'm not trying to say the area is booming," Power said of the rural West during the 1980s, "but people have to sit back and ask, first, what it is they want from the economy. The Main Street business people may think what they want is an ongoing expansion or boom . . . but most of that boom or expansion doesn't do the vast majority of us any good at all. It doesn't add to our economic well-being."

In fact, it's possible for per capita incomes to decline during a boom, since low-paying jobs may outnumber high-paying ones. And it's also possible for unemployment to rise, as persons are drawn from other areas in search of work. Even if per capita incomes rose significantly and unemployment declined, that wouldn't necessarily mean that persons who lived in the area before the boom had more income or were more likely to have jobs.

LIFE IN THE GOOD LANE

Cedron Jones has spent forty-seven years proving it's possible to live a worthwhile life without working full-time for a living. He spends about one-third hiking, bird-watching, or cross-country skiing; one-third taking care of the chores of life; and one-third working. "I don't see any theoretical reason people couldn't live the way I do," Jones said. "What we really need to do is figure out how people can feel worthwhile without having to work."

Many people think they work to earn money for possessions such as a new car or a Gore-Tex parka. But Jones thinks they work because it's the only way they can feel worthwhile. The money and the possessions it buys come with the job. Rather than organizing society around jobs and the profit motive that provides them, Jones would like to see society say, "Hey, why don't we concentrate on making this a beautiful place to be and making it fun to be with one another?"

Jones was raised in San Francisco and graduated from the University of California at Berkeley with a degree in biochemistry. He attended graduate school at Berkeley before going to India in the Peace Corps. He returned to become a graduate student at the Massachusetts Institute of Technology, working for a physiologist using electron microscopy in his research. By 1970 Jones realized he couldn't continue to work as a scientist. At the time the possibility of genetic engineering was becoming apparent. The attitude of scientists was, "Oh man, this is the Brave New Frontier," Jones said. "My attitude was: Jesus Christ, there's no way we as a culture are prepared to deal with things like this."

In December 1970 Jones and his wife, Sarah Taubman, left Cambridge for the West. They lived with friends in Colorado before moving to Bend, Oregon, where Jones spent fifteen months working in a furniture factory. "That is the only period of extended employment I've ever had in my life." By then, Jones and Taubman had caught back-to-the-land fever. Although they didn't know anything about trees or animals and had never held a gun or a fishing rod, they decided they would live on their own land as latter-day pioneers.

After some traveling, they found twenty-eight acres of flat ground on a clay bench along the south side of the Clark Fork River valley near Heron, Montana. When they closed the deal in May 1973, half their belongings were stored at their relatives and the rest were in their Toyota car, parked on land they could call their own, but with no house in which to live. Because they had borrowed to buy the land, they had to find jobs, and within weeks they were living in a Forest Service fire lookout fifteen miles from their land. Jones was the official lookout and Taubman was the alternate. The job gave them income and a place to live. On his days off, Jones built a log shed on their property.

That winter they worked as caretakers at a downhill ski area in Oregon. Again they were able to earn money while their jobs provided housing. "Over those two winters we saved enough to pay off the place," Jones said. They continued working summers for the Forest Service in a variety of jobs. At the same time they built a pottery kiln for Taubman's pottery business and finally a 15-foot-by-16-foot two-story log home. They also rebuilt a washed-out pond and stocked it with trout. They canned food raised in their garden. They read by propane lights and heated their home with a wood stove.

One summer, while Jones was working on a Forest Service trail crew, some of his colleagues were griping about the high salaries Forest Service employees received for working in the office while field employees received meager wages. "I realized that I didn't give a damn, and the reason that I didn't give a damn was that the notion that your life is worth $5.35 an hour is so patently degrading and absurd," Jones said. "I wanted to be clearing trail, and I didn't care if I worked my ass off while some GS-7 sat in an office and made twice as much as I did."

As Jones traveled around Montana to hike, he realized he liked the big sky of eastern Montana more than the rain forest of the west. So in 1985 he and his wife sold their land in Heron and used the buyer's down payment to help buy a fix-it-up home in Helena, and the buyer's monthly payments to help finance their life on the outskirts of the cash economy. Jones works as a volunteer for the Montana Wilderness Association. He also contracts to work part-time for the Natural Heritage Information System, which records information about the state's rare plants and animals. Taubman pots.

"We eat well," Jones said. "We've got a nice house. We've got a car to drive. I play. What I feel I've given up to live this life are new clothes. I buy my clothes at the Salvation Army. I never eat out. We just don't buy pop. I don't go to movies anymore."

He walks to work. They use the pickup truck only when they travel. During their travels, they camp in the bed of the pickup in a simple, homemade camper. One of their biggest headaches is health insurance. They don't feel they can do without it, yet it consumes a large portion of their income. They aren't building retirement benefits, as they might if they were working at full-time jobs. "But I just feel like I'd rather postpone acting under necessity until the necessity's there," Jones said.

Although their income is no higher than that of some families society may consider poor, they are not. "With the right kind of techniques of living, you can still have that positive feeling of controlling your destiny," Jones said. "Being willfully poor is just a totally different game than not knowing anything but poverty." Jones believes his lifestyle is environmentally responsible, but he doesn't judge others who have chosen other lifestyles. A lot of people live with contradictions. They say they're environmentalists, and their lifestyles are incredibly consumptive. "I'm basically concerned with the quality of my life. I want to be proud of the record of Cedron Jones."

Bert Lindler

"Until we know who got the income, we don't know anything about the well-being of the local population," Power said. "Our traditional statistics don't tell us anything about the well-being of the existing population. They tell us something about the expansion of the commercial economy, and local economic well-being is often only tangentially tied to that expansion in the commercial economy."

Residents of the rural West haven't chosen to stay here because of an abundance of high-paying jobs. So they must have other reasons. "That something else is our communities and our landscape," Power said. "That's the wealth that enriches those people's lives enough so that they will put up with the limited commercial economy."

Rural areas with an agricultural base haven't collapsed, despite tough times in agriculture and other natural resource industries throughout the West. "It's because people want to live there," Power said. "They take in their neighbor's wash, they do odd jobs, spend savings, not to give up what the natural and social environment provides them with. That commitment to place stabilizes everything. It means you don't have a Wyoming or an Alaska energy phenomenon, where the population just comes and goes with the price of crude oil."

Traditional economists see low per capita income as a sign of poverty. Power says it may mean that residents are willing to accept less pay in a certain region because the quality of life is higher. He suggests that *real* income may be equal across the nation, if money and quality of life are both taken into account. Power doesn't think communities are likely to benefit by establishing an economic development agency to offer tax breaks or other incentives to lure outside firms into an area. "You get slick, PR types who really only want to go and hang out with other slick, PR types and corporate representatives and wine and dine, and what you get are incredibly marginal firms," Power said.

Often economic development agencies seek firms that will be manufacturing goods for sale elsewhere. Such firms are thought to provide the economic base for the community, since they're bringing in money from the outside. However, such firms also make the community vulnerable to economic shocks from the outside. "The exports, touted as the primary source of local economic welfare, become the conduit through which instability in the national and international economies are imported," said Power in his book, *The Economic Pursuit of Quality*, recently published by M. E. Sharpe. "The more dependent the economy is on exports . . . the more it is at the mercy of random events."

Power believes communities would spend their money more wisely if they provided technical assistance to small local businesses. "We know that in Montana something between one-fourth and one-third of all employment is self-employed," Power said. "We know that those are low-income, very unstable proprietary businesses that are very important to the economy of the state." As the state's economy suffered during the 1980s, more and more Montanans have found that the only available jobs were those they made themselves. "This is the primary adjustment mechanism that Montanans have used during the 1980s to allow them to remain Montanans," Power said. "It's responsible for tens of thousands of jobs. We should do something to support it, especially if it's really inexpensive to support it, instead of trying to offer million-dollar bribes to biotech companies to move from California to Bozeman."

In addition, Power says that efforts to make communities more livable are a form of economic development. Local communities can work to improve schools, control crime, protect the local environment, or foster cultural development. If they do, the community will be better off. The money wouldn't be spent for tourists, or to convince out-of-state businesses to relocate. It would be spent to foster the well-being of the existing residents. "Citizens seeking new skills, environmentalists seeking clean air or water, artists seeking attention to their work, school boards seeking support for their schools, neighbors seeking to protect the integrity of their communities are all engaged in economic activities," Power says in his book. "They are as relevant to the area's development as the downtown business person or the national manufacturing or mining firms that operate locally."

CHAPTER TWENTY-ONE

Weaving the Tapestry of a Way of Life

Colleen Cabot

WE MAY not be able to change the course of nations or even of our home-towns. But each of us can change values and human dominance over the natural world.

Economic activity is narrowly defined as the generation of money to exchange for goods and services. And because economic activity is what often is valued most, the land and the people suffer from spiritual neglect. In the last two decades, land-centered values have regained a stronger voice in human activism and environmental education. Yet I am dissatisfied. My values and my daily life are not yet integrated. I no longer wish to talk about change. I wish to weave my values into a way of life.

A deep caring for wildlands underscores my values. I am looking for some way of making a living that involves dirt and physical labor, expresses my spiritual connections to land, and embraces me in a human community. Landscape gardening and indigenous horticulture draw all these yearnings together, pulling me into occupied territory. Wilderness has always been "out there." Now I wish to bring wilderness into the garden.

My daily choices are grains of sand that one day may wash up on a beach marking the edge of a new culture. Culture is the expression of people enacting

values through personal choice. My pursuit of livelihood is a matter of expressing my deep connection to intimate landscapes. The landscape, Gaia, is alive.
Landscape is the whole fabric of land and my experience on the land: the brisk
wind, the elusive heron, the adamant cliff. Qualities like integrity, which I
sense in healthy landscapes, give me benchmarks from which to measure my
wholeness and balance.

That sense of balance is given to me through direct interaction with the
land. My beliefs and imagination make up my personal internal landscape. To
maintain integrity in my life, to nurture my internal landscape, my economic
endeavors need to be responsive to the rhythms of the exterior landscape.
Economy, in this sense, is the full measure of exchange between myself and my
environment. I inhale and exhale with the plants. I trade my care and labor for
sustenance from the earth. I exchange the excess bounty with fellow humans.
My life ebbs and flows with the seasons, and that rhythm beats in my soul. My
external and internal landscapes thus cocreate two dimensions of my self.

> The wind touches my ear and
> passing through me is changed by
> my spirit. My voice mingles with
> the voice of the land.

> The breath of the land, passing
> through me, creates story. Telling
> story, I recreate the land. Telling
> story again and again, I create a mythological land-
> scape, a landscape reflecting my human spirit
> as well as its own.

I cannot attain this interaction with the land through politics or education.
Nor can I attain wholeness if my life is fragmented into units like a job,
spiritual growth, and physical fitness. I don't want to jog to stay fit. Hiking, I
pass over the land; I don't live with it. I don't want to eat food bludgeoned from
the soil by Safeway. Productive labor that earns my daily bread directly from
the earth in tune with Her rhythms would be more satisfying.

My jobs so far have not engendered this kind of wholeness. Years of wandering in wildlands attuned me to the sacred harmonies in Gaia's dance. Academic training and political activism underscored these profound experiences.
Yet I remain a visitor to wild places. I talk a great line about being part of a
landscape. I have committed to these ideals through my work as a cartogra-
pher, an environmental activist, a director of a field ecology school. But how
can I frame a way of life in which I make daily choices in response to the
landscape of a particular place?

My life must reflect a landscape if I wish to enact my values. To establish an
indigenous livelihood (that is, a way of life native to a place), I am asking

questions like these: Is the basis of the activity responsive to local resources and natural forces? Does the activity enhance the local environment? Is there a local or regional market for the service or product? Does it embrace elements of diversity that will enhance its viability and my continuing interest? The questions are many. Not only do I wish to establish a way of life for myself, I also hope to contribute to my community and culture. Wilderness and culture are contrary notions in the modern vernacular. Humans left the wilderness to establish civilization. Growing a garden is the borderland between the wild and the domestic. I will weave the two together again.

I am a restless sort. While a thread of values strings my days together, it isn't enough. I would pattern my life like the process of weaving. My interests, my values, and my habits would be the weft, woven across the warp of the intimate landscapes of my home territory. I want to live in harmony with Gaia, engaged in vital relationships with people and place. In a private space within a community I would live in health and elegant simplicity, expressing the beauty that flows through me, maintaining variety in my life in an abiding rhythm that harmonizes with the seasons and the land's abundance.

At the moment I am untangling a bunch of threads chosen a bit at random as I fell in love with an appealing color or an intriguing texture. Periods of intense curiosity about animals and soil and clouds have filled my brain with a prodigious array of data. Ecological principles tied all this into a neat bundle of systems. But it was theory. Could I look at a piece of land and see all this "ecology" happening? And what difference did ecology make as I faithfully followed my Day-Timer through job after job? My life seemed chopped into a tangled bundle of yearnings. *Hireaeth* the Welsh call it: longing for the unattainable.

A memory offered a clue. I was thirteen, an avid Girl Scout. Our group trailed a loaded covered wagon through Hole in the Wall country on the southeast flank of Wyoming's Big Horn Range. A truck hauled the wagon, but we walked. It was real enough, walking along the edge of old times. A rancher's wife gave us a glass of cold water when we knocked at her door. Eight or ten people sat around a long table eating dinner at midday. All the men's foreheads were pale. We would camp in a few days in the battlefield of Dull Knife.

After our trail supper, cooked in a big iron kettle over an open fire, I wandered up a draw, looking for the outlaw stronghold. The sudden buzz of a rattlesnake peaked my adrenaline at the same moment the setting sun burnished red buttes with crimson. The sage edged this glory with a cloak of pale gray-green. The air was crystal. Something in that landscape at that moment spoke to me, left me in tears, without words to explain the feeling that knifed through my soul. Inexplicable. Science hadn't prepared me for this.

Recently I stumbled onto a word that embraced the experience. Geomancy: the magic of the land. Experience and language come together in this word. I have felt the power of certain places: striking earth drum song vibrating along the bole of a cottonwood lying prostrate in a desert canyon; being caught in crystalline water trickling through shards of fractured quartz in a Teton saddle, spinning a silver thread a thousand miles along streams and rivers to the surf-rounded moonstones of Puget Sound.

There is no explaining the profound vitality I touched meditating with a jade plant, nor the joyous affection offered by a sycamore. Gaia's spirit emanates from rocks, plants, animals/humans, gathered by the motion of wind and water along features of the land to gild certain places with greater vitality and power. Tapping this essence of place is called geomancy. It happens that way sometimes. We spend years picking up pieces from an intricate puzzle. One day, a batch of pieces falls together. (I will be a geomancer.) There have been so many voices informing my choices, sparking my imagination. Now it is time to give voice to my heart's desire: to let the voice of the land speak through me.

September. I am hiking up the Beckler River in southeast Yellowstone. An image comes: snow is falling and a Great Bear ambles into her winter den. Curled in Gaia's womb, she begins to dream. Memories of the season's last succulent raspberry slide into a recollection of traversing the Pitchstone under a June full moon. Her dreams reach back across many seasons. The bear tidies her life, reweaves lessons from experience, and emerges in the spring newly born of old stuff. Some say the Bear dreams for us all, dreams the world whole again.

The year turns to another September. A friend, a wildcrafter, gathers wild medicinal plants for tinctures and salves. I join her to dig osha. The root of this plant's name is bear. The root of the plant has healed my lungs over the past year. Digging, I can feel the powerful clawed arm part meadow soil.

A few days later I left on a journey taking me into my own winter dream time, to sort the experiences of a lifetime through winter's solitude, to spiral another step toward wholeness. I dreamed of growing medicinal herbs to share the healing they have given me. I want to sit with these plants in the wild and then bring them into a garden that still feels like home to them.

Wild places are the original homes of us all. We, the People, have manipulated the ancestral wildness out of our inhabited places, cutting ourselves off from our true homes. All beings change the environment in which they reside: rock casts shadows, water cuts canyons, puma eats deer, tree gives oxygen. Humans can cast huge shadows that blight the earth. I cannot live without a shadow, but I can live modestly with respect for all beings, and nurturing beauty and wildness in my home.

I spent the winter reshaping torn landscapes, tracing the ghost of desert washes across suburban backyards. In the summer I worked in an organic market garden and a nursery specializing in native plants, and helped friends make gardens. I dream of a greenhouse, round and big enough to house a little café. I would create a beautiful garden, as like a wild home as possible, asking plants to reside with me and give of their bounty in return for the care and respect I give them. In creating a home for plants, I would create a home for myself. Eventually, I wish to collaborate with indigenous varieties of plants adapted to high-altitude situations. Landscaping, organic produce, whole foods: GeoMagic, I call the enterprise. I will be the geomancer. The gardens will grow wilder, and so will I.

Despair is my enemy as I travel into this new country. My history is so entangled with greed and grief that establishing a pattern of harmony in human endeavor seems impossible. Yet my life is one thread in an evolving pattern. If I can untangle my life, live true to my beliefs, take responsibility for my choices, that is one thread untangled. My life has evolved from political action through education into personal action. My choices make up my only true sphere of influence. I am presumptuous to foist solutions on others. But I can live my life. With integrity. In beauty.

> it is too easy
> to yearn after innocence
> it is our task
> to live life
> to shovel the dung
> and heap the middens
> if we are lucky
> we will find simplicity
> and beauty.

CHAPTER TWENTY-TWO

Tourism Beats Logging in Wyoming

Tom Bell

IN THEORY, every U.S. citizen has an equal say in the management of public lands. In fact, residents of small towns dotted across the rural West exert a disproportionate control over those lands. In the past that control has led to roading, logging, mining, and oil and gas exploration. But now, as this story out of the Yellowstone region indicates, some small towns are using their power to oppose extractive activities.

When he came to Dubois, Wyoming, in the late 1960s to take charge of national forestlands around that town, the new district ranger, Harold Wadley, was an experienced timberman and a decorated Marine captain from the Korean War. The overcutting he saw on his new domain shocked him, and he recommended that the annual cut on his part of the Shoshone National Forest be reduced from 17 million board-feet to 1.3 million board-feet.

National forest policy requires that timber be managed so that it can be cut at a more or less constant rate, in perpetuity. The overcutting Wadley saw meant that the timber around the Dubois area would be exhausted in a few years; his recommendation was meant to prevent that exhaustion. In the hue and cry that followed, his superiors caved in to political pressure. He was cashiered as district ranger, and "promoted" to supervisor of the Pine Ridge Job Corps camp in South Dakota. The year was 1970.

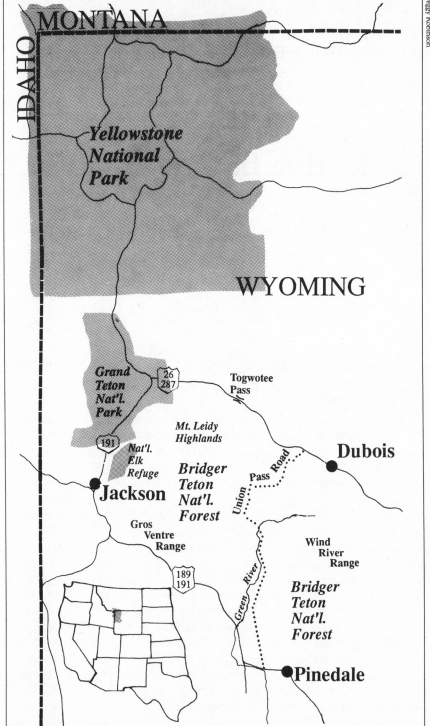

MONTANA

IDAHO

Yellowstone
National
Park

WYOMING

Grand
Teton
Nat'l.
Park

26
287

Togwotee
Pass

Mt. Leidy
Highlands

Dubois

191

Nat'l.
Elk
Refuge

Bridger
Teton
Nat'l.
Forest

Union Pass Road

Jackson

Gros
Ventre
Range

189
191

Wind
River
Range

Green River

Bridger
Teton
Nat'l.
Forest

Pinedale

In a timber sense, time has proven Wadley correct, but politically he was eighteen years ahead of his time. The agency that chose to avoid a fight eighteen years ago by transferring Wadley has now girded its loins and is fighting the war it backed away from then. Today's Bridger-Teton National Forest Supervisor Brian Stout describes the resource decisions he must make as "gut wrenching." They are gut wrenching because they represent an abrupt turn for the agency, from giving almost carte blanche to logging on the national forestlands in western Wyoming to an attempt to preserve surviving stands by drastically reducing logging. The agency's change has had a major effect: the closing in May 1988 of Louisiana-Pacific's (L-P) Dubois mill—an operation many in Dubois saw as the heart of the town's economy and heritage.

Small family sawmills have been a part of all the mountain towns in western Wyoming. Large-scale timbering came to Dubois with the advent of the railroad-tie industry. From the early 1900s until after World War II, millions of ties were cut on the Shoshone National Forest land surrounding Dubois. The ties were floated down the DuNoir and Wind rivers in colorful tie drives to the railroad at Riverton. Better methods of preserving railroad ties and the decline of railroads led the timber industry to turn to lumber and then to building studs. Now the days of large-scale timbering appear to be over.

The fact that Dubois had several years' warning that the closure was coming didn't make the event less traumatic for the town of eleven hundred or for Fremont County and its county seat of Lander. Since 1981 there has been a loss of about twenty-five hundred jobs in the basic industries of uranium, iron ore, and oil and gas in a county that has about forty thousand inhabitants. In addition to the loss in mining, milling, and oil and gas, the area's cattle ranching has been depressed during much of the 1980s.

Coming on top of the other economic losses, the effect of the mill closure achieved outsize proportions. L-P provided about 165 jobs in Dubois and at the associated planing mill at Riverton. About $3 million in wages went with those jobs. The loss of the L-P jobs at Dubois transmitted a painful message to Dubois and to Fremont County—the need to rebuild the economy on a very different base, one that depends on new attitudes and new skills. It is not just the human population that must change if the timber industry is to be replaced. Like the people, the forestlands have also been adapted to a timber economy. Logging and the accompanying road system have altered what was once roadless, prime big-game habitat.

One of the scenic areas near Dubois is the stretch of country between Togwotee and Union passes. Jim Straley, a retired Wyoming Game and Fish Department big-game biologist, says he saw much of the area from Togwotee Pass to Union Pass go from wilderness-type elk hunting to practically nothing. He says that today automobiles drive over miles of road that didn't exist twenty years ago. Long, successful hunting seasons have been replaced by short seasons and controlled permits.

The fate of once-beautiful lands, and the tighter and tighter box the Forest Service found itself in as a result of decades of earlier logging practices, is illustrated by the so-called co-op sale held in 1987 near Union Pass. The co-op sale began life as two planned sales in other areas. But public anger over the location and size of those sales forced the Forest Service to cast about for another site and size. The agency finally settled on 150 acres near the head of Fish Creek, a tributary to the Gros Ventre River. The relatively small co-op sale—150 acres yielding 3.1 million board-feet—was set in an area that had been repeatedly logged and roaded since 1961. What had been prime elk and moose habitat was now a big-game desert. Cover, or trees, for elk was down to 24 percent. The Forest Service's own standard for good elk habitat calls for 60 percent cover.

What was the agency doing cutting again in an area already badly overcut? The co-op sale was an admission that the Forest Service was caught between its commitment to the timber industry to supply a certain minimum cut each year and public and conservationist anger at overcut forests. In so many words the Forest Service admitted that the sale was a bad one. Bridger-Teton spokesman Fred Kingwill told a local newspaper on March 31, 1987: "There will be impacts on what elk are left there, but they're impacts we feel we can live with.

Angus Thuermer, Jr.

Clear-cuts in the Bridger-Teton National Forest

Members of the Jackson Hole Alliance tour a Union Pass clear-cut.

Habitat effectiveness has been heavily impacted by previous sales. It's not much good at all anymore. This new sale will cause some further denigration of habitat effectiveness, but in an area that wasn't worth much anyway."

The Forest Service and L-P had been reduced to bonepicking in already heavily logged lands because they had been cut off, through political and legal action, from the remaining unroaded, uncut forestlands in western Wyoming. Their adversaries were not just state and national environmental groups, but two neighboring communities: Jackson and Pinedale. Jackson is only eighty-five highway miles from Dubois, and much less as the crow flies. Both communities started out as ranching towns with some tourism, but today they are poles apart.

Jackson, the seat of Teton County, lies on the west side of the Continental Divide, surrounded by two national forests, the Jackson Hole National Elk Refuge and Grand Teton National Park. The south entrance to Yellowstone National Park is only an hour's drive away. Its chief commodities are scenery, abundant wildlife, ski slopes, and that Old West, "unspoiled" feel so prized by tourists. Both the town and country have a tourist and visitor economy, although cattle ranching is still important.

The third point of this triangle, Pinedale, is a small community dominated by ranching; and, like Jackson, it is on the west side of the Continental Divide.

It is in the Green River valley, almost directly south of Dubois. The two towns are separated from each other by the most rugged part of the Wind River Mountains. In a lower-key way than Jackson, Pinedale also depends on tourism—it attracts hunters, fishermen, and those in search of scenery. The area also has a few sawmills and, more recently, a booming oil and gas industry.

As in most small communities, it has a long memory; the heavy logging it saw on the forests at the head of the Green River turned many against the timber industry. As a result, while Jackson opposes the oil and gas exploration that Pinedale accommodated, the two towns, and their counties (Teton and Sublette), are united in opposition to timbering, and therefore to Dubois. So when L-P and the Forest Service tried to solve their overcutting problem by moving farther afield, they were met with fierce opposition. Generally, small communities like to live and let live, but Jackson and Pinedale felt that logging based in Dubois threatened both their tourist and their outfitting industries.

Small communities sitting amidst public lands exert disproportionate control over those lands. L-P and its predecessors (L-P bought the Dubois mill in 1974) were able to overcut the lands around Dubois because they had the general support of the town and county. But as the threat to other industries based on the public lands grew, people in Jackson, Pinedale, and neighboring communities mobilized against timbering. County commissioners in both Teton and Sublette counties took positions exactly opposite to those of Fremont County in regard to the timber industry.

Another element in the overcutting involved the nature of the Forest Service itself. The Shoshone National Forest around Dubois was overcut because the industry's desire coincided with a Forest Service philosophy of increased timbering. Many newly trained foresters saw trees only as a commodity. They saw, too, that the forests were maturing and therefore subject to disease and parasites. The Forest Service encouraged the industry buildup by offering, in the post–World War II period, large, cheap sales of the public timber.

The people of western Wyoming saw the results of that policy and in Jackson and Pinedale were incensed by it. A candid 1985 report by the Forest Service, titled "Preliminary Impact Analysis of the Dubois, Wyoming, Community Relative to National Forest Management Decisions," backed up their observations. Three agency economists wrote that accelerated timbering on the Shoshone forest began in the late 1950s. The timber available for cutting had been set at 21 million board-feet a year for forty years. Much of the timber, the report said, existed only on paper, and the figure was dropped to around 5 million board-feet after only ten years.

The situation has also been described by Phil Miller, a former forester who had been in charge of timber sale preparation on the Dubois district from 1960 until 1970. In a letter to the editor of the *Dubois Frontier* on February 12,

1987, Miller wrote: "One year, the Forest Service, using the beetle infestation as an excuse, authorized and financed the Dubois Ranger District to sell 25 million board-feet of timber for logging. The beetles weren't in half of it. From early in the 1960s until about 1967, 15 to 20 million board-feet of timber were cut on the district annually. The big clearcuts began to show."

The Teton forest, later combined with the Bridger National Forest into the Bridger-Teton, also began accelerated harvesting at about the same time, and on about the same scale. Once the Shoshone forest's timber supply was exhausted, timbering was concentrated on the Bridger-Teton. All of the readily accessible timber in the Union Pass area was cut, even though it meant damaging other multiple-use resources. Brian Stout, Bridger-Teton Forest supervisor, told a meeting of the Fremont County commissioners in Lander on May 31, 1988, that the 1979 timber management plan on which the cutting had been based had not considered other resources.

Stout was explaining to the hostile commissioners why his agency was resisting, along with Jackson and Pinedale, the expansion of L-P chain saws into unroaded areas of the Bridger-Teton forest. L-P was demanding sales on the north end of the Bridger-Teton, in the most sensitive areas in the forest. One of these is the Mount Leidy Highlands. The 1985 Forest Service report describes it as the last remaining unprotected "gap" in what has been called the Emerald Chain. The chain includes areas off-limits to logging such as the Teton Wilderness Area; Yellowstone National Park; John D. Rockefeller, Jr., Parkway; Grand Teton National Park; Jedediah Smith Wilderness; Palisades Wilderness Study Area; Snake River Scenic River (nominated by Congress); Grayback Ridge; Gros Ventre Wilderness; and the National Elk Refuge.

To the pro-logging contingent, the creation of all these protected areas has made it all the more important to log areas not protected by legislation or management directives. To others, the existence of large tracts of protected ground is an argument to protect whatever hasn't yet been protected. There are economically based arguments on both sides. The Mount Leidy Highlands are considered an integral part of the Jackson Hole guiding and outfitting industry. The industry remembers that one legacy of earlier logging was the destruction of many guiding and outfitting jobs. In addition, a large part of the highlands is designated Grizzly Bear Management Situations 1 and 2, bringing it under the wing of the Endangered Species Act.

The area is also an important watershed, containing the headwaters of the Gros Ventre River, Spread Creek, and the Buffalo River. It is also an important viewshed. Parts of it can be seen from Grand Teton National Park and from a major tourist road into Jackson Hole, the Togwotee Pass highway. As if that were not enough, Mount Leidy contains elk migration corridors to and from the National Elk Refuge, and the area lies within the Greater Yellowstone Ecosystem.

Another area that could supply timber to the Dubois mill lies at the head of the Green River, within the sphere of influence of Pinedale and the even smaller town of Cora. The past history of timbering in the Union Pass area and at the head of the Green River serves as a reminder of what indiscriminate logging can do. Within the timbered areas, natural forest regrowth ranges from practically nothing to moderately successful. But even where it is termed successful, foresters estimate it will take at least 140 years to produce another crop of trees. So the prevailing attitude—even in an area that ranches and drills for oil and gas—is that logging should be limited to supplying timber for small, locally owned sawmills supplied by sales that do not require much road building.

In response to its own analysis, and to increasing attention from national conservation groups and growing pressure from the communities around Dubois, the Forest Service moved to cut off L-P's access to new timber supplies. But the agency has not had an easy time of it. A draft 50-year management plan was originally scheduled to be released in September 1985. It finally appeared in 1986. Politics, all the way to Washington, D.C., caused much of the delay. Some observers saw the heavy hand of the Reagan administration, as L-P, neutralized in Wyoming, sought help in Washington.

The public showed great interest in the plan. The allure of Yellowstone has been extended to the Bridger-Teton area through the efforts of the Greater Yellowstone Coalition, which helped spread the idea that Yellowstone National Park is simply part of a more extensive ecological region covering parts of Wyoming, Montana, and Idaho. The area the Dubois mill covered was within this Yellowstone area. Comments came from individuals and groups in every state except Rhode Island. Most of the twenty thousand comments—more than for any other plan—focused on timber harvest levels and mineral development; and the majority said they wanted less emphasis on both. Many expressed opposition to new roads and asked for closures of existing roads. A majority expressed concern with the below-cost timber sales that dominated the Bridger-Teton.

The plan drew fire from both sides. The agency's preferred alternative called for an annual cut of only 15.9 million board-feet on the entire forest. That was much less than L-P wanted, but more than conservation groups thought healthy. The reduction was especially drastic on the north end of the forest, in the Mount Leidy area, and that jeopardized the L-P mill. The oil and gas industry also objected, saying the plan was extremely biased against its interests. It objected to a buffer zone next to Grand Teton National Park (in the past, drilling and logging had gone on close to the park boundary), to a ban on exploration in a wilderness study area, and to a ban on leasing in critical grizzly bear habitat.

The flood of comments led to a major rewriting of the plan after the comment period ended in February 1987. Computer modeling and the use of map overlays to show all multiple uses made the plan both more sophisticated and more understandable. This was combined with a genuine outreach effort, in which the Forest Service laid its plan, and its dilemma, frankly on the table.

A complication came in December 1987 and January 1988, when the oil and gas industry and the timber industry filed suits against the Forest Service. L-P's case argued that it should be allowed to harvest much more timber than the Forest Service intended to put up for sale. It was at the trial before Federal District Judge Clarence Brimmer that Bridger-Teton Forest Supervisor Brian Stout said management of forest resources was "gut wrenching." The Bridger-Teton, Stout said, is probably the most complex forest in the lower forty-eight states. Its 3.4 million acres make it one of the nation's largest, and its closeness to national parks, wildlife refuges, and rivers further increases its importance.

After a well-publicized trial, Judge Brimmer ruled for the Forest Service in April. He said increased logging would cause more harm to the region than would occur if the Dubois mill closed. "Tourism, recreation, ranchers and small loggers would be harmed. . . ." He also said that "increased timber harvesting may have unforeseen environmental effects . . . some evidence connects diminished elk habitat with timber harvesting."

The agency then moved to insulate itself from the political pressures of the day. Stout told Fremont County commissioners in May that the revised forest plan was not going to be released until after the November elections. He also said the plan was not going to provide more timber on the north end of the forest than the draft had proposed. L-P went to Washington to request a minimum of 14 million board-feet of timber from the north end. The Forest Service replied that the request would not be considered until after the final plan was adopted. So a legal and administrative wall seems to separate L-P from the trees in Jackson's backyard, in the north end of the Bridger-Teton forest.

But L-P has another option: the Union Pass road. It has been the main haul road for timber coming off the Dubois side of Union Pass. Part of the road between Dubois and Pinedale consists of a 3.8-mile section that is more trail than road. L-P has long wanted to get that section rebuilt so that timber on the Upper Green River and on the south end of the forest would be more accessible. Ranchers, small loggers, and recreationists have resisted, and the road has been an emotional issue for the last several years. Ironically, as a result of the attention drawn to the road, Dubois and Pinedale have decided that an upgraded road would serve them both. Regardless of L-P, many now believe it will be a boon to tourism. The development could put L-P back in business on a reduced scale by providing timber from the south end of the forest, but it would also put the company in direct competition with mills in that area. And the road could also give Dubois a larger stake in a tourist economy.

Officially, Dubois has spoken with one voice on the L-P mill: town and Fremont County officials, as well as community leaders, have fought hard for the mill. But Dubois is not a one-industry town, except perhaps psychologically. Cattle ranching, dude ranching, hunting and outfitting, and small sawmills are still in place. Of late, retirees have discovered the Dubois area, with its relatively mild climate and spectacular scenery.

Although L-P may look on the town of eleven hundred as a company town, not all residents accept that benevolence. Open discussion, however, is not easy in the community. To take one example, in February 1987, the Forest Service scheduled a forest plan "listening session" for Dubois. On the day of the hearing, flyers invited community members to enjoy free beer at the Ramshorn Bar prior to the hearing, and to wear black as a sign of mourning for lost jobs. Also planned was a funeral procession, complete with pine casket, leading from the bar to the high school, where logging trucks would circle the building as the meeting went forward. Other ideas included writing comments on two-by-fours and wheeling them in. L-P chief forester Bob Baker said the events were meant as an antidote to the dull, drawn-out planning process; people, he said, "wanted to have some fun."

The Forest Service canceled the meeting. The general nature of a small town has also inhibited discussion within the community. Mary Back, author, artist, and environmentalist, has lived in the Dubois area for more than fifty years. Like many other natives, she opposed clear-cutting and the roads. But

Bob Baker

she dislikes fighting with neighbors. She says, "We can still smile at each other" in spite of differences.

What comes now, with the L-P mill at Dubois and the associated planing mill at Riverton closed? The best guess is that the Dubois mill will stay closed. The Dubois area's timber is gone for the next century. And gone with the timber is the public and Forest Service attitudes that permitted the overexploitation. Dubois is already planning its future—one in which logging and sawmills will have much less importance. Now that the mill is closed, a serious reassessment is under way. The forested areas may have suffered from decades of logging by L-P and its predecessors, but Dubois is still in the midst of country that 99 percent of America would consider spectacular.

More broadly, logging has cost western Wyoming some loss of scenery, big game and its habitat, and fishing potential. Given enough time, however, the cut lands will recover and the scenery and wildlife will come back. These special lands will become even more important as pressures build on today's national parks. It is only a matter of time until visitor restrictions are imposed in the parks. When that happens, people will be looking for other places to go while waiting for their "turn" in the parks to come up. Union Pass and other recovered areas may then be there to enthrall tomorrow's visitors.

CHAPTER TWENTY-THREE

Butte Comes out of the Pit

Bruce Farling

FOR NEARLY one hundred years, miners in Butte, Montana, rode rickety cages into a dank netherworld where the talk was of drifts, stopes, buzzies, and rock. Or they pushed large machines around a dusty, wind-wracked open pit, one of the largest such mines in the world. They argued about strikes, poor air, crumbling shafts. They discussed death, for mining in Butte and elsewhere was a daily gamble. Men learned to dodge rocks, keep an eye on the powder man, stay on their toes. If they didn't, they could die, or, worse, end up crippled.

The world of the tunnel and pit was theirs, but the whole hill, the town, their jobs, belonged to well-dressed men with soft hands who sat in board rooms in New York, San Francisco, and Denver—men who never let Butte forget who signed the paychecks.

Then, in 1983, the boss walked. The Atlantic Richfield Company, the owner of Butte's old boss, Anaconda Minerals, shut down copper mining in the Berkeley Pit, putting the town's last eight hundred miners out of work. It was the final gasp of one of the country's largest mining and smelting empires, one that had produced an estimated $3 billion in metals over the years. It was done in by low copper prices and foreign competition. From 1979 to 1984, Butte lost five thousand jobs. The closure caused the town's population to drop from thirty-eight thousand to thirty-four thousand. The last shovel had turned in Butte.

By all logic, the loss of its century-old dominant industry and many of its jobs should have laid Butte low. Yet five years later the community enjoys growing prosperity. The number of new Butte businesses is up, unemployment is down. High technology, tourism, education, even some mining, have sparked an economic revival and grabbed national attention.

In June 1988 Butte was named an All-American City by the National Civic League, an urban booster group. Of 870 cities nominated, only 10 were selected. The National League of Cities last year gave the town an award for having the nation's most innovative job-training program. Stories about Butte appeared in *U.S. News and World Report* and *Business Week,* extolling the tenacity of the town and of boosters who refused to call it quits.

How did it happen? In this fiercely union town, where agreement often used to come only after a fistfight, residents generally agree that Butte's emerging new economy is the result of a few local leaders who saw possibilities in a stagnant, crumbling mine town. The main architect, everyone agrees, has been Don Peoples. "Now that I look back at it, one of the best things that ever happened to this community was Anaconda's leaving," says Peoples, chief executive officer of Butte–Silver Bow government.

Fifteen years ago that sentiment would have raised cheers on the picket line and a brawl in the paycheck line. But times have changed. Peoples, the mayor in Butte's consolidated city-county government, says Butte had to learn to get along without being tethered to the Anaconda Company and ARCo. "I often tell the story of how we put our shovel down in Butte," Peoples says. "I always talk about the guy who searched the world, but came back home and found wealth and fortune just by putting his bucket down in his birthplace. And I think that's what we've done in Butte. We don't need to look outside. We don't need to chase smokestacks. We've got all the resources in the world. We're just making things happen."

With Peoples as chief ambassador, the community developed an economic strategy that has helped bring in new businesses. Peoples had refused to let the community destroy its industrial and commercial infrastructure after ARCo folded. And the old mine facilities and commercial buildings have attracted prospective businesses. In addition, Butte wasn't totally dependent on mining. For example, Montana Power employs twelve hundred people, so the town didn't empty out after ARCo's closure, as other mining towns have. That provided an economic cushion during the transition.

Butte's support for Peoples's efforts is shown by its boosterism. Tourism brochures, restaurant menus, and bumper stickers extoll economic development in what locals call the "Can Do City" or "Butte, America." The list of new developments is modest, but growing. A children's psychiatric hospital opened in the fall of 1988, employing one hundred people. After out-hustling several other cities, Butte landed a $2.1 million federal grant to start the state's top truck-to-rail freight transfer facility. With another $2.7 million that it will raise, the community will have a shipping hub to both encourage export of local products and directly employ one hundred people.

Butte's economic development commission is planning construction this winter of a 40,000-square-foot building to house a trade center to display and export Montana-produced products. The community has also purchased a 230,000-square-foot former Safeway warehouse. It is the kind of bargain available in towns that have lost a major industry. Valued at $4.5 million, the building was bought for $700,000. It will house an industrial business incubator and a program that will research how to manufacture products in Montana from the raw natural resources the state now exports.

Butte has also started the country's only municipally owned small business incubator, a project that has helped eighteen new businesses in eighteen months. Jim Kambich, the incubator's director, says the project admits only companies that do not compete with existing Butte businesses. It provides cheap rent, low overhead, shared administrative services, and some consulting donated by local businesses, lawyers, and accountants. Among the incubator's tenants are a computer software company, a home health-care firm, a marketing consultant, and a research company that specializes in a high-technology process used to recover metals from mining ores and mining waste. It has created about seventy-five jobs so far. Peoples calls the incubator a "success beyond our wildest dreams." He convinced the Catholic Diocese in Helena to sell the building that houses the project to the Butte–Silver Bow government for a dollar, even though it was appraised for $200,000. A federal matching grant paid for the building's repair. According to Peoples, it is now worth $1 million.

Butte has also landed several small high-technology firms with the help of the Montana Science and Technology Alliance, a state-run venture-capital program that lent money to promising businesses. Butte's latest catch is an Oregon firm that produces materials for lasers and semiconductors. It hopes to employ fifty people within two or three years. However, a state court ruled in July that the alliance's activities violate the state constitution. That decision could end one method the town has used for attracting business.

The community is also turning its liabilities, such as its 5,700-foot elevation and cold winters, into assets. In 1985 it started construction of a high-altitude training center for Olympic athletes competing in speed and figure skating, hockey, and indoor cycling. The unfinished $9.5-million facility, funded by private donations, is one of only two such facilities in the world; the other is located in the Soviet Union. The training center was the site for last winter's World Cup speed skating competition, which attracted thousands of tourists.

Some trace the roots of the business resurgence back to 1984, when the community, suffering from 20 percent unemployment and little prospect for

David J. Spear

The famous Berkeley Pit in Butte, Montana

immediate relief, tried new-age motivation to get residents pondering things besides food stamps. A Seattle firm was brought in to put on 30-hour work-shops on positive thinking. More than four thousand attended. "It sounds Pollyannaish," Peoples says, "It sounds like something out of the space cadets or something, but this thing, it's really good." Peoples says it helped people both to think more positively about their community and to work together to solve problems.

Butte's success has given Peoples, a second-generation Butte Irishman, national recognition. In 1987, *U.S. News and World Report* ranked him among the country's top twenty mayors and chief executive officers. He has headed Butte–Silver Bow government since 1979 and says he'd like to keep the job for a while longer. He is considered by many to be one of Montana's rising Democratic stars.

The creation and attraction of new businesses aren't the only economic arrows in Butte's quiver. Mining—leaner, more efficient, and somewhat less dependent on absentee owners—has returned to Butte. When ARCo left, it abandoned a huge empire: the mile-wide Berkeley Pit, more than three thousand miles of underground tunnels, a huge ore concentrator, millions of dollars of mine equipment, and a considerable amount of copper, silver, lead, molybdenum, and zinc ore. All ready to go. All ready to be mined. For somebody who liked to gamble.

BEATING SLAG HEAPS INTO TOURIST SITES

Missouri. South Carolina. California. Manitoba. West Virginia. So go the license plates on cars parked at Butte's World Museum of Mining on a warm day in mid-July. The museum, according to its brochure, preserves a "segment of American history that has heretofore been neglected," and brings "to the people a realization of the glorious and ingenious heritage which is theirs."

In other parts of town, many of the museum's attractions would be considered trash and hazardous. There are tons of rusty equipment; dilapidated buildings; an ancient, hulking 100-foot-tall mine headframe; and a backdrop of thousands of acres of mine-tailing scabland—part of the nation's largest Superfund site here, near the headwaters of the Clark Fork River.

Not all of the museum, however, is trash or toxic. It also features an interesting replica of a late-1800s mining town. On this day, though, most of the action is in the gift shop, where an elderly woman in purple stretch pants is haggling with the counter girl over the price of a coffee mug that says "From Montana, With Love." Copper trinkets (more heritage), T-shirts, and ceramic deer clutter the small shop. Platter-size pewter belt buckles pay homage to God, guts, guns, cold dead fingers, and the flag. Some crafty salesman snuck one in to torment dyslexic members of the National Rifle Association. It reads: "Second Amendment Revised—Support the Right to Arm Bears." A man with a Texas drawl shouts to no one in particular: "How many mines y'all got in this heah town? Suppose y'all want to get back to work, huh?" The counter girl smiles.

Business is brisker at the Berkeley Pit Viewing Platform. A tour bus pulls in, disgorging about forty camera or kid-toting tourists. They shuffle through the short tunnel to the platform, which is perched above the mile-wide cavity that is filling rapidly with chocolate brown, heavy-metal-laden water. A few video cameras pan a landscape left sterile by twenty-five years of open-pit mining. Most people stay for just a few minutes. Somebody mentions the Grand Canyon. After staring at the pit for a moment, a man turns to his wife and says: "Is that all there is? It's just a big goddamn hole."

Tourism has become a significant player in Butte's economic revival. Jobs in the "industry" have increased by three to four hundred people since 1983, when ARCo closed the mines, according to Don Peoples, Butte–Silver Bow chief executive. Many of the jobs depend on Butte's history as the West's biggest, and perhaps toughest, mining town. On a plaque at a highway viewpoint overlooking the town, Butte boosters declare: "She was a bold, unashamed, rootin' tootin', hell-roarin' camp in days gone by and still drinks her liquor straight."

Butte has also refurbished a portion of the railroad that once carried ore from the mines to the smelter in Anaconda. An antiquated rail car chugs from the old Kelly mine to the museum, hauling a different lode— smiling, gawking tourists, at $2.50 a crack. After the train ride, many will visit the opulent mansion of one of the old copper barons, William Andrews Clark.

Not every tourist attraction features mining. Sitting twenty-five hundred feet above the town on the Continental Divide, where it can be seen from Butte and the interstate, is the Our Lady of the Rockies monument. The 90-foot-high, bright white statue of the Virgin Mary was placed on the divide in 1985, following a 7-year effort by three Butte men who wanted a memorial devoted to the mothers of the world. According to a brochure published by the group that leads tours to the statue, the monument is "nondenominational," and weighs fifty-one tons; the statue's lips are 3 feet wide. The statue has been praised and ridiculed; critics call it gaudy, "Our Lady of the Tailings," or "Darth Virgin." Gaudy or not, Al Beavis, president of all-volunteer, nonprofit Our Lady of the Rockies, Incorporated, says it will attract sixty-five hundred to eight thousand visitors in 1988. Trips to the statue cost ten dollars for adults, five dollars for children.

Bruce Farling

Missoula entrepreneur Dennis Washington was described by former *Missoulian* reporter Steve Smith in a 1979 profile as having "an exuberant, almost boyish quality that might evidence itself in a youngster who has discovered the neighborhood's largest dirt pile; who is going to get paid handsome for moving it, and who, among his rival playmates, has the largest fleet of bright yellow Tonka Toys with which to do the job." The description was prophetic. In 1985 Washington bought Montana's largest dirt pile from ARCo. The audacity of buying a copper mine when the mineral market was at rock bottom raised eyebrows around the state. Many said Washington would lose the gamble.

They were wrong. Prices went up, Washington cut costs, and the copper and molybdenum his mining company, Montana Resources, Incorporated (MRI), hauled out of Butte's Continental Pit in the first half of 1988 will bring in a $40-million profit. The company projects a $100-million profit for the year. MRI employs 350 people, most of them longtime Anaconda-ARCo workers. According to Peoples, MRI adds $50 million to the state economy, has a payroll of $15 million, and will pay $5 million this year in state and local taxes.

The 54-year-old Washington, who parlayed a $30,000 loan in 1964 into one of the West's biggest road and mining construction businesses, needed help to buy into Butte. But ARCo, which had reportedly lost $750 million since buying the Butte properties from Anaconda Minerals in the mid-1970s, was anxious to sell. With an $8 million loan from the Montana State Board of Investment and another $12 million of his own, Washington went into the mining business.

Butte also opened up its pocketbook for Washington. Montana Power, the town's largest employer, gave MRI a 15 percent discount on power rates. Property taxes on the new acquisition were dropped from $5.2 million to $1 million for a 3-year period. The toughest concession Butte made, however, was its acceptance of the new company as a nonunion operation. Labor leaders roundly criticized Washington. However, after considering its unemployment rate, the town reluctantly swallowed its union pride. Peoples says because of MRI's profit-sharing program, the miners "are making as much as when Anaconda was running the show."

Besides MRI, other mining is starting up around Butte. An Australian-European landholding company bought the underground mines from Washington and turned them over to local miners. Closed since the 1970s, several of Butte's tunnels are now starting to produce ore, employing close to one hundred people. In addition, Pegasus Gold is building a gold mine sixteen miles southwest of Butte. It will employ seventy-five to one hundred people.

Peoples says, "Mining is always going to be important in Butte," and he predicts the industry will employ 750 to 1,000 people within a few years. He says the new companies are more efficient and more competitive than were Anaconda and ARCo, which should result in a more stable mining industry. However, he adds, Butte's future is in diversity, and not just in turning shovels. The recent economic growth hasn't hidden Butte's considerable blemishes. Mining left the town with a ravaged landscape and severe health hazards.

Millions of tons of mine waste are scattered about neighborhoods, children play near abandoned mines, and the water level in the 1,800-foot-deep Berkeley Pit is rising 10 feet per month. Some scientists say that unless something is done within four or five years, the water, which is loaded with heavy metals such as copper, zinc, cadmium, and arsenic, will back into the town's groundwater and surface water.

Mining-related environmental problems are so bad that much of the town has been designated a Superfund toxic waste cleanup area. The Berkeley Pit, soils in the satellite community of Walkerville, and various old mines are part of the enormous Silver Bow complex, the largest Superfund site in the country. A defunct pole-treatment plant located on the south end of the town has been leaking PCBs and PCPs into Silver Bow Creek. It also is a Superfund site.

Environmentalists have long recognized the problems left by mining and smelting in Butte and elsewhere in the upper Clark Fork River basin. "The third world has been trashed, and Montana has been part of the third world because of the copper barons," says Jim Jensen, director of the Montana

Environmental Information Center. Jensen and other environmentalists have criticized Butte for not doing enough to correct the sins of the past. The environmental center has also been critical recently of Butte's economic development leaders for their efforts to bring a $6.8 million vermiculite processing plant to the community. The mineral, which often contains highly toxic asbestos, would be hauled through Missoula and up the Clark Fork River valley to Butte. Jensen says that that exposes other communities and the river to possible asbestos contamination. He adds that it is ironic that even as Butte tries to attract world-class athletes to its high-altitude training center, it risks downgrading the community's air quality with asbestos.

The Environmental Protection Agency has been slow to push for cleanup in Butte. The community's business and political leaders, including Peoples, compounded the problem by resisting the Superfund classifications. They were afraid that the label would discourage businesses from locating there. But some reclamation has occurred recently, most of it by local government. In the last two years $500,000 has been spent building storm drains around tailings piles and reclaiming and converting three mine sites to parks and baseball fields. Rick Griffith, reclamation coordinator for Butte–Silver Bow government, says that is a drop in the bucket, and that there are 150 to 300 mine sites in the town that may need reclamation.

ARCo, which could be held liable for much of the reclamation, spent $3 million recently to remove contaminated soils in Walkerville. Eventual costs could run in the hundreds of millions, spawning a local boom. But to date, only a few local people have been employed in reclamation.

From his office window, David Toppen looks out over a bleak landscape covered with old mine tailings and sees economic possibilities. "A mine dump is another resource," he says. "When we clean it up, it has value." Toppen is vice president of academic affairs at the Montana College of Mineral Science and Technology, popularly known as Montana Tech. His school, which was cited last fall in *Newsweek* as the top small science-and-technology college in the country, has been selected as a state-designated "center for excellence." Using a loan from state coal-tax money for start-up, Montana Tech's center will focus on research in hazardous waste cleanup and metals recovery.

John Driscoll, a member of the Montana Public Service Commission, also sees possibilities in Butte's wastes. Driscoll, whose roots are in the town, says the Berkeley Pit represents an opportunity to convert an enormous environmental liability into an economic asset. "I prefer to look at the pit as a mine," Driscoll says. The metals in the water could be recovered and used, he says, but more important, so could the water. Driscoll says existing technology could extract both commercial-grade metals and clean water from the pit's reddish brown soup. "A lot of states have a similar problem, and they could benefit from the technologies we develop," he says.

Driscoll has been discussing the possibilities of pit cleanup with the Electric

Power Research Institute, the nation's largest utility-funded research center. In January 1987 he put together a conference in Butte on reclamation of the pit's water that was attended by members of the institute and by scientists from both inside and outside Montana. Most agreed the technology was available, but expensive. In an attempt to further the pit-cleaning concept, Driscoll proposed two years ago to spend part of his public service commission time working on the project. The proposal drew fire from his fellow commissioners, people in Butte, and some environmentalists, who said that Butte had bigger problems than the pit.

Driscoll says part of the reason the pit isn't being cleaned is that people won't admit that its rapidly rising water level is a problem. He blames locals who think the EPA will take care of things. "The presence of the EPA in Butte has sedated people," he says. "It has kept local initiative down." Despite apathy and opposition, Driscoll plugs away. He has filed for water rights in the pit and continues to look for sponsors who might be interested in the high-technology reclamation project.

Other Montanans are beginning to look at Butte and neighboring Ana-conda as possible centers for national and worldwide reclamation technolo-gies. Jensen, at the Environmental Information Center, has promoted the idea for several years. "We have the best field laboratory on earth for heavy metal reclamation," he says, referring to the upper Clark Fork River basin, which includes Butte and Anaconda. "What we need is the energy and a plan."

During the spring of 1988, a plan for promoting the area as a center for reclamation technology emerged in Montana's Democratic gubernatorial pri-mary. Frank Morrison, who eventually lost to former governor Tom Judge, proposed borrowing $50 million from the state's mineral severance tax fund to fund reclamation work and a research center in the upper Clark Fork basin. Morrison said the loan would be repaid by suing ARCo for natural resource damages caused by mining in the basin, a move that is allowed by Superfund's program to collect from liable parties. Though Morrison won't be able to try out the program, environmentalists say they will continue to pursue the concept.

For the first time in its history, Butte will determine its own course. How close that takes the community to the past may be too early to tell. Certainly, though, if it doesn't forget its past, it will be less likely to repeat it.

CHAPTER TWENTY-FOUR

Butte Remains a Center of Infection

Don Moniak

THE CITY of Butte, Montana, and its associated smelter town of Anaconda, twenty miles away, are not pretty places. Large vacant lots filled with rubble and noxious weeds are much more common than shade trees and green strips. Butte itself is littered with abandoned headframes, old tailings piles, denuded hillsides, and a devastated riparian area along Silver Bow Creek. Summers are hot, dusty, repelling; winters find Butte blanketed for much of the day with smog caused by wood-burning stoves, industry, and auto emissions from the nearby interstate highway.

In the case of both Butte and Anaconda, you can tell a book by its cover. A century of mining and smelting has left the communities a toxic legacy. Technically, both are mountain towns—over a mile high and close to the Continental Divide. Anaconda has a mural declaring itself a place "where the town meets the mountains," but neither contains much of a mountain climate or atmosphere, aside from mining waste and relics.

It is not surprising that residents of both places frequently travel twenty-five or so miles over the Continental Divide to the Big Hole River area and its clean air and water, green valleys and forests, prime hunting and fishing, and the folksy small rural communities of Divide, Dewey, and Wise River. The Big

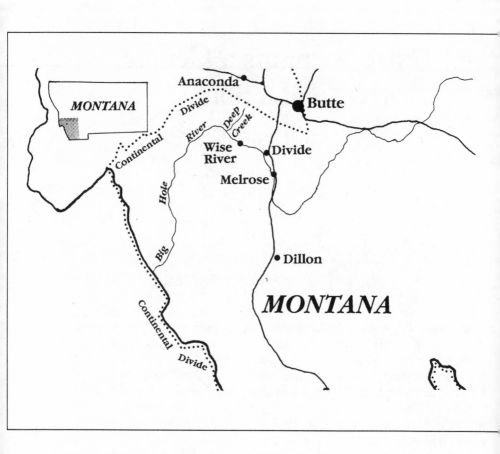

Hole area's recreation economy welcomes the visitors. The growing tourist economy, however, may be a mixed blessing. It raises the question of whether the devastation that radiated outward from Butte and Anaconda, when copper was king, isn't being continued today through recreation and suburbanization.

Butte describes itself as the "can do city," and its recent economic turnaround following ARCo's departure has been applauded across Montana and the nation. But the term "won't do" may be more applicable so far as reclamation and pollution go.

Butte boosters have resisted a Superfund designation, fearing it would taint the city. The flooding Berkeley Pit is ignored, although its waters threaten to seep into city streets in the near future, and noxious weed infestations in and around the city and air quality problems are addressed at a snail's pace or not at all. Not much appears to have been learned from the environmental devastation that has left Butte and Anaconda handicapped now that mining is a ghost of its past self. Don Peoples, the popular chief executive of the city of Butte and Silver Bow County, is striving for a diversified economic base. But that diversification has not yet included cleanup campaigns or long-term strategies for making Butte livable, let alone attractive.

Peoples says he is pushing hard on the EPA to clean up Butte. But in a replay of the past, most leaders and the local press embrace polluting proposals, such as a vermiculite exfoliation plant, despite the dangers of airborne asbestos. The battle over the plant is complete with charges that objectors are "environmental extremists" and a "vocal minority" in a city that illustrates what happens when a place lacks environmentalists and vocal minorities.

Anaconda, a traditional Butte rival, is usually a tad different, and leaders there are looking at the jobs and potential to lure engineering firms that come with Superfund cleanup. But mining adventures remain sacred, and a meeting early in 1988 drew zero opposition to a proposed cyanide-heap-leaching gold mine on national forest land between Butte and Anaconda.

Given this attitude toward their hometowns, it is not surprising that some Big Hole locals wonder whether their area can survive as a combination playground and bedroom for the mining towns. Butte and Anaconda residents are not the only visitors to the Big Hole area—it is increasingly popular with visitors from across Montana and the nation. But residents of the two nearby towns are the largest and most easily identifiable group.

Take the controversial issue of off-road vehicles, or ORVs. An area that still reveres ex-convict and motorcycle daredevil Evel Knievel (a Butte native) is bound to produce a fair share of weekend ORV backcountry daredevils. Summer and winter, the vehicles traveling along the Big Hole on Highway 43 are hauling many more all-terrain vehicles, dirtbikes, snowmobiles, and mobile homes than tents, skis, rubber rafts, and canoes.

The country they head into is by no means untouched. The Big Hole drainage has been strongly affected by the Beaverhead National Forest's very ambitious timber-cutting policies during the past twenty-five years. The Deep Creek drainage, a tributary to the Big Hole River, was especially hard hit by mining. For decades the emissions from the Anaconda stack passed over the Continental Divide carrying enough arsenic to poison forage and cattle in the valley.

As homesteaders lost herds and livelihood, Anaconda began buying them out, eventually consolidating all but one ranch. As for the smelter town itself, seventy-five years of emissions kept vegetative growth at bay for miles around the town. And as the smelter wreaked havoc along the Continental Divide, the first head of the Forest Service, Gifford Pinchot, helped arrange early in this century an extremely large timber sale to stoke the smelter furnaces with charcoal.

Despite this harsh use of Big Hole lands, its recreational economy has undergone steady and, lately, even rapid growth. This is clear from the number of people found hunting and fishing and from the rapidly growing number of hunting and fishing guides and outfitters. The effect of the recreation is more subtle than the flagrant clear-cutting the Forest Service has allowed or the destruction caused by the smelter fumes, but it is visible.

On public land, increased pressure on designated wilderness and roadless backcountry by backpackers, horse users, and motorized recreationists has degraded popular dispersed campsites, particularly around lakes. The degradation has led the Forest Service to take some action. In the West Pioneer Roadless Area, almost 20 percent of the area, or twenty thousand acres, has been closed to motorized travel and has become de facto wilderness in reaction to meadow damage by ORVs. Log fences have been built in areas that have not had livestock for years to prevent damage by ORVs to grayling spawning sites. But most areas are not protected. The Wise River valley, a major drainage for both the East and West Pioneer mountains, is slowly becoming a playground for ORVs, with heavy dirtbike traffic blazing new trails and damaging old ones.

The gravest threat from recreationists, however, is the dreaded knapweed— a tenacious, quickly spreading plant that replaces native forage and turns land into deserts, so far as wildlife and domestic livestock are concerned. The Big Hole is nearly surrounded by knapweed-infested areas such as the Bitterroot and Clark Fork drainages, but thus far strong measures by Big Hole ranchers and public land managers have kept its knapweed under control.

That is a mixed blessing, for as an increasing amount of Montana winter range productivity is reduced by knapweed, the Big Hole valley will feel more pressure from hunters following the big game. Charlie Hahnkamp, a local rancher who has spearheaded the anti-knapweed campaign, says hunting is a major culprit in the spread of weeds, because vehicles pick up weed seeds in one place and drop them in another.

Twenty-five years of heavy logging have left eighteen hundred miles of roads in the Big Hole area, and locals say they are a mecca for Butte-Anaconda residents, who have a reputation for road hunting. The sportsmen reject the weed-spreading tag. Tony Schnoonen, a Butte-area resident, says, "Bad hay is responsible for the spread of knapweed, not hunters and recreationists."

Closing old logging roads would help prevent weed spread, and some roads have been closed. But road closure is opposed by most area sportsmen. Schnoonen says the Skyline Sportsmen group in Butte is opposed to all new

Hikers passing a clear-cut area in the Beaverhead National Forest, Montana

road construction, but it is just as opposed to new road closures. The only issue more controversial than the Beaverhead's logging plan, which proposes 230 miles of new roads to harvest 100 million board-feet of timber over ten years, is the road-closure plan. In the face of increased logging and roading, and the growing use of these roads and backcountry for all sorts of motorized and nonmotorized recreation, the Big Hole area will be increasingly hard put to keep knapweed under control.

There are other threats to the environmental health of the area. On the Big Hole River, regulations are now needed to preserve the blue ribbon fishery. In 1988 the number of miles of no-live-bait fishing and decreased limits have more than doubled and a two-month whitefish season was closed. In addition to the new regulations, fishermen are responding voluntarily, and there is more and more catch and release.

The pressure on the fishery has put Big Hole area ranchers in a tricky situation. Until a few years ago, area ranchers generally supported logging and opposed wilderness. But in recent years many ranchers have turned against logging and sided with wilderness and recreation. Rancher J. B. Anderson says he switched from anti-wilderness to pro-wilderness because "I decided the logging plans were far less attractive. Ranching and recreation go hand in hand here. Ranchers and the fishery both need a steady yield of clean water."

Decreased flows during the past dry years, however, have led to increased grumbling about the irrigation practices of Big Hole ranchers. Darryl Jacobson, the anti-wilderness owner of the Antler Saloon in the tiny town of Wisdom, says if the ranchers "are worried about grayling and trout, tell them to let some water down the river." The last population of river-dwelling arctic grayling in the continental United States is in the upper Big Hole River, and it is a key issue in the timber debate.

At present, recreationists and ranchers are united against the Beaverhead National Forest's roading-logging plans for the upper Big Hole—the culmination of twenty-five years of heavy timbering. But the heavy irrigation practices used by the ranchers along the river, aggravated by bulldozed diversion dams that disturb the river bottom, could create a rift between them and recreationists once the timber fight, and its threat to water and scenery, is settled.

There is a final threat to the wild and rural character of the Big Hole that makes all the other problems look insignificant: urbanization, or, rather, suburbanization. As Butte's economy diversifies away from heavy industry and new people with new values move to the city for jobs, many of them will seek alternatives to a town where the EPA is dragging its feet on Superfund cleanup, and where the legacy of mining and smelting is so visible.

The appearance and possible health problems of living in Butte are in stark contrast to the clean, beautiful, nearby lower Big Hole. Suburbanization is already under way. Some entire ranches and portions of just about every ranch between Divide and Deep Creek, a 25-mile stretch, have 20- to 40-acre parcels for sale. The American dream includes owning 20 acres of the West, with a few horses or cattle grazing on them. The problem is illustrated by the country north of Salmon, Idaho, where subdivided land has led to a decline in open space, severely overgrazed lots, knapweed infested pastures, and a loss of agricultural land. Charlie Hahnkamp, his eye on knapweed, says that control gets more and more difficult as the land is subdivided. Owners are more numerous and more difficult to organize, and are more likely to overgraze the land and let knapweed get footholds all over the valley.

In the Big Hole, the suburbanization is just beginning, but it could be socially and environmentally devastating. The Divide–Wise River–Melrose region is slowly becoming a bedroom community of Butte. Attempts to slow or direct the trend bump into the West's aversion to controls. Efforts at flood-plain management have been strongly resisted by landowners and developers. And ranchers who have bankers knocking at the door are less concerned with the social costs of residential development than with remaining solvent.

Part Four

THE
FUTURE

CHAPTER TWENTY-FIVE

Cutting the Apron Strings

Ed Marston

THE WEST'S immediate past can be painted in broad strokes. In more thickly settled areas, with their denser economies, trends fight and cancel one another. Not in the West. Its spare populations and few economies make for clear trends. The movement of ten thousand people into a state or the creation of a few thousand jobs translates into a boom. The closure of a dozen mines or the cancellation of several large construction projects results in a bust.

Writing about the West's past, therefore, is easy. It can be summed up as a gold rush, the uranium boom, the ski resort boom. In a New York or Chicago or Los Angeles, these activities wouldn't be noticed. In the rural West, they dominate their period. For the same reason of scale, or, rather, lack of scale, writing about the West's future is difficult. One can identify trends, but there is no guarantee that they will continue, for trends in the rural West have no weight to them. Nothing could have seemed more massive than the energy, minerals, and real estate boom of the 1970s, and yet it was destroyed with ease by a change in the global economy and the national administration.

Moreover, it is hard to imagine a region less ready for the twenty-first century. It is still looking around, getting its bearings, at a time when previously prominent landmarks are fading from view. For example, there are strong signs that the global economy may have permanently lost its appetite for commodities, throwing the West's traditional extractive industries into permanent decline. And the other part of the West's economy—the federal presence—is also weakening. Nationally, the treasury is squeezed by huge debt and deficits. Dams, subsidized energy projects, and rural development programs are all under close scrutiny. No longer does the West automatically receive a share of an ever-larger pork barrel.

The separation from the federal government is accelerated by the region's own attitudes. Over the past two decades, the West has elected an increasingly conservative bloc of United States senators. This trend—the replacing of a Frank Church of Idaho by a James McClure or Steve Symms, for example—is driven by several forces. Those on welfare always resent the red tape and social workers that come with the dole. The West's cheap or free access to public land, federally subsidized water, and cheap electricity in the Northwest have created a backlash within the region. This "get out and just send money" attitude has been part of the place since earliest days. The new element is the political importance of social conservatism. Anti–gun control, anti-abortion, a distaste for or lack of understanding of minorities, and general alienation from urban America means the Democratic Party is increasingly alien to the rural West.

The very accent of a Teddy Kennedy grates on Western ears. As minorities, gays, and other groups become more prominent on the national stage, the very homogeneous, very white West feels more distant from that stage. Gubernatorial campaigns in the West are relatively nonideological. There is a job to be done, and voters have a sense of who can best do that job. The result is that Democrats, with their belief in government, occupy a large number of statehouses. But in elections for president, senators, and congressmen, ideological issues are more often the deciding factor.

Candidates can't be elected senator from Utah or Idaho without a strong stand against abortion. They can't be elected in most Western states without being pro-gun. It is also helpful everywhere in the West to be against unions, since organizing to increase wages offends Westerners' idea of rugged individualism. Conservative Democrats are still elected from the West. In states with a large urban population—which mainly means Colorado—you can even (barely) elect a liberal like Tim Wirth. But conservative Republicans in the West don't have to swim against the tide. They don't have to set themselves off from their party. They find the West easier because they are free of the Democrats' pro-union, multihued, big-city image.

So the West's senatorial bloc over the past two decades has come to be dominated by socially and economically conservative Republicans, even though the economic self-interest of the region would predict another outcome. These Republican senators are not free agents. In the 1980s they were of necessity part of the Reagan team, and participated in the efforts to dismantle programs and regulatory structures the West traditionally depended on. They have, of course, some wriggle room. Conservative Western senators continue to unanimously support a large military presence in the West and the building of dams, despite their opposition to a federal presence and subsidies.

But other aspects of the West's dependence on the federal government are expendable. The bloc no longer automatically supports universal telephone service; subsidized or regulated air, bus, and train transportation; regulated trucking; subsidized rural housing and other social programs; and rural electrification. The on-the-ground results of the shrinking of certain governmental functions are described in Chapter Thirty-one.

With some exceptions, then, the West's major political force is helping to dismantle programs and ideologies that support the West and keep it connected to the rest of America. There is larger significance to this severing of national links. Those ties were once part of a larger program. Water, energy, mineral, and rural development were tools to transform the West from a wild region to a rural region to an urbanized region.

There was no master plan, but there was a shared sense of direction, symbolized initially by construction of Hoover Dam, conceived by the conservative Hoover administration and executed by the activist Roosevelt administration and its Interior secretary, Harold Ickes. Now that sense of direction is gone, killed by changing times and the difficulty during the Reagan era of combining social conservatism with liberal governmental policies. The absence of regional direction is most easily seen in the West's senatorial bloc.

For want of a broad program, that group has been reduced to bone picking. Its economic-development energies serve the surviving beneficiaries of cheap or free access to public land: oil and gas exploration firms, logging companies, public land ranchers, and water project builders and recipients. It is easy to blame the senators for bone picking and lack of a regional agenda. But given grassroots insistence on social conservatism, it is not clear that they have much choice.

Wherever responsibility lies, the West approaches the millennium cut off from many national resources, and without the institutions—good education, competent media, citizen reformers—developed regions take for granted. The West will have lots of time to demonstrate whether its antipathy toward the federal government, toward regulation, and toward polyglot America will do it harm or good. Meanwhile, it has been thrown back—it has thrown itself back—on its resources.

What are those resources? Landscape, clear air, and, for those willing and able to conform, wonderful communities and a relaxed way of life. But there are also vast expanses of ravaged land: overgrazed, overroaded, polluted by radioactive tailings, littered with official and unofficial Superfund sites. Wildlife refuges are often toxic sinks; some irrigated land produces more salt than food; and hundreds of reservoirs are either silting up or unsafe. To the original handicaps of the nineteenth century—aridity, harsh climate, difficult trans-portation—are added the bitter fruits of one hundred years of development. Where, a century ago, all seemed possible, now all seems impossible.

If there is a blessing here, it lies in the narrowing of the rural West's choices. Its first, and easiest, option is liquidation. Prices of land and water have dropped to where people from the nation's real economies fly or drive into the region every day to pick up, for spare change, a retirement or summer home, or ranch, or even a small reservoir.

There is a more subtle form of liquidation. The demise of so many rural economies has opened the way for nonrural economies: tourism, retirement and other forms of "lifestyle," and electronic cottages, in which small towns serve as bedroom communities for workers whose work base is elsewhere. These activities are in the rural West by choice, rather than because the region has resources or locations they must have.

Many of those who are in the West by choice came for landscape, air, and recreation, but stayed because of small, livable communities. Those commu-nities now being resettled were established and shaped by people who worked the land, or who provided services to those who worked the land. Those rural activities are in retreat, or have been routed. Inevitably, their loss will mean transformation of the towns they established. A town may be in the Rockies, but if it is dominated by computer-program writers and tourist-industry workers, its character will be urban, not rural. A mix of newcomers and rural people can be healthy, injecting a place with hybrid vigor. But that mixing requires the survival of rural ways of life.

So the question is: Can the West develop new rural activities to sustain traditional communities. Will there be, after the present transition, commu-nities strong enough to resist urbanization? Will there be rural towns strong enough to force migrating urbanites to adapt to the community, rather than vice versa? What tough, demanding land and resource-based jobs are there that need doing?

One answer, perhaps the only answer, is reclamation: deroading forests, dealing with ubiquitous mining wastes, recovering overgrazed land, repairing or dismantling dams, pushing out weeds, restoring damaged streams, detoxify-ing wildlife refuges, and reintroducing wildlife habitat and wildlife.

A regional commitment to restoration would do much for the West as a place; it would do even more for Westerners. Although restoration is rural, it is not a rural activity that fits today's West. Rather, restoration is "rural" in the sense of the Amish, or of Wendell Berry. The massive work of regional restoration cannot be done with the present Western mindset or skills. Com-mitment to this task will require commitment to change from the bottom up.

It is common to meet every suggestion with the same question: How will it be paid for? How can a region unable to build a stable life when it was highgrading mineral deposits and old-growth forests repair damage caused by extraction of a century's worth of wealth? The question is backward. The real question is: How can the West not afford restoration? How can Butte not deal with the flooding Berkeley Pit? How can Leadville and the downstream towns not clean up the Arkansas River? How can Missoula and Flagstaff not clean up their wintertime air? How can communities like Dubois, Wyoming, surrounded by overroaded, overcut national forests, not meet their moral obligation to repair land their mills despoiled?

Once the West decides that the land, streams, and, where necessary, the air must be reclaimed, ways to do it will be found. In places, and quietly, that process is under way. As a first step, a large number of communities has turned to long-neglected, long-abused riverfronts. For the most part, this work goes forward under the cloak of economic development. But it can also be seen as an instinctive urge, now that the 1970s' gold rush is past, to begin repairing the land. The rural West has time on its hands, and some places are putting that time to good use.

Restoration and reclamation also provide a way for the West to emerge as a full partner to other regions of the nation. For example, the U.S. Congress, led by Senator J. Bennett Johnston of Louisiana, is in the process of shoving a nuclear waste dump down the throat of Nevada. There is some justice in this shoving—the West produced and profited from uranium, but the present formula will prove a disaster. Nuclear energy requires a long-term, careful, humble approach. No part of the United States is capable today of caring for the waste; the rural West is least capable of it. However, it is conceivable that the West, through efforts to deal with its toxified and ravaged areas, will develop the society, the skills, and the mentality to handle nuclear waste. It would, after all, be a very Western activity—dangerous.

After Butte has cleaned up the Berkeley Pit, after the BLM and the ranchers have brought the weeds under control, after the West has built a strong educational system and developed a capable, region-wide media, there is no reason to think it couldn't take on a dangerous, necessary national task. So there is more than one way to pay for the restoration of the West, and those various ways will be discovered once the decision is made to get on with the job. If the restoration decision is made, the rural West will clean itself up over the next century.

If the decision is not made, the West will continue its ecological and social decline. Those declines will continue together because they are linked. Unhealthy land reflects unhealthy human communities. Timing is everything, and today is uniquely right for undertaking restoration. Because of the bust, the West has lost those who came here for a conventionally comfortable American life. The bust has left behind a disproportionate number of believers in its landscape, air, and wildlife, whatever other beliefs tend to divide them. The West also has time on its hands, for the old dreams of instant wealth are dead. To paraphrase Rabbi Hillel: If not now, never!

CHAPTER TWENTY-SIX

The Last Place on Earth

Donald Snow

IT NEVER would have occurred to me, but when I heard it, it made sense. We were irrigating about three hundred acres north of Fort Collins, Colorado, out of a big ditch built by Horace Greeley. Newcomers to farming but not to the West, we were hard at the task of healing land farmed by tenants for a dozen years. They had loved atrizine, a chemical programmed to kill everything green except corn. They had loved N-P-K fertilizer delivered in tidy white wagons, hitched to leased tractors and dragged hurriedly all over the fields and then left out by the country road for the dealer's boys to pick up empty when they delivered a fresh wagon.

The soil was thus a mere medium, a sterile red loam ground fine as talcum powder by the plows and harrows, the fat-tire drills and spreaders run by the tenants' hirelings. It wasn't theirs. The owner lived in a residential hotel in town, so it wasn't his, either. The only part of the farm that mattered was the balance sheet. So when the tenants turned to malting barley, and Coors said, "Spray!" they sprayed. Even if there were no weeds left, they sprayed.

We had most of the irrigated land in "green manure" when the first hunters arrived. We were setting ditches out in the chest-high yellow clover when we saw their shiny new Jeep stop on the county road and three men start walking

236

uncertainly toward us. They probably believed that trespassing on foot was more acceptable than in a car. It was June, and they were getting an early start, seeking permission to hunt the little reservoirs and sloughs that ran through the middle of the place. Someone had told them about the new owners, and they were out looking to do things right—by permission rather than theft. They meant well.

All three were "techies"—middle management in town. The New Rugged. Patagonia everything, except for the Vuarnets and Croakies. We were mud-daubed, fly-bitten, hot, and salty as the Dead Sea, which we smelled like. John had on his usual sleeveless undershirt, so his shoulders and pectorals made a strong impression, deepened by all that mud.

After some light chatter, one of them finally popped the big question. He was there to negotiate over a price. They wanted to build a blind down in our swimming hole. They wanted exclusive rights to come and go as they pleased all during waterfowl season. They knew the meaning of closed gates and untrampled fences, and they were willing to pay top dollar.

John's answer was this: No amount of cash would purchase hunting rights on his farm. But they were welcome to hunt in exchange for work. One hour planting windbreak equaled one hour hunting. They could start next spring, since the year was old already. John pointed to the mile-long row of poplar saplings and cotoneasters we'd already put into place. Now it was time to start the conifers. We'd provide the training free, and we'd drill the holes since John wanted no gringos fingering his orchard tractor. They walked off shaking their heads. You'd have thought he'd asked for their firstborn.

I like to tell the story and have, over and over in my head. It has been years since I told it out loud, though, and I've never written it down until now. I like the loopy sense of perspective it brings, the tiny but delicious twinge of power it implies—real power, like that from the Old West, the power of knowledge, the power of men *doing* over men just dreaming.

The historian K. Ross Toole liked such stories too. He tells one something like it at the beginning of *The Rape of the Great Plains*. You remember it, even if you haven't read that book. A well-dressed stranger shows up at a rancher's place one day. The stranger has a big idea about what to build next, what will save this little podunk economy out in the howling prairie. Grass just doesn't get people excited. It's industry, our savior, the stranger represents. He wants the rancher to sell.

He and the rancher talk awhile; then the rancher asks the fellow to judge the distance of yonder mountain. The fellow guesses ten miles. The rancher smiles. Yonder mountain is more than sixty miles overland. The West is not quite as it seems. Never was, never will be. The air is pretty damn clean.

The problem with these stories, though, is as palpable as the pleasure they bring. We landed gentry—I was temporary gentry and only hired, but gentry grows better than grass in the West and never did require ownership—we wear that mud with addled pride. We put those strangers in their place right quick, and among us we carry a million stories about them. I can't tell if it's unfortunate or not that my story is "real." I do know the conversation, such as it was, ended with the pastel backs of three dudes grumbling away toward town. There was no success there for anyone, except a few ducks. In truth, I was as transitory as they. We all are.

The problem is this: Two tiny worlds endlessly come into collision across the West. There's a scuffle, better if it's a good-humored one, lurid if someone goes for the gun, but the scuffle tends to end in a draw. The gentry, we sacred firsterners of the West, hold our moral high ground, which we continue to irrigate. Newcomers, perennially baffled, either beat the holy rolling hell out of us (another Pyrrhic victory for progress, Manifest Destiny, whitefolks), or turn away dazed. Maybe they learned something, maybe not.

I say these worlds are tiny because I mean it. It doesn't matter if K. Ross's rancher is facing draglines while John and I faced only a trio of shotguns and the shattered peace of a dozen Sunday mornings. The end is still the same: new people come to fill up this land. They bring every damn thing with them. That's the story of the West—always was, always will be.

People who smile like ozoned Rashnishees while they mutter soporifics about "clean industry" miss the point worst of all. We don't make such choices in the West. We, the citizenry, the leadership, even the Mormon presidency, don't select one kind of growth over another. We get both and all and nothing simultaneously. That's also the West. The Forest Service doesn't decide to halt logging because someone announces plans to build a ski area. First they log off the ski area, then they turn to their real pleasure in life, which is logging the rest of it. People still graze cattle and ride trail bikes right across the Bureau of Land Management uranium digs. Because that's the West, a land of dreams and dreamers, still the last place on earth. Its very landscapes haunt us. It has haunted us as far back as early-nineteenth-century Europe. It haunted some deluded coot—maybe the Queen, I can't remember—to dream up Cibola, the Seven Cities of Gold. That was in the sixteenth century.

It haunted Jefferson enough to send two living video cameras up the Missouri until they ran out of river, then on to the Columbia, then back. Lewis went nuts. It haunted the 26-year-old Bodmer for the rest of his days. He ran out of paintings, going back to his dreamlike works of the West again and again until he died. It haunted N.P. "National Park" Langford and his artist friend Moran until Yellowstone's "natural curiosities" were ossified into America's first preserve.

It must have haunted the hell out of Brigham Young, who, sick and hallucinating, could not have known all that water in the Great Salt Lake was salt. Look what that wrought. It haunted D. H. Lawrence and Georgia O'Keeffe, Robert Pirsig and Robinson Jeffers and Joseph Wood Krutch. It haunts its own spawn so thoroughly that the best have to leave in order to

continue loving this hostile place enough to scream in its windblown face:
Bernard DeVoto and Donald Worster and Wallace Stegner.

It haunts all who are not so jaded and somnambulant from the cities that we
can no longer feel and see. We straddle a crack, a suture, in the white Navajo
sandstone, the fossil dunes that form the parietal bones of the canyon head,
and we follow the little crack until it widens, and then begin our descent into
the dark brains of the canyon. We lose our minds as we go; we can hardly
believe there is such a place left on this exhausted earth. And yet here it is. We
drive the Datsun right to it.

The West is a land of dreams, and we cannot and should not hope to stop
the dreaming. I want to finish my sad-dude story another way. I want them to
say yes, a hesitant, ponderous yes. I want them to come back, not next spring

Charles Higley

but next week—we can give an inch too. I want to show them the beautiful windbreak we planted, which they walked through without noticing. I want them to see what those trees mean to the pheasants and the geese, what they mean to the soil we are grasping so hard to hold against the irresponsibility and stupidity of an earlier decade.

I want them to know another meaning of the hilarious verb, to break wind. I want to trust them to drive John's tractor and mount the heavy yellow auger and learn to fasten the power takeoff to the shaft at the proper angle and replace the shear bolt when the screw catches a rock. I want them to join me in my tiny empire of water because I never did want to be the emperor, and I'm not happy there, isolated in simpleton superiority. I might even want them to bring me a duck, just one duck, and stick around while we sear it hot in the propane roaster and eat it rare and bloody with a bottle of decent wine. Yet we continue to tell our stories, we self-annointed, tiresome educators of the "general public." Out West we chase culture a whole lot harder than it chases us.

Telluride, Colorado, July 1986. I sit under a giant tent erected in the city park. I am on a panel with nine others, and we and the assembled conferees— those left over after the International People have talked for three days—have just finished hearing a rousing list read to us by Edward Abbey, the only man in the West who can hold my interest with a list.

Our panel represents the Regional People who have the unseemly job of making the conference theme, "Reinventing Politics," trickle down to the grass roots, the home front, in the wake left by, for instance, Jane Fonda's husband. No one made us do this. We are there with our egos on our sleeves.

I spent part of the previous day writhing in my seat while several speakers whipped the crowd into a thoughtful frenzy about just what kind of economy would be good for the West Slope. No one had bothered mentioning that the economy that permitted our being there in the first place, in safety and ease, with all the elegant feasting and sky-prayer we could bear, had been pretty fair and still was, and perhaps the people who built it should gain even a grain of our recognition. Most had given it their lives.

The tent stands within viewing distance of Telluride's mine-mill tailings heap, left over from when the word *telluride* had a nearly alchemical meaning. There had been many nasty remarks leveled at this pile, as if the pile needed more grief than it already owned. The nastiness stemmed, of course, from the majority there, for whom the word *mine* brought up demonic images. (I was reminded of certain folktales wherein some inanimate object, some useless, improbable mound of something, has to suffer the shadow-grief of a village until the object takes on a name, then a personality, then finally does something positive about its plight, like standing up one night and collecting itself and pillaging several villagers as they dream.) That merely amused me until a shy older woman rose to the microphone and suggested that since the leaders of this thoughtful and uplifting discussion were obviously so bright and droll, and since most of them worked for the same "high-altitude think tank" in a town nearby, why not design the West Slope exclusively to accommodate more think tanks, until these became the actual spine of the regional economy? When I sensed a general bobbing of heads among the dozens who did not get the joke, I decided to take on the burden of the tailings.

So now I'm on a platform in the tent, ready to launch my highwire act. By the time my turn comes, I've already heard most of my own points, my own tailings masquerade, from the other panelists, who have spoken generally with the good sense of Westerners and know of what they speak.

I spend my talk quoting Wallace Stegner and plagiarizing Charles Wilkinson's "Lords of Yesterday" thesis. I give a precise recitation of the ways in which the West continues to be dominated by the resource laws, policies, and attitudes of the nineteenth century, sometimes grown over or warped, but unmistakably there, bedrock. In this pressurized litany of Future Trouble from the Past, I have, of course, discussed the doctrine of prior appropriation—the bedrock law of Western water rights, which gives the first user of the water first right to it.

At the end of my talk, the moderator calls for questions. The first one comes from a newcomer to the Colorado West Slope, a reinventor of local politics, who says, in a question, to me: "That's interesting, but I don't think I caught all of it. Who is the Doctor of Prime Association?"

Windbags have always floated over the giant terrains of the West, huffing and puffing about the future of civilization. Their moorings are always tied down in San Francisco or New York or, usually, Washington. We still don't know quite where the West begins; it ends before any coast. That should not justify our isolation, but should instead invigorate us to end it. We can take at least some small comfort in the fact that if we don't know exactly where we are yet, the windbags know even less.

Our schemes continue to remain small, and for that we are blessed. But our dreams must be great, greater than before. They cannot be the dreams of only those who come to live well by leaving it all alone. The trick now, the trick of the future, is to learn to dream together, here in the backslack in this failing empire of water. Here with, and not against, the ones who have already given their lives. When the dudes call again, I'll look 'em harder in the eyes. If they're wearing Vuarnets, I'll ask if they won't take them off.

CHAPTER TWENTY-SEVEN

Mining's Diminished Future

John Leshy

Beginning with Coronado's sixteenth-century search for the seven cities of Cibola, the lure of mineral wealth has played a special role in Western history. From the fabulous, frenzied "rushes" of the nineteenth century through the uranium boom following World War II, mineral activity has left its mark on the West.

Until recently, mining was regarded as an unqualified good. But as the twentieth century has unfolded, the assumption that mining is the highest and best use of land has been increasingly questioned, by environmentalists and by the communities that apparently stand to benefit from the mining. This change of attitude makes the question "Does mining have a future in the West?" a real one.

Mining is fundamentally different from other natural-resource uses. More than with most enterprises, it is a gamble. The importance of luck is being reduced by science and technology, but the hunch is still very important. The rewards can be enormous. Congressman George Julian, a major player when federal mineral policy was established around the time of the Civil War, said: "The business of mining . . . sharpens the faculties and dulls the conscience." Because its "prizes are often rich and suddenly gained," it "gives cupidity its keenest edge." Little wonder then that the symbol for today's Arizona state lottery is a cartoon mining prospector.

Unpredictability does not end with discovery. Minerals are not renewable, and that means mining enterprises are finite and less stable than those dependent upon renewable resources. The speed with which bust has followed boom has sometimes been astonishing. Numerous spots around the West exploded to several thousand residents within months of a strike and then emptied overnight when the deposit was depleted.

Any migration is a gamble, but a miner's gamble has a harder edge. It is not just that his migration is often to remote areas. In that sense he is not so different from the homesteader. And both miner and homesteader labor long and hard under difficult conditions. But unlike the homesteader, the miner's commitment is less to a place than to a deposit, his dream less of building a home than of becoming wealthy overnight. This further undermines the stability of the mining culture and dependent communities. It is no surprise, then, that the "boom and bust" syndrome, and boomtown social ills like alcoholism and divorce, tend to occur more frequently in mining towns than in other communities.

This internal instability is aggravated by outside markets. Historically, the price of many minerals has widely, even wildly, fluctuated. The emergence of a global market for most minerals in the last few decades has made things worse, as Chilean copper, Canadian uranium, and Australian bauxite have played havoc with the demand for output from U.S. mines.

Another characteristic of mining, its environmental destructiveness, is inherent in wresting a resource from the earth and processing it into a usable form. It alters landscapes and fouls air and water. Some impacts can be controlled, but some cannot.

In the years since the California gold rush, mining has gradually changed from an individualistic endeavor to a much more complex, sophisticated one. Most early ventures were small, owner-operated, often poorly capitalized, pick-and-shovel operations. These still survive in substantial numbers—mom-and-pop explorationers, whose roots go back to the early prospectors. Relatively few make much of a living at it, but they are as close to romantic figures as the mining industry has today. By early in this century, these smaller operators had been largely supplanted by industrial miners—more systematic and sophisticated, and employing higher technology in exploration and development. Their most obvious characteristic is scale—wide-area exploration and large open pits. They are also organized along more conventional capitalistic lines, with sharp divisions between management and labor.

These mines took root in the second half of the nineteenth century. With absentee owners, mostly, and large numbers of relatively poorly paid workers laboring in harsh conditions, they were the first places in the West the labor movement gained a toehold. The bargaining power of unions, along with government regulation, modern mechanization, and other technological advances, has improved the lot of the miner. But in the process, he or she has become much more a conventional industrial worker than a romantic figure. Mining can still be hazardous, but exploitation has been muted by the trappings of the modern welfare state. The "company town," where miners owed their souls to the company store, is gone.

The miner of legend—whether as the lone explorer or the pick-and-shovel laborer working under hazardous conditions—has just about disappeared. Some of the myth of these earlier days survives in the public mind, but the miner never captured the American imagination the way the rancher did. It is hard to imagine a grimy, tired miner reaching for a Marlboro, even with spectacular peaks in the background, or to expect Hollywood to make a movie about an "urban miner."

The cowboy, like the miner, was also a low-paid worker, laboring under harsh conditions. But he worked the land's surface, nomadically, caring for animals, and in many ways his life was genuinely romantic. In theory, the miner shared some of this—he led an independent life in the outdoors, often amid spectacular scenery. But the reality was different.

The history of mining shows how little attention the typical prospector or miner paid to his surroundings. A few got captured by a place or landscape. Robert Stanton lost a bundle trying to wrest gold from the elusive sands in the bottom of Glen Canyon along the Colorado River at the turn of the century, yet he was entranced by the region for the rest of his life. But he was the exception; most prospectors and miners were too confined by their struggles, and too consumed by the search for riches. This is not remarkable—environmental sensitivity is linked to economic and physical security; when you are trying to make a living from the earth under uncertain conditions, appreciating your surroundings is unlikely to be a priority. The instability of mining, its physical destructiveness, and, finally, the failure of mining to capture the public imagination have all set the stage for contemporary conflicts over mining's future.

The differences between miners and environmentalists are fundamental because they are competing for the same landscape. To the environmentalist, nothing insults the natural balance and beauty quite so much as mining. And its effects last. Long after a mine shuts down, it can produce windblown dust that lodges in lungs and obscures vistas, toxic chemicals that foul streams, disruption of underground aquifers, and land subsidence.

On these issues, environmental sensitivity has largely prevailed. As a society, we have made the decision to prize more highly our natural surroundings. Many industrial mining operations have responded to the challenge; some are proud of their environmental sensitivity, and there seems to be no turning back to the days when such damage was irrelevant.

But while today's mines are better neighbors, and mining towns more desirable places to live and work, these are often not enough to tempt many localities to welcome them. Even communities that came into existence as mining towns, like Crested Butte, Colorado, now harbor substantial, even overwhelming, sentiment against new mines nearby. Part of the resistance is environmental. But perhaps a more basic reason is cultural. Many have fled to the mountains (where, of course, minerals are often found) to escape industrialism, and they are horrified at the prospect that it will follow them. The "not in my backyard" attitude that plagues all sorts of industries today is aggravated by the peculiarities of mining—the instability, the lure of sudden wealth, the rootlessness.

There is an irony in the resistance that mountain towns, many now oriented

Ed Marston

Paonia, Colorado, coal miners in the late 1970s at the now-closed U.S. Steel mine

toward tourism, offer to mining. In many cases tourism followed mining and simply took over—at bargain prices—the homes and infrastructure mining had built, as occurred at Aspen and Telluride, Colorado; Park City, Utah; and many other places. That few miners stay long enough to reap the rewards of this transition is consistent with the fact that the initial discoverer of a mineral deposit rarely captured much of its value either.

In the resistance to mining, only recently—after a long evolution—have its cultural aspects come to be regarded as relevant. Not until the turn of this century did the idea take hold that the government had anything to say about whether and where mining might take place. Nearly all mining in the West is found on federal, or formerly federal, land, and the government's tacit acquiescence to the trespasses of the forty-niners in California's Sierra Nevada range firmly established the policy of turning its mineral land over to prospectors and developers on demand. That policy was later formally ratified by Congress in the Mining Law of 1872.

That law is still in effect. It is the last remnant of free access to federal lands that was the driving engine of nineteenth-century westward expansion. Its scope has, however, been substantially diminished by withdrawals of federal land and by removals of certain kinds of minerals from its ambit. Fossil fuels and most fertilizer minerals must now be leased. Sand and gravel and other common substances may be sold, but only at the federal government's discretion. An overlay of environmental regulation and resource planning by federal land-management agencies has also weakened the 1872 mining law. Still, enough of the old mining law policies of mineral self-initiation and privatization survive to rankle those who prize other uses of the public land. And that fight between mining and other uses has focused new attention on the possibility of reforming the mining law.

In the end, however, whether the Mining Law of 1872 is formally jettisoned may not make a great deal of difference. The change in values will likely prove durable, and increasingly confine where and how an industry will be allowed to operate. If, for example, the long-anticipated oil shale boom comes to the Colorado Plateau, it will likely involve substantial advance planning, up-front financial aid for social services, tight environmental controls, and other features nineteenth-century miners would find unbelievable.

While still a potent symbol, the protection the 1872 mining law once gave the industry is increasingly proving hollow. Like all laws, it is at the mercy of larger social currents, and the culture of the West—and political power with it—is evolving away from mining. Signals of this change abound, as when citizens in and around Douglas, Arizona (a town founded by and named for a Phelps-Dodge magnate), opposed continued operation of the firm's copper smelter because it was seen as blighting the town's trade and tourism, or when the state of Idaho sued mining companies to clean up decades-old, but still-polluting, mining residue. The Reagan administration, the most pro-mining and anti-regulation one within memory, had little discernible impact on that evolution.

This is not to say that mining will disappear. But the process of opening new mines will be increasingly difficult, and those that run the gauntlet and begin operations will scarcely be given free rein, as in the past. To borrow a lawyer's phrase, in the court of Western public opinion, the burden of proof has shifted from the opponents to the proponents of mineral development, and with that shift, the golden age of Western mining has passed.

CHAPTER TWENTY-EIGHT

Whither the Colorado Plateau?

Raymond Wheeler

UNTIL THE early 1980s southern Utah was a battleground between those who favored extractive industry and those who favored preservation of the land. Now the struggle is between those who see benefit in industrial tourism, typified by Lake Powell and its several million annual visitors, and those who see benefit in the more modest, home-grown tourism centered around the region's beauty and its small communities.

What kind of a place might southern Utah be if it were not run by a handful of powerful businessmen? What kind of an economy might be possible if outsiders were welcomed rather than scorned? What kind of future might be possible if the political leaders of Moab, Monticello, Escalante, and Kanab would recognize and accept that the surrounding public lands are a scenic resource of international significance, that the silence and wonder that they hold is not merely a powerful economic asset but something more valuable still—something worth preserving and protecting forever whether or not it can turn a profit every day of the year?

Here and there throughout southern Utah, I discovered the answer to those questions poking up out of the ground like the first green shoots of spring. Ever since 1979, Sagebrush Rebels have been preaching a kind of doomsday gospel—a fire and brimstone prophecy that the residents of Moab would be doomed without a mining economy to bring in the bread. But when the doomsday cry went out, someone forgot to tell Robin and Bill Groff.

During the 1970s, the Groff brothers were miners. Bill worked as an underground miner and a helicopter pilot for exploration companies; Robin was a mining engineer. By 1980 both brothers were making twenty thousand dollars to thirty thousand dollars per year. Then with the bust, they were out of work. "We'd been here for a long time," recalls Bill, "and instead of uprooting and moving somewhere else, I somehow talked Robin and my father into opening a bike shop."

In July 1983 the Groffs opened Rim Cyclery with a capital investment of forty-five hundred dollars. Today it is a booming success. "They're not making millions of dollars," says Moab resident Craig Bigler, "but on the Moab scale, they're doing well."

Like so many southern Utah businesses, the bike shop is rooted in the magic and beauty of the land. In recent years the country around Moab has become a mecca for mountain biking, and the nearby Slickrock Bike Trail, originally designed as a motorcycle play area, now draws ten thousand mountain bikers a year. But the success of Rim Cyclery is also attributable to the skill and energy of the Groffs. There is, says Craig Bigler, a "symbiotic relationship" between the family and their customers. "These guys are miners. Bill is a redneck. And that, perhaps, makes it easier for him to get along with bikers who are yuppies or would-be yuppies or something. Somehow they just really click.

"If a couple of hotshot bike-shop owners had come down here and opened one up, it probably would have failed. It had to be indigenous—yet somehow there had to be an openness to these kind of people coming in that hardly any of the leftovers from the mining industry could possibly achieve."

After visiting the shop several times in the spring of 1987, I noticed that a great many Moab residents and visiting bikers came there simply to hang out. There is a special energy in the place, the very same kind of energy, in fact, that I felt radiating from Alfred Frost, the pinto-bean farmer who began backpacking at age sixty. If there were just one word for it, the word would be *joy*.

I asked Robin Groff whether he would go back to mining if the uranium market revived. "No. Probably not," he replied. "I enjoy what I do down here. You make all the decisions here—right or wrong. I enjoy that a lot more than midlevel management. The thing about a small business is you do everything from emptying out the garbage cans in the morning to filling out your financial reports in the afternoon. And everything in between—work on the floor, fix the bikes, and if a tool breaks, fix the tool. Make the coffee—everything. I like that."

Norm Shrewsbury

Suburban Moab, Utah, and the La Sal Mountains

Ninety percent of Rim Cyclery's business is from out of town, yet the Groffs have an extraordinary sensitivity to the needs of their customers. "If they're happy, they come back," says Robin. "And we try real hard to make everybody happy. When people bring in a broken bike off the street, we try to get it up on the stand right away to fix it for them. Most people are down here having a vacation, and they've driven five or six hours to ride in this area."

That attitude is repaid by a consumer loyalty that can only be described as fierce. "We have people from Vail that bring their bikes down here to be serviced," Robin told me. "People just keep coming back. We're actually competing with Denver, Phoenix, and Salt Lake City bike shops."

After the shop was destroyed in a fire, the Groffs received calls and letters of support from bikers all over the country. "There was a guy in Chicago who called us and said, 'I heard you guys burned down. I'm coming out there on vacation. If you need help, I'll spend my whole two weeks there, helping you.' That amazed me," recalls Bill.

Surely the Groffs must be some kind of fluke. Two former uranium miners hustling to provide quality service for out-of-state tourists? "I don't think it's unique, other than that we work hard at it," says Robin. "It's just a matter of realizing what's going on in the world. It took about six months to realize that the mining industry was not going to come back, and it was either move or find something else to do. And if you look around, it doesn't exactly take a soothsayer to see that Moab has resources—and that's the scenic beauty. Other than Jackson Hole, Moab's one of the only towns in the West that sits at the entrance to two national parks. It's a renewable resource."

Coming from a former Moab mining engineer, that is indeed a profound statement. Even more profound is what came out next: "Moab has not catered to the tourist business at all. People come here, and they go to Arches and Canyonlands national parks during the day; they come back in the evening, and there's nothing to do. They have money to spend and no place to spend it. There's a lot of room for entrepreneurs that want to provide a service to these people."

It is indeed ironic that while Moab residents have been leaving town for lack

Raymond Wheeler

Robin and Bill Groff

of employment, tourists stream through, wallets bulging with money, "and nowhere to spend it." I asked Robin Groff to explain this paradox. Why has the town not moved swiftly to fill the need? "The government, the older sector of town—they were involved with mining all of their lives. They feel that we need industry in here to make this a viable community. I think we do need some light industry. But you're not going to attract it the way the town is right now—it has nothing to offer, basically. It's off the beaten track. There's no railroad, no highway. I think we need a more grassroots approach to develop a recreation industry."

While Sagebrush Rebels are searching for the next massive taxpayer-subsidized construction project or the next real estate or mining-claim speculation deal, a few of their neighbors are prospering the old-fashioned way—through hard work, ingenuity, and a love for the beauty of the land and for cultural traditions that by far predate the first big mining boom of the 1950s.

In Blanding a firm called Cedar Mesa Products produces hand-painted pottery for sale to tourists. In 1982, its first year, the store grossed more than $90,000. Today the firm, owned by Blanding native Joe Lyman, brings in well over $500,000 a year. In many ways Lyman and his pottery shop epitomize the enormous untapped economic potential of southern Utah. Lyman produces a product that draws on Native American cultural tradition. He employs thirty Navajo and Ute Indian artists, and his attitude toward his employees is revolutionary: "Why should I hire these people and force them into my mold?" Lyman asked *Utah Holiday* magazine in a recent interview. "Instead, I'll put them in an environment where they can succeed."

Recognizing that many Navajo and Ute Indians are torn between cultures, Lyman goes out of his way to provide them with flexibility on the job. He pays them by the piece and allows them time off when they need it. "They can come and go when they want, leave when they want, take two or three weeks off when they want, and still have their jobs."

Melvin Heaton is a native of Moccasin, Arizona, population seventy, where his family has lived since 1886. As a boy, Heaton grew up riding bareback, herding cattle, and performing as an extra at the movie ranches in nearby Kanab. Like many southern Utah natives, Heaton has supplemented his income from ranching with a government job, working for the National Park Service at Pipe Springs National Monument. All his life Heaton has nurtured three loves: horses, Western history, and the spectacular landscape of the Colorado Plateau. In 1976 he hit upon an ingenious means of combining the three. As a bicentennial event, Heaton organized a group ride over the historic Mormon pioneer trail between Pipe Springs National Monument and Saint George, Utah. As icons for the event, Heaton designed and constructed two

Melvin Heaton, canyon guide

Conestoga wagons. Public response was overwhelming. Some 250 people signed up for the ride.

When *Arizona Highways* published a story on the event, about twenty-five hundred people wrote for more information. Heaton promptly took out a $26,000 loan and began building more wagons. Today he makes his living as a guide. In addition to the Honeymoon Trail ride, which Heaton rides once a year with one hundred people, thirty horses, and ten covered wagons, Heaton runs guided horsepack trips that are among the most ambitious of their kind anywhere in the world. His "Three-Park Spectacular" winds 230 miles across the heart of the Colorado Plateau, threading the narrow slot canyons of the Paria River, traversing the forested ramparts of Bryce National Park, skirting the cliffs and domes of Navajo sandstone bordering Zion National Park, slicing through the Vermilion Cliffs, and finally winding among the plateaus and volcanic mountains of the Arizona strip to the brink of the Grand Canyon.

Heaton's success is attributable to his native skills, his ingenuity, and a powerful marketing tool—the Colorado Plateau. "People who ride all over the world have told me that you can't find this kind of country anywhere else," Heaton says. His clients include a French trail-riding association that makes annual excursions to places such as Kenya and Argentina. But in the canyon country of southern Utah, Heaton's clients have found something unique. "We can ride for five days on this route," says Heaton, "and never see anybody."

When doomsayers began lamenting the fate of the Western rancher, someone forgot to tell Melvin Heaton the bad news. In addition to guiding, Heaton draws income from ranching and film-production work. His pack trips are so profitable that he runs just four a year. He spends much of his time in the backcountry, scouting new trails for his clients. His net profits from guiding alone exceed $25,000 per year.

By Moab standards, Ken Sleight is a one-man chamber of commerce. Between commercial river trips in Grand Canyon and horse-pack trips in the Escalante canyons, Sleight somehow finds time to manage a bookstore and a guest ranch. Indeed, in his younger years, Sleight helped organize the Escalante Chamber of Commerce and served as its first president. Yet for thirty years Sleight has been an outspoken environmentalist and a target for the wrath of Sagebrush Rebels. In 1979, when Sleight was campaigning against a Trans-Escalante highway, Rebels ran his pickup truck off a cliff.

Like many who have spent their lives in the outdoors, Sleight radiates infectious joy—except when he is discussing the development of Lake Powell. Sleight was one of the first environmentalists to oppose the flooding of Glen Canyon, and for twenty years he has watched, with increasing dismay, the transformation of Glen Canyon into one of the West's most intensively developed recreational playgrounds.

"All along the bank of the reservoir it's polluted," he says. "Writing on the wall, they're desecrating Indian ruins—writing on Rainbow Bridge itself. You can't hardly get off your boats to camp on a beach; it's all covered with human excrement."

With more than 2 million visitors a year, Glen Canyon National Recreation Area is the most popular outdoor tourist attraction in the state. When Sagebrush Rebels talk about tourism, Lake Powell is what they have in mind. This kind of tourism is easy for Sagebrush Rebels to understand, since it is little different from the mining and power plant projects of the 1970s. This is industrial tourism, wholly dependent, now and in the future, upon large construction projects. This is campgrounds, marinas, gas stations, stores, restaurants, ferries, RV parks, airports, motels, and, most important of all, condominiums, which is to say, whole cities.

The distinction between industrial tourism and the tourist trade plied by Joe Lyman, Melvin Heaton, and Ken Sleight (let us call theirs "dispersed" tourism) is a distinction of economic caste. While dispersed tourism creates jobs in the small towns ringing the wilderness core of the Colorado Plateau, the industrial tourism of Lake Powell creates wealth for those who are already wealthy.

As usual, most of it flows out of Utah into the corporate coffers of Del Webb Corporation, the Phoenix construction giant that built Sun City and operates a fleet of casinos in Las Vegas. "We're subsidizing Del Webb," says Ken Sleight. "The government puts up a lot of things, campgrounds and so on. And then Del Webb puts money into restaurants and promotion." Not the least of the Lake Powell subsidies is the proposed paving of the Burr Trail—Garfield County's link to Bullfrog Marina on Lake Powell. San Juan County is also providing subsidies to Del Webb Corporation on Lake Powell. When Del Webb announced plans for a new motel at Hall's Crossing, San Juan County promptly awarded Del Webb its annual allotment of tax-exempt industrial revenue bonds to stimulate investment in the project.

Why would San Juan County pour its resources into Del Webb Corporation rather than into the small towns of Blanding, Monticello, or Bluff? That is a question San Juan County Economic Development Board director Peggy Humphries has asked herself more than once. When county commissioners asked her to allocate a large chunk of her $43,000 annual budget for a brochure depicting Lake Powell as the geographic center of San Juan County, Humphries balked. Del Webb Corporation, she observes, has an annual advertising budget of $2 million and annual gross revenues of $40 million. "Why should I emphasize Lake Powell, for heaven's sakes? I have a hard time promoting that. I'd rather promote Arches or Canyonlands than Lake Powell. If you're pulling a boat, or if you're going to the lake, everything else is going to be secondary." Reminded that San Juan County benefits from sales tax and transient room-tax revenues generated by Hall's Crossing Marina, Humphries replies, "Yes, but you'd have a hard time convincing a motel owner in Blanding or Monticello. And I can definitely see their point."

The massive complex of corporate tourist development surrounding Lake Powell has transformed the small towns of Moab, Monticello, and Blanding from destination points into "pit stops," says Sleight. "We're being bypassed. We're putting our emphasis on Lake Powell instead of on our small towns."

Elsewhere in southern Utah, industrial tourism follows a familiar pattern. Taxpayer dollars help to subsidize the creation of golf courses, new roads, and the expansion of water, sewer, and power systems. Then the real estate and construction barons move in and begin building condominiums. At present, at least three southern Utah towns—Moab, Kanab, and Springdale—are moving to construct golf courses. For Springdale, the new golf course has been a traumatic affair. To acquire property for the golf course along the Virgin River, the city council condemned the "backyards" of a number of longtime residents.

"A lot of the old-timers in town feel like everything is being taken out of their hands," says Springdale restaurant owner Michael Parry. "All of a sudden, it's big money talking here, and people, especially a lot of the old-timers, feel a sense of helplessness." Parry's business, the Bit and Spur Restaurant, has a reputation as one of the finest restaurants in southern Utah. It was one of the few businesses in town to take a strong public stand opposing the golf course. "I just hate to see this town slide downhill," says Parry. "You can see this town going the way of Sedona and Taos—places that are completely out of touch."

On a bright November morning after the summer tourist trade has quieted down, Springdale regains for a moment its native charm. Morning sunlight rolls down 3,000-foot cliffs of rose-colored sandstone, and a cool fall breeze sends cottonwood leaves scuttering in the streets. But this tranquillity, one must remember, is soon to be lost—buried under condominiums, RV parks, billboards, putting greens, helicopter tours, convention centers.

"What's the use of doing a quality project here if you're going to be surrounded by trash?" asks Parry. As developers move in, natives like Michael Parry are quietly moving out. "I've chosen to leave," he says. "I'm tired of being angry about it. Springdale was my last move in southwestern Utah. I will come here as a tourist, but I probably will never live here again."

The last thing former economic development expert Craig Bigler wants for Moab is the kind of prosperity that he sees in the town of Saint George. "Prosperity?" says Bigler, "I think it's hideous. Saint George is built to defy the environment, rather than to be compatible with it or take advantage of it."

The problem with industrial tourism, says Bigler, is not merely that it destroys the beauty or tranquillity or the culture of a community like Moab. What is worse is that industrial tourism can hook a community or an entire region on an addictive cycle of deficit spending. To pay for the expanded infrastructure needed for industrial tourism, communities like Saint George have "begged and borrowed money from the state, from the federal government," says Bigler. He says they are like junkies, always looking for the next big hit. For Craig Bigler, it is a syndrome that is all too familiar.

"The liberals—Lord, I know, because I was part of it—had this attitude that growth is good, and as long as you can make growth happen, then things are going to be okay. But what they never faced up to is the costs imposed by that growth. For streets, for water, for schools, for police—these things increase disproportionately, and so you have to have more the next time around. And then you still have to have more to cover your costs. You always have to have more. There's never enough."

What in the hell do people like Craig Bigler and Michael Parry want, anyway? They don't like the mining economy because it destroys the beauty of the landscape. But they don't like industrial tourism either because it can so often be equally destructive. If they are opposed to mining and opposed to industrial tourism, what then aren't they opposed to? "The only thing that will work for a small town in southern Utah, in my mind," says Bigler, "is a minimalist approach where you say, 'Hey, we don't want to have the kind of development that requires these kinds of massive investments. We only need two grocery stores in Moab. We only need one or two hardware stores.' You either accept limitations, or you're stuck with this endless need for growth.

"You can't just grow, willy-nilly, without exceeding the capacity. And there's really a capacity to how many people can live here. There just isn't space. This valley is so narrow. Where would you put the freeways? The noise, the congestion, would be horrendous."

What Bigler wants, in other words, is for the town of Moab to do something revolutionary—to do what few other communities in the nation have been able to do since the arrival of European immigrants on the American continent: to live within its means. Rather than finding creative new ways to feed growth, Bigler wants Moab to learn to control growth.

In 1986 Bigler completed a study of Moab's economic development prospects. In his report to the community, Bigler urged the townspeople to "establish Moab/Grand County as a diversified, four-season destination resort area" by creating for the town a "destination resort image . . . to attract investors and employers who want to own property and/or live in such a place." At the end of our interview, I asked Bigler whether creating such an image for Moab would not destroy the charm, the very character, of the town.

Wheeler: Are you possibly creating the seeds of your own disaster? Is that a paradox?

Bigler: Uh huh.

Wheeler: Building up momentum, making Moab an attractive place to visit and an attractive place to live. Creating pressures for development that will create a Moab which is bigger than you'd like it to be, personally?

Bigler: Uh huh.

Wheeler: So how do you get around that paradox?

Bigler: (*Silence.*)

Wheeler: Cross that bridge when you come to it?

Bigler: Yeah. I've fussed with it an awful lot. If you want Moab to be just like any other urban area, then you let it grow, willy-nilly, endlessly trying to go back and recover from the mistakes of the past. Or you orient the growth and development so that you get a very specific, selfish clientele that wants it for itself, drives the prices up so that no one else can afford it—which is the Vail route. Or you oppose all kinds of development and you control growth through poverty, which is what we're doing now. We can't afford to grow; we're not growing. That's the preference of a lot of people in this town. The "minimalists" and the retirees.

Wheeler: Is that your preferred alternative?

Bigler: (*Silence.*)

Wheeler: Off the record?

Bigler: (*Silence.*)

Wheeler: You're in a bit of a bind, Craig.

Night had fallen around Bigler's house. A warm, gusting spring wind was shaking the windows and stirring the cottonwood leaves. As I stared down into a beer mug, watching the bubbles rise off the thick bottom, I realized I had at last found the path to the future of the Colorado Plateau. The future will be precisely what we who live here are willing to believe it can be. With the collapse of the mining economy and the rise of the environmental movement as a political force, the Colorado Plateau is up for grabs.

CHAPTER TWENTY-NINE

For Whom the Bell Toll Rises

Ed Quillen

A CENTURY AGO rural communities lived or died depending on whether a railroad was built through them. After World War II, interstate highways played a similar make-or-break role. Today access to good telephone service will determine the economic fate of many Western towns. A couple of years ago, every time you turned on the TV set, you were assaulted by ads that urged you to save money with MCI or to stick with AT&T. The discount-store fliers promoted cordless telephones and answering machines. You read breathless articles that explained how personal computers could be connected to a telephone line, fetching information from almost anywhere. If you lived in a rural area, however, most of this could have been happening on Saturn. Long-distance companies battled for a market share in the cities, but out in the boondocks, your long-distance choice was simple: expensive AT&T or costly AT&T.

If your local service came from a party line, you didn't dare use a cordless telephone, because party lines use different ringer signals than private lines do. The cordless phone could beep for someone else's number, and ignore yours. Answering machines, a necessity to small enterprises, present that problem and another: sometimes they don't hang up once the message is taken, which ties up the line even though no one is talking. In many states it's illegal to use an answering machine on a party line.

As for the "electronic cottage," it's a shack if it's on a party line. Computers and modems aren't yet smart enough to hang up if the neighbor picks up the line and announces a pressing need to report a barn fire. And the migrating bytes get scrambled by the interruption.

The telecommunications revolution got under way with the court-ordered breakup of AT&T on January 1, 1984. Although society was supposed to benefit, if you lived outside a metropolitan area, there wasn't much of anything you could call a benefit. Instead, you got the same old service, except you had to pay a lot more for it. Your monthly base charge for local service kept climbing. On top of that, you got stuck with something called an "access charge"—$6 a month if you had a business line; for residences, $1 a month in 1985, doubled to $2 in 1986, and raised to $2.60 in 1988.

But there's more to it than that. The changes in the telephone industry will present a major challenge to rural areas that want to prosper. Pundits say America is moving from an industrial economy to an information economy. What that means to rural areas is that the old wisdom about the sources of economic growth is no longer wisdom. Traditional industry deals in heavy goods that must be transported. Keeping costs within reason requires the right location. It has to be near bulky raw materials—coal, ore, and such. Bulk commodities require appropriate transportation, like waterways and railroads. An industry's other suppliers—smelters, foundries, stamping plants—should also be close by. Likewise its major markets, so that it's convenient to ship products to the majority of its customers. There are a lot of good reasons why the American steel industry developed primarily between Chicago and Pittsburgh, and why they built so many cars in Michigan.

But what of an information-based industry? It's hard to define, and harder to generalize about. But consider Mark Emmer, who lives about four miles away from me, in an old farmhouse on eight acres not far from Salida, Colorado. He's the president of Catspaw, Incorporated; for all practical purposes, he is Catspaw, a firm that writes custom computer operating systems, and that developed, supports, and sells the SNOBOL4 programming language for personal computers.

Mark's raw materials are information. His products are ways to organize that information. Nothing he sells weighs more than a few pounds; United Parcel Service and Federal Express easily handle all his transportation requirements. His customers are scattered across six continents. The resources he needs are likewise scattered everywhere. Those resources are people who have developed algorithms Mark could use, or experts on a certain chip's registers and instruction set. Mark's enterprise brings in money from elsewhere, most of which he spends in Salida, thus stimulating our retail trade, real estate market, and all those other economic indicators that chambers of commerce are so fond of watching.

Catspaw could set up shop anywhere—as long as the UPS truck will come by, and as long as there's good telephone service. Mark sends and receives much of his work with a computer connected to a telephone line. His customers call, sometimes from Paris or Manila, for information and to place orders. His isn't a business you could run on a four-party line, although for almost three years, he tried to. He had to wait that long, and then pay $1,200 to Mountain Bell to install a new cable, before he could get a single-party business line.

As a free-lance writer, I, too, need good telephone service. There's no way I could deliver a timely weekly column to the *Denver Post*, 150 miles away and generally two days by mail, if I couldn't connect my computer to my telephone and deposit my work straight into the *Post's* computer. Nor could I have done much of the research for this article if I hadn't been able to reach the computerized information services that provide details I couldn't find in the local library.

Those two enterprises can easily be multiplied, even in this remote little town: other writers and computer programmers, people who tie fishing flies, a maker of upscale fly-fishing reels, sculptors, artists, artisans. We all bring in money from elsewhere and spend it here. We all require, to varying degrees, good telephone service, because our clients and customers are scattered. Telephone is the only quick way they can reach us, and often the only way we can get the information—"raw materials"—that we require. We need state-of-the-art communications because our competition is not some retailer down the street, but everyone else in the world who does what we do. It isn't enough to be accessible to Salida; we've got to be easily accessible to New York and London.

We're invisible to the local chamber of commerce and its boosters of economic development, because we don't have smokestacks or payrolls. Another reason that we're not apparent is that we aren't organized—people who like to go to meetings and elect officers don't run solitary cottage industries. But I'd be glad to wager that we're the only growing segment of the local economy. Further, I believe we are the most plausible way for most rural areas to prosper in coming years. The major asset of many rural communities is that they are cheap to live in, which is vital when your cash flow fluctuates so violently. Many relatively isolated little towns are also congenial places to live and work. So long as our cottage industries can stay in touch with the rest of the world at competitive rates, using current communications technology as it develops, we can operate far from metropolitan areas.

That pleasing scenario, however, is threatened by the changes in rural telephone service in the wake of the breakup of AT&T. To understand why rural telephone systems face a dismal future that could wreck the best opportunities for rural economies, we have to look at the history of AT&T—an example of practical socialism put together by that avatar of capitalism, J. P. Morgan.

A century ago the telephone industry was highly competitive; every promising city might have two or three companies. H. L. Mencken recalled that the *Baltimore Herald* of 1904 sported six phones on the city-room wall—one for each company that provided local service. AT&T brought that down to one. The AT&T of recent memory had several divisions, but only two concern us here. AT&T Long-Lines handled long-distance. Local service came from a "Bell Operating Company." There were twenty-three of them; their names all ended in Bell, as in Mountain Bell or Pacific Bell. Most were wholly owned by AT&T; in all Bells, AT&T held a majority of the stock. This was the Bell System. It did not serve all phones in America; only 80 percent were directly linked to a Bell Operating Company. About 15 percent were served by the Big Five independents: GTE, United, Continental, Centel, and Alltel. The other phones in America—almost all in rural areas—were served by 1,432 tiny telephone companies.

During the early days of this century, AT&T sought a total monopoly— every telephone in America. Even then, it controlled the long-distance network. Wherever an independent company was flourishing and AT&T wanted to move in, the independent quickly learned the facts of life. He could sell out to AT&T. Or he could try to stay in business. But his customers wouldn't be able to connect to the AT&T long-distance network, while the customers of his new competitor, an AT&T subsidiary, could call long distance. In that reformist era, AT&T looked like a predator. By 1913 an agreement had been reached. AT&T would no longer try to acquire local telephone exchanges. It would make its long-distance service available to the remaining independents. But AT&T would maintain a monopoly on long-distance service, and it would also undertake to provide, within reason, "universal telephone service."

As propounded by Theodore Vail, the man who led AT&T to its near-monopoly position with the financial backing of J. P. Morgan, universal service means that anyone who wants a telephone can get one installed. The customer pays a minimal price for local service—that is, the five or six dollars per month we used to pay. The customer then has access to the long-distance system.

Where AT&T offered local service through its subsidiaries, the company could implement universal service on its own. But what about rural areas, generally served by independents? On a per-customer basis, rural areas cost a lot more to service than urban areas. A mile of line in town might serve five hundred paying customers, whereas the company might have to run ten miles of line to serve only one rural customer. Yet a mile of line costs pretty much the same to install and maintain, no matter how much or little income it produces. The same exchange machinery that could handle ten thousand lines in a city

Marge Higley

might serve only six hundred lines in a little town. The city exchange could generate fifty thousand dollars a month in income, as opposed to the hamlet's three thousand dollars—but the capital and operation costs were virtually identical.

Where Bell companies served expensive rural areas, they also served profitable urban markets, so they could average those costs. But the rural independents couldn't. As per its agreement, AT&T couldn't take over those companies, but it was still obliged to provide "universal service." AT&T met this obligation through a process called "the settlements and separations pool." You've always heard that long-distance service subsidized local service; the settlements pool was the mechanism for that subsidy. This subsidy procedure was an effective application of the socialist maxim: "From each according to his ability to pay, to each according to his needs."

Businesses make about 85 percent of the long-distance calls in America. Long distance was priced out of proportion to cost, but AT&T could get away with this because it had a monopoly on long distance. The substantial excess went to the local operating companies to keep rates low for personal telephones. It might have cost your local company thirty dollars per month to install, maintain, and amortize a line from the exchange to your house, along with your share of the requisite switching equipment, support staff, and so on. But you paid only six dollars per month. The other twenty-four dollars per month was made up by what was, in essence, a tax on business to make sure that individuals could afford telephone service.

In 1981 AT&T collected about $30 billion in long-distance revenues. Of that, it kept only $12 billion. The rest went into the pool to be returned to local operating companies. Pool income provided a substantial share of their income. The average proportion was 44 percent, and for rural independents 63 percent.

That sounds generous, but you have to remember that AT&T owned the local operating companies that handled 80 percent of American telephone calls. In effect, the giant company was taking money out of one pocket and putting it in another. And in the process, some change—about $4 billion in 1981—fell to the floor, to be picked up by the independents. How much an independent received from the pool was not a function of how much long-distance business it provided. Instead, AT&T examined the independent's costs; the pool then provided enough money to make sure the independent stayed in business while paying its stockholders a reasonable return.

Rural independents had other sources of income, such as local charges and Yellow Pages, and they could get cheap long-term financing through the Rural Electrification Agency (REA). The REA got into the telephone business in 1949. Back in 1924, about 40 percent of rural households had telephones, although most of them were linked to primitive barbed-wire networks where a farm wife served as a part-time operator, running the switchboard when she wasn't hanging laundry or milking cows. Even those systems lost money and began to vanish, to where only 24 percent of farm homes had phones by 1949. So the REA, while continuing to promote electricity on the farm, began financing rural telephone systems. Some rural systems were organized as customer-owned cooperatives, like their electric counterparts, while others remained private companies.

The REA would underwrite loans for both types, and both could use other REA services, such as setting technical standards and testing vendors' offerings in a laboratory. In 1983 the combination of REA low-interest, long-term financing with a guaranteed income from the AT&T settlements pool meant that rural telephone companies were financially healthy, even though their local rates were quite low in comparison to the cost of service. As the president of one such company explained to me, "You could borrow money at 5 percent from the REA. And AT&T would guarantee you a 12-percent return on your investment. All you had to do was maintain what you had, upgrading as necessary. In those days you would have had to work at it to lose money with an independent telephone company."

That ended on January 1, 1984, when AT&T was broken up. The major effect, so far as we're concerned, is that the Bell Operating Companies and AT&T Long-Lines are no longer part of the same company. Whereas most of what AT&T had once paid out of the settlements pool just went to other

AT&T divisions, that money was now forever gone from AT&T's coffers. Further, AT&T faced competition from Sprint, MCI, and others, in the long-distance market. It couldn't set rates arbitrarily high and use the excess to subsidize universal telephone service. Hence, no more guaranteed money from Ma Bell for rural independent telephone systems.

How much a local telephone company gets from the pool is now determined almost entirely by how many long-distance calls its customers make. To help make up for the loss of guaranteed income from the settlements pool, the Federal Communications Commission (FCC) implemented those "access charges" in 1985. In theory, that $2.60 per month is what you pay for the privilege of being connected to the long-distance system. But you have to pay it whether you make long-distance calls or not. The money goes straight to the local telephone company, just like your monthly charge for basic service. It's actually an increase in rates for basic service.

It was done this way, through the FCC, to avoid hundreds of hearings before the public utilities commissions of fifty states. But even at that, local telephone companies have been seeking rate increases at a furious clip, because they have to recover more of their costs from all users as less comes in from long distance. Our telephone system is changing from paternalistic socialism to an "if you want it, you pay your share" operation. The remaining subsidy mechanism is the Universal Service Fund, financed through an access charge levied on interstate long distance calls. It provides operating subsidies to rural telephone systems whose costs exceed a certain percentage of the national average. However, no one I talked to is sure how it works. I heard figures ranging from 110 percent to 150 percent as the minimum, and the varying formulas for payments were complex. Not one rural telephone manager knew how much, if any, his company could expect from the fund.

One effect of this uncertainty is that rural telephone companies are cutting costs by laying off employees. Maybe it's a desirable trimming of corporate fat, but it might also mean that service could get worse. Suppose it takes the company days instead of hours to repair your line after a lightning zap or backhoe attack. Is your business better off this way? Let's see what else this means to rural telephone customers.

There are other long-distance services besides AT&T; MCI is the biggest of the competitors. MCI's rates are lower than AT&T's. But most of us can't use MCI. MCI advertises that you can call any telephone in the country through its system, which is true. But you can't use MCI to place a call unless you're in a metropolitan area. Why? Certain AT&T people I talked to wouldn't go on record, but they suspected that MCI is "skimming the cream" off the long-distance market. MCI will serve the profitable urban areas, while leaving the expensive rural markets to AT&T.

I asked various public-relations people at MCI about this, as well as what the company's plans were for expanding into rural markets. Over eighteen months all I heard were runarounds and unkept promises that "we'll call you back on that."

What does this apparent MCI strategy mean to us in the country? Nothing good. If MCI keeps its costs down by skimming the cream, it will gain a metropolitan market share from AT&T. To remain competitive and in business, AT&T will be forced to lower its rates for urban markets. That money will have to be made up somewhere—and rural areas are a captive set of pockets within AT&T's reach. Our long-distance rates will go up. That makes it harder for me to compete with a writer in, say, Denver. I already use long distance more than she does, because when she's working on an article she can reach a lot more people with a local call than I can. And when my rates climb and hers don't, I've got to charge more or work cheaper. Eventually I'll either find some other line of work or be forced to move. If the latter happens often enough, it's going to hurt rural economies in the place where they're most competitive right now—their attractiveness to cottage industries.

There are, of course, other long-distance companies besides MCI, and some of them serve rural areas. Most are known in the trade as "resellers." They don't own transmission facilities; they lease capacity, generally from AT&T. In effect, they're retailers, and AT&T is their wholesaler. Using one of those—I have friends here who swear by Northwest Telcom—is considerably cheaper than AT&T. But the price difference is primarily an artifice of regulation that will disappear sooner or later. In the meantime, it's a good way to drive local rates even higher.

Those companies can undercut AT&T by substantial amounts—40 percent is typical—because even now the long-distance company doesn't get to keep most of your long-distance toll. The long-distance company pays the local company for access. In rural areas AT&T pays a lot more to the local company because AT&T benefits from a convenience established when there was only one long-distance company. To place your call through AT&T, you just dial "1" and then the number. Using another service means dialing a dozen digits before getting to the number you want to call.

Because the non-AT&T carriers do not have the "1" convenience, in rural areas they pay about 45 percent less to the local phone company than AT&T does. The FCC set that up so that competitors would have a fair chance in the market—they may not be as easy to use, but they could offer savings. In cities most of that price differential has vanished. As soon as their exchanges were switched over, so that you could select a long-distance carrier that you would connect with every time you dialed a "1" first, everybody started paying the same percentage to the local phone company. That's why MCI's price advantage over AT&T has dropped from 45 percent to less than 10 percent.

Why the difference between rural areas and cities here? Most cities have modern electronic-switching exchanges that work like big computers; they were easy to convert to multiple long-distance carriers. In rural areas (especially those served by the former Bell Operating Companies), the exchanges are often old-fashioned stepper or crossbar systems, clicking arrays of electromechanical relays. These antiques still function reliably, but they were designed to function easily with only one long-distance carrier. Using more than one means dialing a lot more numbers. Anyway, once your exchange is modernized, you won't save much money by using a competitor instead of AT&T. And if you use a competitor in the interim, you'll be delaying the day your phone company can modernize your exchange. Your discount long-distance calls won't provide as much income to the local company, and thus there won't be as much money for modernization. Without that modernization, more of your friends and neighbors will be stuck with party lines, which won't work with answering machines, cordless phones, or computers. You won't get call forwarding, call holding, and other changes that can turn your telephone into a better tool.

These days, you get what you pay for. If you pay less, you're going to be getting less. However, there remain some charming inequities in rural telephone service. I get my service from Mountain Bell, the biggest division of gargantuan US West, and we still have party lines around here, along with that ancient mechanical exchange. My neighbors down the river in Howard are served by tiny Eagle Telecommunications. Although they're spread all over some rugged countryside, they don't have party lines. Their exchange is modern and digital, with the accompanying bells and whistles. They pay less for telephone service than I do, even though it must cost more to provide their service.

A rancher over in the Powderhorn valley between Gunnison and Lake City wanted a phone. That's Mountain Bell territory, and he got a bill of $47,597 for his first dial tone. He had to pay the full cost of extending the line. In Eagle's territory the same rancher might have paid only $100 or so for installation, despite similar costs to the phone company.

Why these differences, in both price and quality, between Bell and independent service? Because the independents can finance their capital investments through the REA. And the REA, conscious of its mission, requires them to treat all customers alike. It costs Eagle Telecommunications about $150 to install a phone in a trailer park in town; at a ranch up the remote Sheephorn valley, that might be $6,000. But the installation fee to the consumer won't reflect the company's costs, it will be minimal. Because Eagle can borrow more cheaply from the REA than Mountain Bell can from the capital markets, Eagle can afford to modernize its facilities more quickly.

Further, Mountain Bell's customers subsidize Eagle's, thanks to the way that money from within-state long-distance calls is divvied up. If someone from Howard calls Colorado Springs, Eagle gets substantially more of the toll than my Mountain Bell exchange gets if I call Colorado Springs. So rural telephone service can be both good and affordable—for the moment, and in places.

The independents and co-ops sweat blood with every federal budget. The Reagan administration always proposed to eliminate the REA's loan programs for rural telephone systems. Congress restored most of what the phone companies said they needed, but the administration kept whittling away. The loan programs' days may be numbered; with every census, the rural proportion of the population, and thus our representation and political clout, declines.

Rural telephone executives say loan programs are important because rural telephone companies have difficulty borrowing money in traditional markets. Phone systems are capital-intensive and take a long time to amortize; the small-town banker is unlikely to be able to lend $1 million over twenty years for a new digital exchange. Going to bigger capital markets means competing with investments that can pay better returns.

The REA's laboratory and technical standards division is also important to independent telephone companies. They can't afford to maintain their own labs to test vendors' equipment. If they all tried to set technical standards, there wouldn't be standards, so they're content to let the REA determine minimum acceptable signal voltages and the like. And that's another thing the Reagan administration wanted to get rid of. Therein is the national political threat to rural telephone service, although it affects only the co-ops and small independents.

The local political climate can work against the Bell companies' rural customers. In 1986 Mountain Bell proposed vast improvements in its rural service to Coloradans—eliminating the 753 eight-party lines, upgrading most of the 48,941 four-party lines to single party, and installing modern electronic exchanges. Since it can't get REA money, Mountain Bell proposed financing this by raising all Colorado customers' rates by fifty-two cents per month for fifteen years. Similar proposals had been approved elsewhere in Mountain Bell territory, such as Idaho, but Colorado regulators wondered why the urban 80 percent of Mountain Bell customers should pay more for phone service to benefit the 20 percent out in the country. The improvement plan was approved, but Mountain Bell was told to make rural customers carry more of the load.

Other changes in the wind could hit all of us who don't live in cities. Principal among these is something called "toll-rate deaveraging." As things work now, the time period being the same, any 850-mile call costs the same as any other 850-mile call. That might be over a busy route, such as Chicago to Denver, or it could be from Pine Bluff, Arkansas, to Pine Bluffs, Wyoming. Obviously, it costs the long-distance company substantially less to handle the Chicago call, but interstate long-distance rates, regulated by the FCC, concern only time and distance, not the true cost of the call.

MCI, to a large extent, evades this inequity by refusing to serve the Pine Bluffs of this land. And AT&T says it is opposed to deaveraging, just as it remains committed to universal service. But recall that AT&T has to compete with the MCIs. If AT&T starts losing its share of the profitable markets, it will have to start pricing long-distance service more in line with actual costs. In which case you're unlikely to hear any more AT&T opposition to toll-rate deaveraging.

This has already been started in New Mexico for intrastate calls, which are regulated by the states, not the FCC. Customers pay different amounts for a 10-minute, 100-mile call during business hours, depending on both the local carrier's and the long-distance carrier's costs. Those costs, and thus the rates, even vary in direction. It costs more to call from Espanola to Albuquerque than from Albuquerque to Espanola, everything else being equal.

Deaveraging is favored by big business, by far the biggest user of the long-distance network. Why should Megacorp pay ten times the true cost to keep its Denver and Chicago offices in touch just so a writer in Salida can afford to talk to an editor in Paonia? Even now, if Megacorp gets too fed up with this situation, it can set up its own communication system, via satellite or other microwave links. This is called bypassing, and it alarms telephone companies.

Ron Nichols

Even the local exchange carriers hate the idea. If Megacorp goes through regular long distance, the local carrier collects healthy access charges that help keep its exchange running. If the bulk of a Megacorp office's communication goes through an in-house telephone system and an antenna on the roof, there also goes substantial income for the local carrier.

If enough of that occurs, the local carrier has to make up for lost revenue with a general rate increase. Some people won't be able to pay those rates, so they terminate their service. Monthly costs remain pretty much the same, though, so it's time for another rate increase. More individuals drop off, and more businesses start looking at bypassing a telephone system that gets more expensive by the month. It's the death spiral usually discussed in connection with electric utilities. This scenario gives nightmares to the management of the local phone company.

On a very local level, phone service presents another political problem that can divide communities. Vocal telephone customers come in two categories: Hustler and Granny. I'm a Hustler. I need the best phone system I can get. Naturally, I don't want to spend any more than I have to for that service, but I'm willing to pay what it takes. Granny lives down the street on a pension. She'd be satisfied with a four-party line, and she never calls long distance. She doesn't need call forwarding because she rarely goes anywhere. Improving phone service means raising her bill for services she doesn't need. And when they have the hearings, she'll remind me that she's on a "limited income," as if anyone had an unlimited income. If Granny wins, rates stay relatively low, but service deteriorates. If Hustler wins, the town might have some hope for a future, but the people who built the town just got priced out of telephones.

Many states address this problem with a "lifeline" service of minimal rate and reduced service; California taxes within-state long-distance calls to finance its service. Some local phone companies let people opt for measured local service, wherein you're billed for the time you talk. That gives Granny a low-cost option, and yet intense users get a modern system. You'll be seeing more such proposals in the future. Affordable universal telephone service is no longer a national priority. Fortune 500 companies won't help you have a phone at home any more, and they don't see any social or other obligation to finance any more of the long-distance system than what they use.

We'll have to pay more for telephone service, both local and long distance, than we're paying now. No matter how eloquently the rural interests present the case for continued subsidies, words can't overcome the hard economics of emerging deregulation. Certainly, we can lobby to protect our peculiar subsidies, just as every other special-interest group does. Toll-rate deaveraging is inevitable, but the longer we can postpone it by protesting, the better off we are. The low-interest loans and other telephone services provided by the REA are doomed by demographics. Even so, concerted letter-writing campaigns might postpone doomsday for a few years.

Political maneuvering aside, the best we can hope for is that our telephone service will be good. It can't be cheap, but it ought to be reliable, and our exchanges should offer everything that metropolitan exchanges offer. Without that link to the rest of the world, modern cottage industries—perhaps your town's best hope for economic growth—can't function. You won't get new ones, and those you have will eventually migrate.

As technology improves, making that connection will become simpler, even in places that don't have telephone service now. The telephone may appear to be ubiquitous, but it isn't. It may be no surprise that 98 percent of Alaska lacks telephone service. And even in the forty-eight states, there are 413,000 square miles—Texas and Montana put together—without telephone service. A half million people live in this phoneless zone, which comprises big chunks of Nevada, Montana, Oregon, Arizona, and Idaho, as well as parts of twenty-one other states. They're so far from existing lines that no one can afford to serve them.

Radio waves can go where wires don't. Rural radio-telephone systems, however, are technically quite different from the mobile cellular-telephone systems employed by Audi-borne yuppies in cities. Generally, the phone company runs a land cable, with capacity to handle several calls at once, as far as feasible. At the terminus, there's a switching system and a radio transmitter and receiver. The households within fifteen miles or so have telephones with numbers and dial tones; they function identically to the familiar telephones, except that they're connected to a little antenna in the yard. Service like this costs two or three times more per month than traditional service, but those who have it say it's a vast improvement on no phone at all. In conjunction with Motorola, Mountain Bell has one such service functioning in an upscale mountain suburb near Woodland Park, Colorado.

Another wireless system, "Ultraphone," now serves nine ranch families in Platte County, Wyoming. Until late 1986, making a call meant a 35-mile roundtrip to Glendo. Each installation cost $4,852, but there weren't any complaints.

It's possible to take the fixed radio telephone concept a step further. If you can put a dish in the yard to receive television signals from a satellite, couldn't you figure out some way to transmit to and receive from the communications satellites that handle telephone signals? There are several ways, as it turns out. The FCC is considering proposals from a half dozen companies. Technically, all work pretty much alike. I talked to people at Sky-Link in Boulder, Colorado, to get specifics on their proposed system, which they said could be operating by 1989. It would mean a dish in the yard, aimed at a satellite. The other earthly end of the connection would be a terminal in a city chosen by the user. The rural telephone would become part of that city's telephone system. Calling anywhere else would involve long distance through the regular network.

Consider a rancher in the sparsely populated Nebraska sandhills if Sky-Link's plan is approved. He can use CB radio for reaching his neighbors in an emergency. But he does most of his business in Omaha—purchasing equipment, selling cattle, and so on. With his dish in the yard and a phone in the house, he gets an Omaha dial tone every time he picks up the phone, although, if he wanted to call Denver or even Valentine, that would involve a long-distance call from his Omaha number.

A novelist in the wilds of Montana could get a Manhattan line, simplifying his dealings with agents and editors. A Denver executive could stay in touch with the office, even from the remote weekend cabin he bought "to get away from it all." A high-tech homesteader wouldn't have to worry about any utility lines, because the satellite link demands so little electricity it could be powered by a solar panel and a storage battery.

An installation would cost two to three thousand dollars, Sky-Link officials estimate. Then would come a monthly charge of twenty-five dollars or so for using the satellite system. On top of that would be whatever the land-based telephone company in a distant city charged for a monthly line.

There are more possibilities, some of which sound like comic-strip fantasies. It is comforting to know that there are a lot of smart people who do care about finding ways to make sure rural America doesn't get cut off from urban America. Our future, however, is in our hands, not theirs. If we're willing to pay while insisting on service that comes close to the state of the art, the countryside can be a thriving place, no matter what happens to crop prices and federal assistance.

CHAPTER THIRTY

Balkanized, Atomized Idaho

Pat Ford

A COMBINATION OF technological change and free market ideology has led the nation to abandon not just railroad and bus lines but its long-held commitment to universal transportation and communication. What can be seen in Idaho describes the balkanization process and its consequences for the rural West. As the impostor called deregulation burst from Washington, D.C., in the late 1970s and early 1980s, Idahoan Perry Swisher watched his state's transport and telephony bounce in its turbulent wake. Long a phrase maker, Swisher called the new approach theology, the Gospel of the Beltway. In a speech to some of the new creed's seminarians at a college of business administration, he proposed its Genesis: "In the Beginning, there was a free market in which all transactions occurred in innocence. Enter government, the snake, with regulation, the apple. . . ."

Swisher has been one of Idaho's three public utilities commissioners since 1979. He is known for his bluntness. Heads snapped around the table when he told a committee of the 1988 Idaho legislature that one provision in Mountain Bell's telephone deregulation bill was "grand theft." Theft, "robbery," and "a rip" are his synonyms for deregulation of basic services. A million people can call themselves Idahoans, but Swisher is one of the few whose life has earned the title. He knows this state as you know your backyard. As an Idahoan, deregulation implies something larger, which he calls balkanization.

Idaho is, first, its geography. Distance, dryness, mountains, and canyons—the common Western isolators—determine much and influence everything. Two communities twenty-five miles apart may be two or three times that by wire and road. Connecting a few hundred people here with a few hundred up and over there is hard, expensive, unprofitable work. Aggravating the natural pocketing are unnatural boundaries. Idaho shares with Montana the nation's only state-line segment to follow John Wesley Powell's advice—put political divides on watershed divides—but the rest of its borders atone for that lapse into sense. Idaho's northern Panhandle—narrow, surveyor-straight, 400-plus tough miles from the populous, dominating Snake River Plain in the south—should be anything, geographically, but Idaho.

Idaho became a state in 1890, but the real creation of a unified community and polity has been long, hard labor. Some recall not just the growth of a skeleton—roads, tracks, wires, docks, canals—on which "Idaho" might be made flesh, but the indispensable enabler of it: federal policy and state and federal money.

In Idaho, the memories of skeleton building aren't that old. Writer John Rember noted: "I remember the summer of 1956, when we watched with something like patriotic awe as the Rural Electrification Administration planted the first power poles in the soil of Sawtooth Valley. I was only five, but I can remember sensing, perhaps for the first time, the great expanding outside nation those poles represented. We had been invited to join it. People outside the valley walls cared about us, we who lived in this remote place and were included in their progress."

A bit earlier and some miles south, ODeen Redman watched his family's Albion Telephone Company and its scattered customers connect to the outside through that same REA. Albion served a few hundred farmers, ranchers, and villagers dusted over two thousand square miles of south-central Idaho and a slice of Utah. Thanks to federal low-interest loans and technical support, Redman watched a modern system of exchanges and lines rather quickly replace their primitive one, giving them access to the nation and world.

Perry Swisher's memory goes further back. He was born on a ranch in southwest Idaho's vast Owyhee Plateau, well before paved roads, power poles, and affordable telephones reached it. "You live that far out," Swisher's former colleague Conley Ward says, "and all sorts of things people take for granted are wonders—bridges, roads, telephones. You realize how fragile they are if that national compact is withdrawn."

Swisher lived forty years in Pocatello, east Idaho's railroad town, where trains—after delivering the paper he printed his newspaper on—branched out to tie Idaho to itself and its fellows. He went to the Idaho legislature in the 1950s, when it saw transport as important, and the state raised its small share of funds for the costs of Interstates 15, 84, and 90. He was city editor of the *Lewiston Tribune*, north Idaho's best newspaper, when the first decent north-south state highway was completed, and when Lewiston built an inland port linking Idaho to Pacific Ocean shipping.

Today, Swisher stubbornly bears witness to this work, and the national compact supporting it, to the ahistorical urbanites he finds in federal agencies, corporations, and business schools: "Until this generation, universal accessibility was a conscious goal of national and state policymakers, and the private sector. A dynamic of progress was that it included the ability to get from here to there—when walking or riding, shipping or ordering, flying or catching a train, mailing a letter or sending a telegram, making a phone call or turning on your radio or television. From the digging of the Erie Canal to the first orbit in space, making access universal had equal standing with the beliefs embedded in the Bill of Rights." Until this generation.

The little town of Grace lies 40 miles southeast of Pocatello. The 6-mile branch connecting Grace to Union Pacific's mainline is a lifeline for the one hundred growers in the Farmers Grain Cooperative. Last year, as the coop was shipping out 22,000 tons of wheat, barley, and malt barley, Union Pacific quietly put the old, deteriorating line on its notice-of-abandonment list. By 1990 Union Pacific will be able to ask federal permission—since deregulation, it doesn't need state permission—to drop the line. Union Pacific says it won't abandon if the line is profitable. That's the only real criterion now, and the judgment is essentially the company's.

"How is the Interstate Commerce Commission, from desks in Washington, D.C., going to know what six miles of decaying track means to a hundred Idaho farmers?" Swisher wonders. "These are Reagan appointees. They don't listen to people." Since the Staggers Act deregulated railroads in 1980, one-fifth of Idaho's trackage, five hundred miles, has been abandoned.

Albion Telephone: sixty years ago, ODeen Redman's family brought telephones to a place the Bell System didn't want to go—remote, barely peopled Great Basin country, emphatically high cost. Today, it's the same: AT&T, Sprint, and US West are not out fighting for market share in those two thousand square miles. But with the REA and a regulatory scheme that pooled and averaged Albion's costs with the broader system, a few hundred people had affordable modern telephone service.

Thanks to Congress, the REA survived yearly Reagan administration attempts to eliminate it. But in 1986, after the courts and Federal Communications Commission deregulated telephones, Redman filed with the Idaho PUC to raise Albion's basic service rate from $6.20 to $35 a month. That's the price to rural users of the withdrawal of a compact that saw the national telephone system as a whole.

It is not just telephones. Swisher says: "Trunk airlines served four, sometimes five, airports in our state of scarcely a million people before deregulation.

Now they serve two, sometimes one. Dozens of Idaho communities lost scheduled common carrier service with truck deregulation. After bus deregulation in 1981, public need was no longer a factor in bus routing. Greyhound crosses Idaho now only for the reason a chicken crosses the road."

An old woman in McAmmon can't rely on the bus to take her twenty miles to the doctor in Pocatello. A shipper in Parma can't find a live body to help him corral three freight cars to start his onions on the way to the processor. From cubicles in Washington, D.C., these are invisible events. "Changes in daily lives seem tiny," Swisher says. "The increments are large. Old folks move to the cities; small towns erode. But there's a continent-wide inversion: the phenomena of the Information Age"—his voice has an edge—"blanket them from view."

Swisher's seat on the Idaho Public Utilities Commission (PUC) puts him in the ring on these events. Established in 1913, the same year as Grace's branch line, the PUC oversees Idaho operations of privately owned utilities and common carriers. That includes seventeen telephone companies (from Albion to AT&T), six railroads, and several hundred motor carriers. From 1976 through 1986 (and perhaps since; it is early to tell), the PUC was the best public body in Idaho. Its energy regulation was a national model. Swisher came on in 1979, joining a young attorney named Conley Ward. One year later Richard High, a farmer and Republican legislator of Swisher's age, joined them. These three served together until 1986, through the years when deregulation—especially the Bell breakup in telephones—both narrowed the PUC's powers and greatly expanded its job.

All are remarkable men, but Swisher is uniquely arresting. There is a voice in the late poetry of Irishman William Butler Yeats—passionate, profane, chained to the body's decay, angry-edged bitter, blunt-edged cruel, yet schooled, hammered, musical. "A wild old wicked man." This is something like the voice and presence of Perry Swisher. He is sixty-three. His large body moves unevenly from early polio and age. Not long ago a good chunk of his insides was removed. Something in his eyes and jaw suggests an old, smart fish. Thin gray and white hair is tame only in the official photograph. He smokes and swears continuously.

Within, an omnibus of a mind: fact-insistent, elliptical, reflective, flinty, eloquent. And always pushing, provoking. By turns Swisher frightens, inspires, and infuriates environmentalists, reporters, businessmen. In 1988 he prodded the national meeting of energy regulators into a panel on the greenhouse effect. Underlying all is an Idaho encyclopedia. PUC attorney Mike Gilmore says: "There's not a town in this state he hasn't been in, and can tell you who ran it twenty years ago, the best place to eat, the people to talk to. When he hears a case, he knows instinctively what it means to the logger, the widow, the farmer. He just knows." An uncommon regulator; along with Ward and High, uncommonly competent. But in the areas of transport and telecommunications, they have mainly employed their talents to contain damage and sound alarms.

The rail network and Idaho's access to it were in place when Swisher was born. Agriculture, timber, and mining all depended on rail. Even today 60 percent of Idaho's lumber is shipped by rail, as is more than half its potatoes and wheat, and half its onions.

What follows from today's progressive decline? "The Staggers Act coincided with the opening of the Cyprus molybdenum mine near Challis," Swisher says. Ore concentrates from the state's largest mine are today trucked 110 miles to the railhead at Pocatello, paralleling much of the way the rusting tracks of the abandoned Mackay branch. Among the results: five times more fuel consumed, higher freight costs, and broken pavement Idaho can't afford to fix.

The Camas Prairie Railroad, co-owned by Union Pacific and Burlington Northern, is a vital link for northern Idaho farmers and sawmills with the main lines and Lewiston's port. It is on the notice list for abandonment. The branch line from northern Idaho's Silver Valley mines west toward Spokane is on the list this year; the branch east, into Montana, is already gone.

Portions of Union Pacific's Boise Group branch lines, which funnel farm and lumber products to the main line and between processing plants, will appear on the list in 1988, and are for sale. The PUC will protest these abandonments, but the railroads and Interstate Commerce Commission will make the decisions.

The events force a question: Do the railroads really want to keep their Idaho customers and attract new ones? There was once, Swisher points out, a strong party involved in this question—the public, through state and federal regulation based on a conscious policy of reasonable access. He has watched American railroads too long to miss their many other problems. But now, as a deregulated regulator, as a reduced representative of Idaho, he can't do much to help. The PUC retains some power, and an activist PUC can move into areas that may or may not be its purview.

But Swisher can, and does, act quasi-officially. He jawbones the companies and unions and pesters Idaho's congressmen to consider the future worth to their state of a new national commitment to a modern, high-speed rail network based on universal access. As an Idahoan, he can keep mulling with local and state leaders how to hold on to what remains. The Camas Prairie Railroad is temporarily making a little money, thanks to shipments from a Grangeville sawmill. That gives breathing space to consider whether Lewiston's Port District should be able to buy a branch line, as Washington ports can. Or whether the state should be able to buy it, as South Dakota is. The Camas line's magnificent high trestles and wilderness-edge destinations suggest tourism possibilities. Whatever Union Pacific and Burlington Northern decide, it may be that the people of north-central Idaho can somehow keep the line alive, supporting farm, timber, and travel economies.

To deregulation's priests and parishioners, Swisher offers a last warning about the law of unintended consequences. "Our kids and grandkids will not forgive us allowing the railroads to die." And their reaction, when it comes, may match in fervor and extremity what the deregulators have done. "In yet another generation, American rail deregulation could eventuate in nationalization of the railbeds. A gift from free-market ideologues to the twenty-first century, and all in the name of free enterprise."

Ask Idaho PUC member Conley Ward about Ronald Reagan's Federal Communications Commission—and stand back. "The most benighted, misguided federal agency I've ever seen"—voice and gesture rising in anger, astonishment, and a kind of soldier's glee—"in thrall to a utopian vision without one whit of reality. By any normal layman's definition of insanity, those people were insane. What a crew."

Crew chief was Chairman Mark Fowler, a former disc jockey whose on-air handle had been Madman Mark. Wholly appropriate, Ward thinks, to both Fowler and his senior staff. Their utopia was complete deregulation of telephony. Swisher, Ward, and High fought underdoggedly to keep Idaho free of it, and a part instead of the human compact called universal telephone service.

The Idaho PUC joined most states in urging that joint responsibility for backbone costs remain in place, with a new formula through which all long-distance carriers contributed to them. This approach promised some stability and commitment to universal service. But the "conservative" FCC was intent on radical change, and long distance was their wedge. These were Beltway conservatives; AT&T, Sprint, MCI were real; Albion Telephone Company was not.

"AT&T fed them the old self-serving industry argument," Ward says, "the same one they'd made in the twenties—that long-distance subsidizes local service. Academics and think-tankers joined in. The FCC bought it." The access charge became the biggest in a series of FCC orders that steadily moved backbone costs from long distance to local exchange customers. The Idaho PUC didn't buy it. "All through those years," Ward recalls, "we'd go to conferences and hear industry and the feds intone their mantra: Toll is subsidizing local. They said it so often and so loud that legislators, reporters, even state regulators came to believe it. They were shocked when we asked for evidence, and doubly shocked when we concluded it wasn't so. Local ratepayers were paying roughly their fair share."

For Swisher, it was simply theft, a massive transfer from Idaho to populous corridors, homes to businesses, local exchange companies to cream-skimming long-line carriers. Abetted by government: "To the FCC, people were no longer people, but 'cost causers.' Abstract economic cogs."

Talk to the people running Idaho's small phone companies, and you begin to suspect a hidden rule beneath these events: Deregulation emanating from Washington, D.C., will, in rural Idaho, do the opposite of what was intended.

"You know, this is all supposed to make things easier for businesses," Jeff Adams says drily. Adams runs Project Mutual, the small phone co-op serving Minidoka County, along the Snake River just north of Albion's territory. "What it's done is greatly expand our administrative burden—paperwork, consultants, attorneys." Albion's Redman has a current case in point: "The FCC just changed the whole accounting system we've used for decades. We had to hire one new person just to deal with that alone. Obviously our customers will pay for it."

Competition presumably caused the Bell breakup. But when Adams and Redman discuss Idaho's telephone landscape today, the word "monopoly" keeps coming up—AT&T's practical monopoly on north-south long distance in Idaho, Mountain Bell's on southern Idaho's east-west. Deregulation's major competitive effect has been to discourage it.

Mountain Bell dominates Idaho telecommunications, serving the more than 70 percent of the state's people who live on the Snake River Plain. Pacific Northwest Bell serves the Lewiston area just north. There are twenty "independents." Most, like Albion, serve small, remote areas, but one, General Telephone of the Northwest, or GTE-NW, serves all of Idaho from Moscow to Canada, and is the second-largest company in the state. Albion and GTE-NW, from remoteness and ruggedness, respectively, serve very high-cost areas. Mountain Bell and Project Mutual are relatively low cost because of flat terrain and greater densities.

Before the breakup, a state settlements agreement tied the pieces together. Backbone system costs were shared between local exchange and in-state long-distance service. Long-distance revenues were pooled, then allocated on a formula giving high-cost companies a bigger share. GTE-NW received $24 million more from this formula than it billed in long distance, Mountain Bell roughly the opposite. The aim was affordable basic rates and uniform long-distance rates. To both Redman and Adams, this agreement was their "partnership" with the Bell System.

The partnership is over. Idaho was split into three "local access and transportation areas" (LATAs)—southern Idaho, GTE-NW's service area, and a slice between, largely served by Pacific Northwest Bell. Suddenly, calls crossing these lines, interLATA calls, could be carried only by AT&T or its competitors. In Idaho, that means AT&T. Conversely, AT&T was banned from competing within LATAs; the southern Idaho one quickly became known as "Mountain Bell's LATA."

For the independents, it was a mess. Project Mutual, Albion, and their fellows had been dealing with one entity on long-distance settlements—Mountain Bell. Suddenly they had complex and shifting administrative dealings with four: Mountain Bell, AT&T within and without Idaho—"from our end, it may as well be two different companies," Adams says—and the FCC's new administrator of interstate revenue arrangements. But the real chaos was in finances. Mountain Bell and AT&T could no longer share costs or revenues. Long-distance revenues once collected by independents now flowed to AT&T. Mountain Bell, administrator and primary revenue source for the old toll pool, refused to share revenues anymore across LATA lines (that is, with GTE-NW). The pool collapsed at the same time that the access charge and other FCC orders were steadily shifting costs once borne by AT&T to in-state companies.

The partnership became a melee. Mountain Bell and AT&T—big, rich, starting the new ball game with essential monopolies and protection from their only short-run competitive threat (each other)—sought maximum deregulation and basic service run-ups to keep rates in their separate long-distance markets low. The high-cost independents began seeking huge rate hikes of 300 to 500 percent to cover their lost dollars from settlements. Threats emerged that had been stilled for fifty years—service area raids, deaveraged long-distance rates, withdrawal of long-distance service (competitors have a way of folding).

The PUC worked five years, and is working still, to piece something coherent back together that still honors universal service; often, says Commissioner Dick High, "without the foggiest idea if we were doing it right." The PUC's tactics varied, but its strategy stayed constant: to keep rates more or less even across the state. Despite that effort, sparsely populated areas saw hefty rate increases. But the PUC's efforts did prevent the $60-per-month rates that for a while threatened rural telephone users. As part of its tactics, the PUC reinvented an Idaho toll pool, renamed a Universal Service Fund; it was ratified by the 1988 legislature. In effect, Mountain Bell's basic rates become the norm, with Albion's or GTE-NW's guaranteed to be no more than 25 percent higher.

This state-level regulatory grind—there was much more—was laced with frustration. Time after time in PUC case orders, one finds statements such as this: "The rate increase that we approve today has its origin in federal policies. The deregulatory trend on the federal level—whether in airlines, railroads, busses, or telephones—has primarily benefited the populous corridors on this country's coasts or along the Great Lakes. The sparsely populated rural states like Idaho have borne the brunt of the costs of these policy changes. It is beyond our jurisdiction and authority to reimpose what we believe to be the logical remedies to these detrimental federal policies."

Real change impelled the cutting of the Bell pie. Technology opened competition in parts of the telephone business. Swisher contends the regulatory structure could have met that challenge. "Regulation is alterable, reducible, improvable, transferable," capable of adjustment to times and technology. The Idaho PUC has voluntarily deregulated much of trucking, some of telephony, and indirectly, much of energy in Idaho. He insists that PUC deregulation has encouraged competition, not chaos.

The fruits of good regulation can be seen in southern Idaho: it has what US West calls the best non-metropolitan communications network in the country: universal one-party service, a fiber-optic spine, and end-to-end digital services by 1991. It is the kind of modern rural infrastructure needed to help counter balkanization. Modernization was done by regulation: the PUC granted rate hikes to cover the first parts of it and agreed to drop an excess earnings investigation against the company in return for the digital upgrade, a pledge to not charge ratepayers for most of it, and a pledge to seek no basic rate hikes for two years. Whatever the strengths of regulation, however, the genie is out of the bottle. After five years of huge consequence from the court's order, the FCC's encyclicals, and natural corporate rapacity, regulators can't meet the challenge in telephony or railroads. Congress is the place for remedy. Swisher is not sanguine.

Balkanization is a constant force in the geographically fractured West— physical, social, and political connections age and break. But why has the federal government in the last decade so aggressively promoted it? Much was the by-product of ideological pursuit, hard to correct because the ideologue doesn't listen. Listen to New York's Senator Patrick Moynihan describe the David Stockman economic crusaders: "A coterie of half-educated ideologues who seized power in such matters, being ideologues, prove impervious to experience . . . conservatives have displaced liberals as starry-eyed advocates of exotic economic doctrines."

The PUC saw the same in the FCC, and ICC—people with no historical or rural perspective, who didn't know what they were doing to Idaho and couldn't be made to know. But the deeper reason, which allowed these zealots to keep their places and win more than lose, was and is the national policy vacuum. Congress did not act. And closer to home, Western senators and congressional representatives didn't unite to speak for and defend their people and states.

In brief letters to each other, the PUC kept citing effects of deregulatory actions on Idaho, and Idaho's congressional representatives kept repeating, formulaically, the Reagan slogans. Only Jim McClure, the senior senator, had some grasp of the issues; he voted against bus deregulation, for instance. But he, and, even more, the others, read the telephone issue mythically—government versus the free market—or politically—Republicans (them) versus Democrats (Ward and Swisher). The railroad issue does not seem to even have been noticed. All voted routinely for bills labeled deregulatory, and none grasped, much less articulated, the pattern of result in Idaho.

There's a more practical matter than ideological blinders. "Congressmen spend their time getting elected today, not making policy that might rile contributors," Swisher says. "There's more turnover in the Politburo these days than in the U.S. House of Representatives." Federal balkaneering slowed as the Reagan wave faltered and key actors like Mark Fowler left government. The steady efforts of state regulators forced more pragmatism on the FCC, and the industry moderated as well. Swisher thinks the new administration will be more practical, and more humane, than Reagan's.

But the drift will not change significantly without new policy. Swisher says, "Only a new national policy can bring a working modern rail system back to Idaho. In telecommunications the facts are different, but the need's the same." In the vacuum, balkanization will be at work. "Financially and legally, it's an unstable system now," ODeen Redman says of Idaho telephony, but describing the transport network too. "It will be volatile for a long time. I don't know whether my little part will survive or not."

Swisher understands that technological trends hold potential to give rural people and communities options heretofore impossible. But, he insists, those options could easily flow only to the rural rich, bypassing the rest. Public regulation, or its lack, will have much to do with the outcome. Characteristically, Swisher widens the perspective further when trying to divine the future. Reagan deregulation is a part of a larger, deeper trend called balkanization. But an atomized West is a symptom itself of something larger. He suggests it with a few brush strokes and leaves you seeking purchase on his meaning: "Hundreds upon hundreds of thousands of the GTE-NW population, town or country, are cruising, like kids on the city couplet or a small town's Main Street. They jog. They watch and listen to cassettes and discs. They do not vote. They do not go to the meeting. They do not write in."

CHAPTER THIRTY-ONE

Building the Masau Trail

Betsy Marston

MANY CONSERVATIONISTS and archaeologists rejoiced in New Mexico in the fall of 1988 after President Reagan signed an appropriations bill that includes several million dollars to enhance the state's heritage. New Mexico and other southwestern states are in a race with time as the remains of ancient Indian civilizations are eliminated or threatened by looting, encroaching suburban sprawl, off-road vehicles, or neglect. Some people, however, had a vision of what the southwestern part of New Mexico could become. They saw cultural and interpretive centers that would draw tourists to the whole range of Native American history. Instead of a scattering of sites that bore little relationship to one another, they envisioned a coherent approach.

The National Park Service and Forest Service took active roles in promoting expansion of park facilities in the less well traveled part of the state. And thanks to federal money available in the fall of 1988, that cooperative effort will be called the Masau Trail, named for the Indian god Masau, who welcomed Indian people to earth from the underworld. According to legend, Masau's footprints were as long as a man's arm.

The Masau Trail will link Indian settlements through signs on major highways. Giant footprint signs will mark Pecos National Monument, Aztec Ruins,

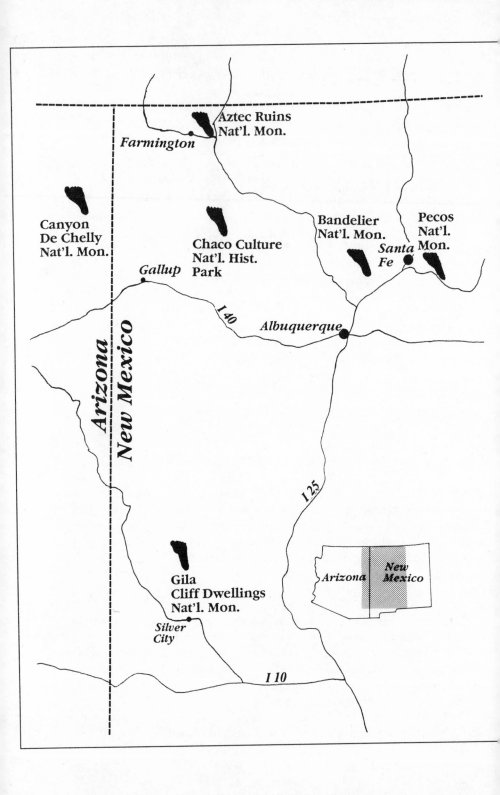

Gila Cliff Dwellings, El Morro, El Malpais—the nation's newest national monument—and other park service centers, including Canyon de Chelly in Arizona.

Jeff Bingaman, Democratic senator from New Mexico and sponsor of the Masau Trail bill, said the many projects just funded will begin to protect the natural, cultural, and historic heritage of the state. Bingaman, who was born in Silver City, New Mexico, in the southwestern half of the state, has introduced a half dozen bills that focus on everything from preserving Spanish colonial history to linking nineteenth-century forts in a "Boots and Saddles" tour. In the remote rural areas of New Mexico, Bingaman says he sees its economic future tied in large part to its past.

Another ardent supporter of the Masau Trail concept is Andrew Gulliford, director of the Western New Mexico University Museum at Silver City. The museum is in the heart of prehistoric Mimbres culture, which produced exquisite pottery that has been dug up and dispersed to museums and private collectors around the world. The appropriations bill just passed includes paying $150,000 for a park service study—recently completed—that recommends a national museum in the Silver City area. Gulliford says it is unfortunate that there is now no center for Mimbres study in the valley where the ceramics were produced. Although the museum he directs displays 80 of its 300 Mimbres pieces, it hasn't the funds to adequately study and research a culture that left beautiful pots but very little else telling us about its people. Gulliford adds, "While everyone is now paying attention to southwestern artifacts, they are not necessarily paying attention to the laws." Looting is a major threat, he points out, as Mimbres pots can command up to $30,000.

National Park Service Director William Penn Mott, Jr., has the final say on what kind of museum Silver City gets, which agencies will share in its administration, and when a center will be built. But for Senator Bingaman, Gulliford, and members of the county archaeological society, what's key is that the area which produced remarkable cultures such as the Mimbres will soon celebrate and house the best work the Mimbres produced.

The people of the Mimbres Valley in southwestern New Mexico disappeared about one thousand years ago. We call them the Mimbres people because *mimbres* is the Spanish word for the willows that shelter the river valley where they lived. They built pit houses and left no direct descendants, but they did leave a legacy of extraordinarily painted black-on-white pottery.

The Mimbrenos fashioned hemispherical bowls from coils of gray ware, then slipped the interiors with a fine, white kaolin clay. They painted designs on the inside surfaces with a black iron-ore paint, and used the bowls in daily life as well as in nearly every burial. Mimbres pots found in burial sites usually have a small hole broken in the bottom, suggesting that the Mimbrenos "killed" the

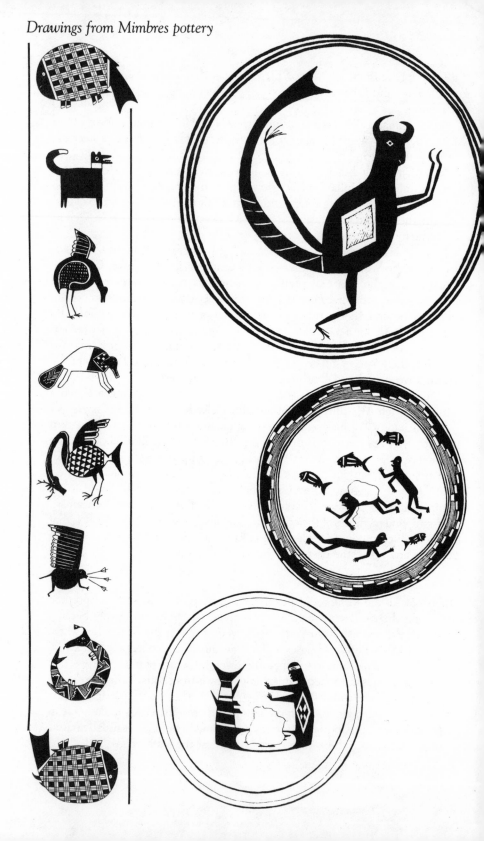

Drawings from Mimbres pottery

from *Mimbres Mythology* by Pat Carr

function of the vessel before placing it over the head of the deceased, perhaps so that the human spirit and the spirit of the bowl could be joined.

Sometime between A.D. 950 and 1150, Mimbres motifs evolved from geometric designs to images of fish, mammals, reptiles, birds, amphibians, insects, and humans. But their "picture pots" didn't stop with renditions of daily living and the surrounding natural world. The Mimbreno artists painted mythological heroes, strange fantastical creatures, and frivolous composite beings such as turkeys with skunk's feet, dragonlike animals with bird bodies, and humans with fishtails.

Mimbres pots give us a vivid picture of their life and culture. Author Pat Carr believes they tell us even more. In *Mimbres Mythology* (Texas Western Press) Carr links the myths and folklore of the Pueblo peoples of the Southwest with the stories appearing on Mimbres bowls. According to Carr, Mimbres story scenes reflect folktales told in nineteenth- and twentieth-century Zuni, Tusayan, Tewa, Hopi, and Navajo cultures, and represent a part of a continuous body of Pueblo literature.

Carr also tells us that the myths reflected in Mimbres pots give us an idea about their outlook on life. One observer called them "the laughing artists of the Mimbres Valley" because in their stories justice and goodness prevail.

Following are several Mimbres myths, taken from *Mimbres Mythology*.

In one tale, the Little War Twins fought the Cloud Swallower—an evil monster who lived high in the mountains and swallowed every passing cloud. The twins killed the monster and rescued rain.

Spider Woman, the grandmother of the Little War Twins, created human beings and taught Pueblo women how to weave. She could fit behind an ear and would whisper advice on love or gambling. The twins often caused trouble by not listening to Spider Woman's wisdom. Once they stole ceremonial rain-making objects and played games with them. Their grandmother asked them to stop, but they paid no attention, and a great flood resulted.

The underworld, a place of moral and social disintegration, was full of unfinished creatures with goggled eyes, webbed feet, and membranous ears. The people ascended into the second cave world, and then the third, and at each stop they found a brighter place.

While the wandering people searched for the center of the earth, they came upon a vast and swiftly flowing river. The waters terrified the children, who began to change into aquatic creatures. Their mothers were startled and dropped them into the raging waters. The children changed into fish and swam.

When the people finally emerged, Kokopelli, the humpbacked flute player, or locust in animal form, led them in their wanderings over the earth. Carrying his flute, or prayerstick, and with his hump full of precious seeds, he symbolized power and fertility. Again and again Kokopelli was tested on behalf of the people, and through these challenges gained the world for humankind.

The Little War Twins, the elder and the younger, also led the people in their wanderings. They made the mountains, rocks, and canyons. Stories tell that while searching for their father, the sun, they encountered many tests and trials.

CHAPTER THIRTY-TWO

Working Toward a Rural Future

Jon Christensen

LIGHTNING FROM a late-afternoon thunderstorm flashed on the white adobe walls of the old trading post in Los Ojos, New Mexico, as three weary sheep traders settled accounts after a successful auction. The room smelled of rain, wet earth, and wool.

Lyle McNeal, a breeding specialist from Utah State University, was on his way into the downpour, bundled in a damp corduroy rancher's jacket, with a gray Stetson pulled over his head. He dawdled and joked with Antonio Manzanares and Maria Varela, who run the livestock growers' cooperative in Tierra Amarilla, a valley of rich green pastures surrounded by mountains. The friendly banter settled on *The Milagro Beanfield War* and the movie's portrayal of life in northern New Mexico.

If anyone wants to find the real action, "this is it right here," McNeal joked. "Joe Mondragon and Ruby Archuleta. Right here in this room." Manzanares and Varela shook their heads and smiled. The latest sale was one of their best ever. They had just moved 110 head of specialty sheep—churro, cormo, and karakul—at a better price than they had averaged before. They were tired but seemed pleased to humor McNeal, whose help in reinvigorating their breeding stock had been essential to their success.

McNeal's comparison of Manzanares and Varela with the characters of *Milagro* was on target. Maria Varela is a dynamo, fortyish, usually dressed in jeans and a sweatshirt, and always on top of the action. Antonio Manzanares, a handsome 36-year-old, stands square-shouldered, his hands in the pockets of a well-worn jeans jacket. Together, the two have brought new hope to this depressed valley—but not through anything as dramatic as diverting water from a resort or standing off developers with shotguns.

Tierra Amarilla has had its share of battles between traditional Hispanic residents and Anglo newcomers. Much of the surrounding territory was part of a 600,000-acre land grant given to the first settlers of the region by Spain and Mexico. But in 1860 Congress turned the Tierra Amarilla community land grant into a private holding, and, soon after, the land was sold to a wealthy Santa Fe land baron. Ever since, descendants of the original settlers have been fighting to regain land they believe was stolen from them.

Throughout the last century, Spanish-American vigilantes torched the haystacks of Anglo ranchers who bought land within the Tierra Amarilla grant. In the late 1960s land-grant activists led by the charismatic Reis Tijerina stormed the county courthouse in a hail of bullets to protest the lack of action on their ancient claims. Today on a hill above town, another group of land-grant claimants is holding out against developers in a shepherd's camp bristling with weapons, surrounded by signs reading *tierra o muerte*, land or death.

Ganados del Valle, a nonprofit organization in its sixth year, has taken another path. It has worked to revitalize a tradition of weaving that nearly passed away during the last generation. A restored century-old trading post in the quiet village of Los Ojos serves as headquarters for the organization and as a workshop and store for Tierra Wools, a weavers' cooperative. In a back room four young women shuttle yarn and trade stories across handmade looms, while another spins a fine white wool. In the showroom out front, bold designs of the Rio Grande weaving tradition show on rugs, ponchos, jackets, and shawls. Under one roof, Ganados del Valle unites this region's traditional Hispanic culture with competitive, hard-nosed business sense and an entrepreneurial awareness of specialty market niches.

Maria Varela first came to Tierra Amarilla to work for the land-grant movement in the late 1960s. Back then, she took direction from a council of village elders set up to reestablish traditional decision making in the erstwhile land grant. "We had a romanticized view of an old form of cooperation," she said. "And they had all kinds of ideas about what they wanted . . . to grow potatoes, raise pigs, get their garbage collected, pave the highways, and start a medical clinic." The group decided to start with a potato farm, but the idea didn't work. "The decision was more symbolic than economic," Varela said.

After failing at a number of agricultural ventures, including raising hogs and cattle, Varela helped raise money to start a community medical clinic. Two months after it opened, the center was firebombed. "Somebody was scared the land-grant movement would get a toehold through the clinic," Varela said. The attack galvanized the community and Varela. Although she knew little about running a business, let alone a rural medical center, Varela agreed to stay on and manage the clinic. She learned about business on the job. She also slowly learned to diagnose the community.

Rio Arriba County has always suffered high seasonal unemployment. Young

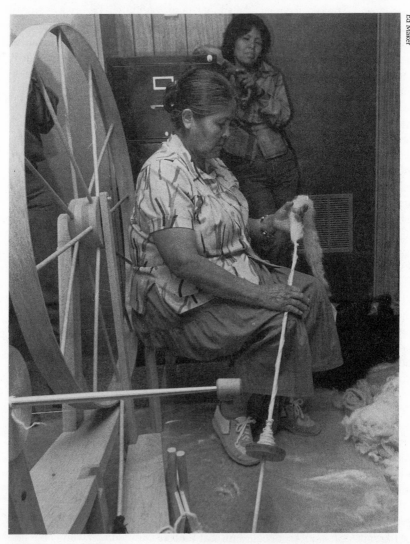

Navajo weaver Nellie Pino

people follow a simple, mean rule: grow up and get out. Varela saw Tierra Amarilla becoming a community of old men and women. "I saw the culture going through stress as more and more pastures were emptied of livestock," she said. When Varela consulted with state government officials about the potential for economic development, she said their attitude was to "write it off, or put in a ski resort." Conventional wisdom said Tierra Amarilla was in the wrong location—72 miles from a bus run, 100 miles from freight lines, and 160 miles from the nearest airport—for anything but recreational development.

In fact, the area had already been proposed for recreational development. Nearby Heron Lake and El Vado Reservoir, created when the Rio Chama was dammed, were popular with anglers and campers. Summer homes for professionals in Santa Fe and Albuquerque began to dot the valley. Developers sought to build a ski resort in the dramatic 2,000-foot cliffs of the Brazos Mountains east of town. With new development, Varela said, residents worried that land prices would rise, that agricultural water rights would be usurped, and that local people would be stuck with the minimum-wage jobs of a tourist economy.

Around that time Varela accepted a scholarship at Amherst in Massachusetts to study for a master's degree in rural development and economic planning. "Getting out of the valley, reading, and talking to other people really helped me," Varela said. "I began to look at economic development, agriculture, and culture as really tied together," she said. "I discovered that sometimes the best new ideas are old ideas. This is a livestock-based community," she explained. "That's not just a romantic ideal; it's a deeply rooted culture that provides much more than just subsistence."

Varela began discussing her ideas with Antonio Manzanares, one of the few young men continuing to raise sheep for a living in Tierra Amarilla. He told her that plenty of things could be done to improve the local livestock economy, ranging from pooling flocks for summer grazing to finding better markets and a higher price. First, they had to break through the isolation that kept local prices ten to fifteen cents per pound lower than the average. They found a company that held auctions by phone and that could sell their sheep for top dollar whenever local growers could pool flocks to make the 400-head minimum.

After a couple of years of growing cooperation among local growers and improving sales, "people started asking us when we were going to start an organization," Varela said. "Then we knew it was time to formalize it." Ganados del Valle was set up as a cooperative, with a vote for every member, under the auspices of a non-profit organization that seeks funding to provide training and advice for both the husbandry and weaving projects.

Ganados del Valle has since become one of the top five employers in Rio Arriba County. More than thirty local families have used the organization's livestock-shares program, revolving loans, and cooperative grazing and marketing efforts to increase their flocks. Sixteen local women have been trained in traditional Rio Grande weaving techniques. Working full-time, they can bring home a decent income, Varela said, producing and selling their wares through Tierra Wools. The Los Ojos trading post is now a popular stop for tourists traveling through Tierra Amarilla to the lakes and the scenic narrow-gauge railroad out of nearby Chama.

The hostilities between local residents and outsiders still surface. Investors are once again promoting the Brazos Mountains ski resort. Local residents have fought all the way to the state Supreme Court a developer's plans to divert water from agriculture to his project. And on a hill overlooking town, a local family and a group of heavily armed land-grant activists refuse to leave land owned by an investment company. The company wants to sell the property for vacation homes and condominiums.

"It's nothing new," said Manzanares. "It's still the same struggle that has been going on here in my lifetime and way before then. But now it's more defined. It used to be just defined as a land struggle, Anglos versus Spanish-Americans. Now we're feeling more development pressures on land and water. Now it's a lot of other things. We're trying to build an economic base using our own natural resources," said Manzanares. "It's not unlike the struggle those guys are having up on the hill, just on another front."

Varela said she saw the need for people with different approaches to preserving land and water rights to work together. "First there are the people who mobilize around petitions against diverting water from agriculture. Then there are the people on the hill who have decided no one will push them off the land. The role of Ganados amidst all of this crisis reaction," she said, "is to make our land and water productive. We have to do something productive, or the kids will continue to leave this community. It's the popular thing now to stand up to developers," Varela said. "But you can't just stand up to the developers and say, 'No, no, no!' You have to say, 'This is what we want. This is what we're going to do. So get out of the way.' "

CHAPTER THIRTY-THREE

Letters from Home

High Country News Readers

BECAUSE WRITING about a region and its people requires at least psychological distance, observers and commentators must always separate themselves from their subjects. So, although *High Country News* and most of its writers are physically located in the rural West, it is no exaggeration to say that this book is not written from home, but is a communication sent home. It is observation and analysis by people who have chosen to pull back and, at least during the act of writing, look at the West the way a surgeon looks at a belly before making the incision.

The challenge for writers is, of course, to achieve the proper distance. If they pull back too far, they produce bloodless analysis. If they stay too close, their work will lack the perspective needed to reflect the region and its situation.

Judging by the mail from "back home" the newspaper version of this series received, most of the essays and articles struck a more or less appropriate balance between distance and closeness. There is not enough space to print all of the letters the issues provoked. But we thought it important to print the following representative sample.

The letters challenge and amplify facts, but for the most part they are concerned with the attitudes of several articles toward ranching and agriculture. The Poppers' article, which forecasts the continued decline of life on the Plains, and Tom Wolf's attack on Wyoming ranching attracted the most emotional replies. But Raymond Wheeler's articles on Utah's desert and canyon country also caught their share of fire.

In Response to Raymond Wheeler's Four-Part Series

Dear *HCN*,

I greatly enjoyed the first of your series "Reopening of the New West" and am looking forward to the rest of the series. I have a comment to make about your introductory piece about the rural West being an artifact of the 1800s, and a correction to offer concerning statements made about me in Ray Wheeler's article.

First, while I thoroughly agree with your analysis, living as I do in the heart of rural southeastern Utah, I somehow can't share your conclusion that the situation is now changing, and rapidly. Although the mineral industry, one-third of the ruling triumvirate, is now in a temporary slump, the other two triad members—grazing and logging interests—are still firmly in the saddle. They control this state's political structure, and its federal land administration agencies, with an iron fist.

While those who would like to bring about change are here in the little town of Moab in considerable numbers, and are presently making a lot of noise decrying the old ways of seeing and doing things, they are far from gaining control of the social-political infrastructure that has dominated Moab and Grand County since 1877, when the town of Moab was first established.

I have carefully watched this aspect of the community for more than two decades, hoping to see signs of change for the better, but to date the key local indicators—the composition of the Grand and San Juan county commissions—have not changed a bit. While commissioners have changed, from individuals who are functionally illiterate to others who are shrewd as foxes, they all sing the same old tune of redneck violence. Yet without this basic change there will be no "reopening" of southeastern Utah.

Right now an election is coming up, but the only hope for replacing, for example, Grand County Commissioner Jimmie Walker, is Merve Lawton, a man who has been active in mining all his life. In San Juan County, of course, the situation is hopeless. It will thus probably take at least one more Grand County election to make any fundamental change of direction in Moab, even though this region could, should, and must convert firmly to a generally conservationist philosophy, with tourism, recreation, and retirement as its economic base.

I discussed this situation in considerable detail in the original text for my

1986 book, *Utah Canyon Country*, but most of what I wrote was edited out by the book's publisher.

My second comment is about the part ascribed to me in Ray Wheeler's article. The article's background is basically correct, but I did not, as Wheeler said, promise those threatening me and my family that I would "never speak out again." I did not communicate with those violence-prone people directly in any way. What actually happened is this: Immediately after the first phone call threatening to blow my home and family to shreds, I alerted several federal agencies, including the Bureau of Alcohol, Tobacco and Firearms (BATF), which has jurisdiction over the licensing of explosives. This led to a BATF investigation that quickly brought the then-common "recreational" use of mining explosives within and around Moab to a screaming halt. No more evening "fun" blasts that rattled every window in town. No more blown-up phone booths.

After my phone tap caught two Atlas Minerals people red-handed, I agreed with the county attorney not to press charges for the federal crime of making telephone threats if he would take action to get Atlas Minerals to stop instigating violence. Between the phone-tap catches and whatever the county attorney said to Atlas, things calmed down after another drunken, threatening phone call or two with bar noises in the background, although I was still given police protection for several days.

Thus, while I made no overt promises to anyone, there was a form of tacit agreement between myself and the county attorney that I would henceforth cease effectively to have full U.S. citizen rights—no freedom of speech, no political rights, no environmental activism, no right to make citizen comments on federal draft environmental impact statements, no say whatsoever in the political-social affairs of the town, county, and state in which I resided.

This situation still applies, and those who really run this town and county have subtly but emphatically made it clear to me that the edict is still in force. While elsewhere I am well known as an author, with some fifteen books and a host of other publications about southeastern Utah to my credit, effectively I am still a nonperson in Moab. I truly know the feelings of the "outsiders" you described so graphically in your article. I have lived with them daily for the last ten years.

Of course, there is some chance that this letter, if published, will bring on more threats, but I thought perhaps your readers should know the truth about my longstanding situation, and that little has really changed in the southeastern Utah sector of the Old West. The "New West" isn't here yet, and isn't even in sight.

F. A. Barnes
Moab, Utah

Dear *HCN*,

I have just completed reading "War on the Colorado Plateau" by Raymond Wheeler. If the entire article is as libelous and untrue as what Janet Ross supposedly told Mr. Wheeler, then your publication is the epitome of "yellow journalism."

At the BLM meeting referred to, I did say that those were the things the people were saying in their anger and frustration at what Gene Day and others were doing. I did tell Congressman McKay and the governor the same thing and said that if the bureaucrats did not give more consideration to the rights of the local people, I feared that talk might turn into action.

Another inaccuracy is that I own five thousand acres of mining claims in the heart of the unit. The mining claims that I own in that area were completely outside of the original WSA. Later it was completely dropped, and only about two years ago it was put back into consideration, and the area where my mining claims are were added on the fringe, not in the middle.

Another interesting part of Mr. Wheeler's article is his reference to Mr. Dave Foreman lobbying for The Wilderness Society. Mr. Foreman is the author of a book on how to sabotage grazing, mining, timbering, road construction, and other equipment and activities. He is also a leader in Earth First!, the extreme environmental group that does advocate and commit vandalism, destruction, and terrorism. It is interesting why Mr. Wheeler makes no reference to that. I'm sure it is too much to expect an accurate and fair article from your publication or your authors.

> Calvin Black, Chairman
> San Juan County Commission
> Monticello, Utah

Raymond Wheeler replies:

When I wrote that Cal Black owned mining claims "in the heart of the unit," I was referring not to the final Mancos Mesa Wilderness Study Area (WSA), but to the original Mancos Mesa "wilderness inventory unit," as depicted on BLM's Utah wilderness inventory map of April 1979. Black's mining claims lie at the head of Moqui Canyon, deep in the heart of that 115,000-acre unit.

At each stage of the inventory, BLM reduced the size of the original Mancos inventory unit by further constricting its boundaries. Yet in late 1979, when Commissioner Black ordered a San Juan County road crew to destroy a BLM barrier blocking vehicular access to Mancos Mesa, some two-thirds of his 5,000 acres of mining claims remained inside the wilderness inventory unit as it was then defined. BLM did later cut the entire Mancos inventory unit from wilderness study. Only after that decision was overturned by the Interior Board of Land Appeals did the agency finally establish a 51,440-acre Mancos

Mesa WSA. The new WSA boundary neatly excluded at least 80 percent of
Black's mining claims. Coincidence? Perhaps.

Commissioner Black suggests that his statements in an April 12, 1979,
meeting with BLM staff were not threatening in nature. If so, the public record
of that meeting, on file at the BLM office in Moab, is misleading.

A BLM staff report from Janet Ross reads in part: "Calvin Black, County
Commissioner, was the chief instigator of negative and occasionally violent
feeling toward BLM in general, as well as its staff. . . . He said, 'We've had
enough of you guys telling us what to do. I'm not a violent man, but I'm getting
to the point where I'll blow up bridges, ruins, and vehicles. We're going to start
a revolution. We're going to get back our lands. We're going to sabotage your
vehicles. You had better start going out in two's and three's because we're going
to take care of you BLMers.' BLM wilderness inventory team leader Paul
Happel said, 'Mr. Black, I hope you are not threatening me?' Cal said, 'I'm not
threatening you. I'm promising you.' "

Dear HCN,

In his article "Stroke and Counterstroke," Raymond Wheeler charges that
the Utah Wilderness Association (UWA) is too accommodating to nonwilder-
ness parties and as a result is ineffective. I believe this is a wrong appraisal of
the UWA's role in wilderness preservation in Utah. The UWA has been in
existence for ten years, and for roughly the first five years was nearly alone in its
defense of Utah wilderness. During those early years it was the UWA's dogged
groundwork that brought the Utah Forest Service wilderness bill to passage.
This was a remarkable achievement in a state which, at that time, had
probably the most antiwilderness political climate of any state in the nation.
The UWA did it with a grassroots organization that simply overwhelmed
political opposition.

The UWA was the first organization to come up with a detailed, researched,
and defensible proposal for wilderness for BLM lands. The UWA challenged
the Bureau of Land Management's pronouncement on Wilderness Study
Areas. Through an appeal, the UWA forced the BLM to reinstate 800,000
acres of BLM lands back in the WSA column. The UWA document for this
appeal had over one thousand pages. This appeal was successful because of the
detailed, on-site study that the UWA had done at each and every WSA. No
other organization could have won that appeal because no other organization
knew the land like the UWA did.

The north slope of the Uinta Mountains, in northern Utah, is now under
attack by industrial interests. The UWA is alone in its defense of these
beautiful lands. The UWA has been successful in stopping or moderating a
number of timber sales, and is leading efforts to stop encroachment of oil wells
and roads into unroaded areas on the north slope.

On grazing issues, through the UWA's quiet lobbying, the Forest Service has retired several livestock grazing allotments in the High Uinta Wilderness Area. I visited one of those areas last summer and, with the absence of domestic sheep, it was brimming with elk and moose. The UWA documents grazing mismanagement in the Uintas and elsewhere in Utah and steadily lobbies the Forest Service and BLM decision makers to reduce the damage caused by grazing.

The essence of the UWA's approach to wilderness preservation is communication and education. The UWA has good relations with political, BLM, and Forest Service people throughout the state. On many issues the UWA goes straight to the decision makers for a hearing. They can do this because they already know these people personally and have a working relationship with them. This personal communication is a key reason for the UWA's successful lobbying efforts. In education, the UWA regularly makes presentations to civic and business groups. This gets the pro-wilderness message out to influential people who would otherwise not hear it. Through its education efforts the UWA has helped bring about the dramatic growth in public support for Wilderness in Utah.

I am a member of the UWA, Sierra Club, The Wilderness Society, and the Audubon Society. I have lived in Utah for thirteen years and during that time have followed the local conservation scene. I believe that for the local Utah scene the UWA is the most effective organization for the preservation of wilderness.

Roger W. Arhart
Salt Lake City, Utah

In Response to "Discouraging Words in Montana" and "The Fate of the Plains"

Dear *HCN*,

First, I would like to say that the last two years here in eastern Montana have been very profitable for my father and me. As a young cattle rancher with only ten years' experience, I've found that big profits the last two years have been a welcome change.

The articles I wish to comment on are "Discouraging Words in Montana" and "The Fate of the Plains." The feeling I was left with after reading these two features was of total despair in the region and certain depopulation and desertification. I felt empty until I opened my account books and noticed the ample profits I have worked hard for over the last few years, and then I stepped out on my porch and viewed a landscape with grass and trees that are still alive after a record drought.

In "Discouraging Words in Montana," only one man who built a business was interviewed, Nibs Allen, and he knows it can still be done. The main reason for peoples' troubles in the Plains is artificially high land prices caused by environmentally unsound, expensive government subsidy programs and tax laws. Another trend mentioned was absentee corporate ownership of the plains. This trend is changing and would never have happened had it not been for extremely lucrative tax shelters for the wealthy that have recently been changed. Just this year three very large corporate farms in this region have been sold—all to local young people and neighbors for reasonable prices. Depopulation is more related to advances in communication and quicker, easier travel than to any other factor. The Plains' successes are best characterized by Nibs Allen, "Those people who tend to business and manage well will do well."

In "The Fate of the Plains," extremely one-sided views appear with people proposing drastic solutions, but not one of these people's area of knowledge is in biology, soil, or range sciences. This article mistakenly assumes that all of the Great Plains region is in terrible environmental condition and that desertification is eminent.

At a Range Research Symposium conducted at Fort Keogh Experiment Station in Miles City, Montana, a panel of professors and researchers issued a statement in the published summary that read, "In spite of local problem areas where range conditions are not what they should be, rangelands in North America are in the best condition they have been in 100 years." So while range condition is not in the pristine state it once was, most areas of range are slowly recovering. The knowledge and scientific know-how are now available to rejuvenate the Plains and leave agriculture and other users somewhat changed but still in place. Changes must be made, but make them with knowledge, not emotions.

In this article you mention two people who have grand plans for the Plains, but they know very little about the original ecosystems that flourished in the Plains, outside of a few vague generalizations. I am speaking of Robert Scott, whom I have met, and Bret Wallach, whom I have not. Only about one rancher in ten in eastern Montana is in financial trouble, which is not much different from the rate of failures for small businesses.

The farming of the Plains is about half a disaster. If the highly erodible half was put back to grass the way it belonged, many of the erosion problems would be over and the other half would be profitable. Much of the land damage to northern Plains lands was done directly in response to government crop subsidies by sodbusting land speculators hoping to capitalize on subsidy-based, inflated land values. The 1985 Farm Bill went a long way toward correcting this problem with its Conservation Reserve Program, sodbusting and swampbusting programs, and payment limitations.

In closing, the situation is tough, but not nearly so bad or irreversible as these articles portray it. Our secret to survival has been frugality and conservation, not the least of which has been a very good rest rotation grazing system.

When the land finally gets cheap enough (as it is now) that young people can make a business work, I hope the federal government doesn't bid up the price so high that they can't get into business. The Plains can be a beautiful, profitable place to live as long as we listen to the people with the knowledge and facts and not the utopic pipe dreams based on fanciful generalizations of people with no scientific background and who make their homes very far from here!

Let the Plains region develop on its own and don't try to blend it to fit any grandiose schemes, and the results will create much less hardship and much less expense to all parties involved.

> Lon R. Reukauf
> President
> Prairie County
> Range Committee
> Terry, Montana

Dear *HCN*,

We were struck by several points in Lon Reukauf's letter about our article "The Fate of the Plains." He criticizes us and two authorities we cited—Robert Scott and Bret Wallach—for excessive pessimism about the future of the Great Plains. At the same time, he admits that Plains farming "is about half a disaster," which is essentially our argument. That is, we turn out to agree.

We also agree with Mr. Reukauf that the Agriculture Department's Conservation Reserve program could help restore much of the Plains grasslands, although it would be useful if the proviso that the reserve can cover no more than a quarter of any one county were lifted. The Reserve and Buffalo Commons we proposed may, in fact, converge over time.

Yet Mr. Reukauf also argues that the only relevant professional background for studying or dealing with the Plains are "biology, soil, or range sciences," as conducted by people who live in the Plains. We believe that this approach is somewhat parochial. It slights the contributions of such fields as history, economics, climatology, and mining, among many others. Moreover, Mr. Reukauf's approach would disqualify the contributions of past giants such as John Wesley Powell (who lived mostly in Washington, D.C.), Hugh Hammond Bennett (Washington and North Carolina), Walter Prescott Webb (Texas), or Frederick Jackson Turner (Wisconsin and Massachusetts). An impractical standard.

We admire the flinty Plains independence and the hard-headed Plains civic-mindedness of Mr. Reukauf's letter. He is clearly a person who will survive under nearly any Plains conditions and thrive under most. But we still think that the region is in deep trouble, as is the bulk of its rural population. Dismissing all but a few back-grounds and anyone who lives elsewhere is not the answer.

Deborah Epstein Popper
Frank J. Popper
Rutgers University
New Brunswick, New Jersey

In Response to " 'Wyoming' Is Dead—Long Live 'Wyoming' "

Dear *HCN*,

Reading Tom Wolf's piece the first time through left me confused. I thought that I'd missed the point. The second reading clarified things. I came away mad. If Tom's intention was to bring out some higher truth about the romantic vision of the West in his critique of Gretel Ehrlich's book, he failed, at least for this reader. He lost me in literary illusions (*not* allusions). The piece was masterfully obfuscatory, full of splendidly written mist. He said that he simply wanted to hold Ehrlich to a higher standard of truth about "Wyoming" (the ranching West) than what he saw in her book, *The Solace of Open Spaces*. The substance of his critique seems to be that Ehrlich's Wyoming is a romantic and pastoral place, far removed from the "rape and rapaciousness" that he implies characterizes the ranching industry and therefore the state of mind that is Wyoming. He says, "Ehrlich accepts a rapacious, brutally exploitative extractive industry [ranching] in terms of its own self-serving myth. Wyoming's caste system is based on the social pretensions and political realities of cowboy mythology, as is made chillingly clear to anyone who . . . attempts to question them. It is one thing to pull on your Tony Lamas in the morning; it is another to feel a cowboy boot crash in your face."

Excuse me? "Rapacious, brutally exploitative extractive industry"? "Caste system"? Tom, is the only good rancher a dead rancher? Wyoming (the state) is my home, but I've been away for a while. Perhaps all of the ranchers and ranch hands (yes, Tom, women can be ranch hands) that I knew who tried hard to be good stewards to their land have passed on to the hell Tom seems to think that they so richly deserve. Or maybe I was just co-opted by "official Wyoming" like Gretel.

I liked *The Solace of Open Spaces*, but I saw it only as one woman's view of the ranching West, not the be-all and end-all truth. I think that ranching can be a good and honorable way of life too, unlike Tom.

What was most upsetting about the piece, though, was that Tom claimed to be a champion of "women and nature," who he says are the downtrodden and abused victims of the ranching industry. Yet he succeeded in trashing Ehrlich, whom he portrays as a mindless romantic (albeit he grants that she is "hands down the best writer Wyoming has ever seen") co-opted by the rapacious ranching industry to write a simplistic pastoral view of Wyoming.

So what is going on here? The most charitable reason I can imagine for Tom's incredibly violent and angry critique is that he was carried away by the power of literary criticism. The least charitable isn't worth mentioning. After all of the women- and "Wyoming"-bashing, does Tom at least offer some corrective vision? I'll let you hear it from Tom's words: "I dream of a newly imagined Wyoming, where the female and nature achieve literary enfranchisement as a truly androgynous corrective to Ehrlich's all-too-traditionally-male cowboy." Say what, Tom?

Susan J. Tweit
Arnes, Iowa

Dear HCN,

Having myself just finished a critique of Gretel Ehrlich's work for another journal, I was surprised and pleased to read Tom Wolf's more thorough, thoughtful, and eloquently expressed " 'Wyoming' Is Dead—Long Live 'Wyoming.' " Wolf's article unveils the true consequence of cowboy mythology faster and better than any I can remember. Gretel Ehrlich may be Wyoming's best writer, but writing from the perspective of her chosen ranching reality, she does more harm than good to the real West. This West is far more important than a dramatic setting for the cowboy lifestyle.

How long can we blindly clutch to cowboy mythology while the real cowboy clutches the throat of the rural West? Please consider Tom Wolf's words again: "Perhaps we need not let the endlessly celebrated, endlessly lamented death of 'ranching as a way of life' deceive us into missing the real death. It is the healthy, natural ecosystems in Wyoming that are dying." Do we care?

Lynn Jacobs
Tucson, Arizona

Dear HCN,

I was very disturbed by the article you ran called " 'Wyoming' Is Dead—Long Live 'Wyoming.' " I am sorry Tom wrote it. He's capable of better. I am sorry you printed it. Your standards should be higher. During about half the article I couldn't understand what he was trying to say, and the other half made me mad. As a person who appreciates clear and straightforward language, I was confused. As a person who loves Wyoming and our agricultural heritage, I was angry. As a member of the High Country News Board of Directors, with my name on your masthead, I was ashamed.

I have read The Solace of Open Spaces, the book about which Tom says he was writing. I felt that sometimes Gretel Ehrlich let her creative use of language and her romanticism get the best of her. In reacting, I'm afraid Tom let his anger (I'm not exactly sure at what) get the best of him. In order to retain my high regard for your editorial judgment, I must conclude that you were really hard up to find some words to fill your extra pages. Next time you are that hard up, I know I can do better for you.

Lynn Dickey
Sheridan, Wyoming

Dear *HCN,*

How regrettable that you selected Tom Wolf to review Gretel Ehrlich's fine book, *The Solace of Open Spaces* (or did he volunteer?). Wolf demonstrates, and has previously proven in other writing, that he is embittered against Wyoming, particularly Wyoming ranchers. Wolf's reviewing a book about Wyoming is like Custer's reviewing a book about Indians.

Wolf's perception of Wyoming and its people is obviously very different from Ehrlich's. Ehrlich says she came to Wyoming seeking solace, to discover her inner self; she found resurrection. Wolf, in a piece in *Northern Lights* [a magazine based in Missoula, Montana], says he came to Wyoming to save it, to educate the natives in the provinces into seeing the "true" light; he was apparently chewed up and spit out, but lives to seek revenge. Considering their different missions, it is no wonder they saw Wyoming from different viewpoints, but Wolf's criticism of Ehrlich's book seems to stem not from the book itself, but from Wolf's previously drawn conclusion that the only good Wyoming rancher is a dead one.

Nancy Curtis
Glendo, Wyoming

Dear *HCN,*

I appreciated Tom Wolf's thoughtful critique of Gretel Ehrlich's *The Solace of Open Spaces.* I read the book when it came out; I loved it. Here, finally, was someone who described my home as it really was. Later, I reread sections and was surprised by the pasteboard quality of Ehrlich's human characterizations. The West seems to inspire creation and recreation of a "noble savage" myth, trotting out—by God—the Virginian as the type for Wyoming men.

Sensitive and silent, "The Wyomingan" doesn't need words to express himself—they would only hamper his sensitivity. And this characterization of Ehrlich's is too dangerous to Westerners to let it stand without challenge. She would have us believe that those of us whose vocabulary is limited are necessarily more tender or sensitive than those of us who have an adequate supply of words with which to express ourselves.

I have never seen this increased sensitivity coming from a stunted vocabulary in the people of my home state (or elsewhere in the West), but I have often seen its reverse, the Billy Budd Syndrome: people who lack the words to say how they feel will resort to violence to demonstrate those feelings. To her credit, Ehrlich does recognize the violence, but she chooses to romanticize it as did Oscar Wilde:

Yet each man kills the thing he loves,
By each let this be heard . . .
The coward does it with a kiss,
The brave man with a sword!

And when enough brave men have killed enough beloveds, they're bound to find out that nothing is left. Wyoming is dead, killed not by a sword, but by a second-rate literary device.

As long as outsiders can sell us a romance that passes but poorly for our true lives, we will continue to think ourselves tender when we savage someone with a funny-color hat. I'm disappointed that Ehrlich chose to stereotype her characters so thoroughly, but I'm most disappointed that her "Wyomingan," a mere literary construct, could strike such a responsive chord in people I've always valued for knowing themselves better than that.

Nancy Banks
Hyde Park, Utah

In Response to "Butte Remains a Center of Infection"

Dear *HCN*,

I would like to point out one grievous error in Don Moniak's article on Butte. He mentions twice in the article that little or nothing is being done in Butte about reclamation, cleanup, and eradication of noxious weeds. My group, Northside Neighborhood Association, and several other groups in Butte have been actively involved in Butte's cleanup campaign since the spring of 1985. I have approximately two thousand hours as a volunteer invested in cleanup, organization, and education of the populace on the subject. I am surprised that Mr. Moniak did not learn of our efforts since we have been involved and sometimes financed by Butte–Silver Bow, State of Montana, and Headwaters Resource, Conservation and Development Office.

Obviously, Mr. Moniak had a particular slant in mind for his story on bad-mouthing Butte. Investigating any further than he did would have put quite a hole in his story idea. There is an old journalism saying, "God help the dog who chews on the bone before he pulls it all the way out of the ground." So, since Mr. Moniak has pulled up a live bone, as it were, I would appreciate a retraction on this particular part of his story, or, better yet, another story.

Nancy Foote
Butte, Montana

In Response to "Mining's Diminished Future"

Dear *HCN*,

I was a little surprised to read about "mining's diminished future," wherein John Leshy asserts that "the golden age of Western mining has passed." Apparently Leshy is unaware of the current gold-mining boom in the basin-and-range region of Nevada and Utah.

Disseminated gold deposits are being found in virtually every range in the region, and open-pit mining is proceeding full-steam ahead. I won't belabor this note with details (Leshy can contact any chamber of commerce in Nevada if he wants to know particulars), but mining interests once more run the show in this region, and "whether the Mining Law of 1872 is formally jettisoned" would *indeed* make a great deal of difference.

I got the impression that Leshy thinks the West comprises the ski-retirement resorts of the Rockies, where vein-type deposits were exhausted and replaced with recreation industries. Please inform him that there is a lot of beautiful land west of the divide that is still threatened by mining interests and unprotected by fashionable environmentalists.

D. Madigan
Elko, Nevada

John Leshy replies:

My observations were aimed at the West as a region, not particular parts of it. I am aware of the gold-mining boom in the basin and range. Nevertheless, it seems to me the big picture is as I have painted it; mining interests generally have a much tougher time than they used to in finding acceptance for their enterprises.

As for the point that jettisoning the Mining Law would "*indeed* make a great deal of difference" to gold mining in Nevada, if gold were subject to a discretionary leasing system, perhaps mining might not occur on such a scale (at least the mining companies would pay rentals and royalties to the federal treasury). But oil, gas, coal, and a number of other minerals have been subject to such a system for nearly seven decades, and I can't recall many instances where lease requests have been refused.

I'm not saying the legal system is irrelevant to mining, but it's not all powerful either.

John D. Leshy
Professor of Law
Arizona State University
Tempe, Arizona

And Kudos

Dear *HCN*,

In 1975 we moved to Halfway, Oregon, following the lead of Tom Bell, who had founded *High Country News* in 1970. Tom and I were elected to the local school board about 1977. We were elected because the voters and the teachers couldn't get the "good old boys" to listen. Three of us then tried to hire a disciple of Dr. William Glasser as high school principal. The superintendent wanted to hire a football coach who'd gone to school nearby and who had the "eastern Oregon philosophy." Our candidate had a beard and was from Los Angeles. Looking back, I'm astounded at my naïveté. It is probably a blessing that our candidate was voted down four to three. The community would have chewed him up in a year.

Your description of the schools in the small-town West was so similar to our experience that I thought Tom had told you about it. This is my way of congratulating you on the current series. It is seldom that a publisher will speak the truth about the culture of the Rocky Mountains.

> Dave Olson
> Portland, Oregon

Dear *HCN*,

I just wanted you to know that I'm devouring your current series on the Rocky Mountain West. Ed Marston's articles in the two should be required reading for anyone considering moving here. I've copied them for wider readership and to hold on file because many people are curious about our lifestyle here.

We moved here twelve happy years ago. But we have our own resources, in terms of money, friends, and work. And the Big Surprises were the power of the religious right, and the militant attitude of the "Four-Wheel Drivers, Miners, and Polluters," which you have touched on very neatly. In fact, I can't think of anything you left out.

I was at the Colorado Environmental Coalition meeting here, and met a Boulder psychiatrist who wanted to know what Buena Vista was like to live in. I spent several minutes trying to characterize it, and all I needed were copies of your articles.

> Barbara Whipple
> Buena Vista, Colorado

Afterword

Ed Marston

Reopening the Western Frontier originally appeared in four newspaper issues published over two months. While the series had been planned and developed for a year and much of the material was in hand before the first issue was printed, it is also true that significant holes remained. The issues took shape really in the days before going to press, and it was not until the series was complete that I could look back and see what it was that the editing and writing had brought us.

One discovery came shortly after I'd sent the final issue to the printer. I was the keynote speaker at the third annual meeting of the Southern Utah Wilderness Alliance (SUWA) outside of Moab, Utah, at Ken and Jane Sleight's Pack Creek Ranch. Had I been invited to talk at SUWA's second annual meeting instead of its third, I would probably have given some variation on my "The Land Is Empty" talk, which emphasized the vastness of the region, the concentration of most people into a few metropolitan areas, and the opportunity for conservation presented by land unencumbered by people. But I discovered in the course of the talk to SUWA on that beautiful fall day that the experience of editing the four special issues had changed me. It had convinced me that the fate of the West's lands lies largely in the hands of its thousands of small communities.

The cultures of those small towns, I told the SUWA gathering, are still dominated by an extractive way of life. They remain in the grip of habits and lifestyles and beliefs laid down by one hundred years of mining, milling, and logging. The culture formed by a century of extraction does not highly value education, lacks a middle class and therefore a citizen reform movement, and is willing to sacrifice land and wildlife to economic needs. Those needs are determined by the fact that the young people in most small communities have not been brought up to take their places in modern America. The communities have come to depend on the well-paying jobs extraction offers to unskilled high school graduates, and to unskilled high school dropouts. The tourist industry and entrepreneurial opportunities created by the communications and information age, which have found a foothold even in rural areas, are out of their reach.

Directions can change, however; the precipitous decline of extraction has opened many small communities to change. There is now a chance for them to move in other directions, and to take the public lands with them. The openness to change will remain as long as extraction stays supine. But should the market for energy and minerals recover tomorrow, most small communities will immediately snap back into old patterns. They will take up old ways because year after year the rural West's high schools will continue to graduate students who had assumed back in kindergarten, along with their parents and community, that formal education and a wider worldview were unimportant to them. They had assumed all they needed was to keep their grades high enough to qualify for wrestling or football. The push to prepare for a larger world was lacking because they knew they intended to go into the mines or mills or construction work after graduation and service in the armed forces.

At the end of my talk to SUWA, which more or less developed the theme of the opportunity and obligation presented to conservationists to help these places change, a questioner asked: So what? These are communities that raped and scraped the land. Why worry about them? SUWA's job is to save the land in southern Utah that the communities didn't get around to destroying. There is no obligation to help such destructive places.

It also seemed to be the audience's question. They had spent the day considering whether a southern Utah wilderness bill would get through Congress, a lawsuit to stop the widening and paving of the Burr Trail, and the growth of a strong environmentalist constituency in Salt Lake City, six hours away. A suggestion that SUWA should undertake a social reform effort that could take decades seemed irrelevant or in questionable taste.

A swifter speaker than I might have had an answer to the question. My reply was to ask for the next question. I did not know how to answer the original question with words. I have always taken it for granted that the small working communities of the West are wonderful places. Their devil's bargain—a trade of landscape and wildlife for extractive jobs—is no worse than many bargains American cities have struck, including the places most of those at the meeting call home. If the terms of the bargain can be altered over the next fifty years by some in-migration of newcomers and by some changes of values, then everyone and everything will be better off. That is the moralistic answer. There is also a practical one.

I am convinced that environmentalism cannot hold the land without also holding the communities. I don't care if Salt Lake City grows to 10 million residents, and all of them become fanatic mountain bikers and wilderness fans. We will still lose the landscape and the land unless those who live in southern Utah wish to protect it. Certainly a stronger tourist economy should be an important part of southern Utah's future, but it will not by itself protect the land. Look, for example, at Yellowstone National Park. Nearby Cody, Wyoming, insists on development at Fishing Bridge, no matter how many grizzlies that development kills. West Yellowstone and the other gateway communities were furious over the fires of summer 1988 because they disrupted their mono-economies.

The same situation is found elsewhere. Estes Park, Colorado, gateway to Rocky Mountain National Park, is the largest threat that park has. If the extractive economies and way of life are shoved out of the way to establish a tourist economy without other changes being made, we will simply have traded threats. Moreover, whatever happens with tourism, a resurgence of extraction is always a threat, unless the local communities are themselves insistent on protection of land, air, and water. In general, careful mining and milling need be no more damaging than tourism.

No matter what, protection of the land requires healthier local communities. Education, the growth of citizen reform movements, and creation of competent local and regional media are long-term, slowly accomplished tasks, but they are the only ways to get the job done. We must take this long, hard road because it is the only way to make better communities, and we can't hold the land without the communities.

Index

313

Also Available from Island Press

The Challenge of Global Warming
Edited by Dean Edwin Abrahamson
Foreword by Senator Timothy E. Wirth
1989, 350 pp., tables, graphs, index, bibliography
Cloth: $34.95 ISBN: 0-933280-87-4
Paper: $19.95 ISBN: 0-933280-86-6

Crossroads: Environmental Priorities for the Future
Edited by Peter Borrelli
1988, 352 pp., index
Cloth: $29.95 ISBN: 0-933280-68-8
Paper: $17.95 ISBN: 0-933280-67-X

Down by the River: The Impact of Federal Water Projects and Policies on Biodiversity
By Constance E. Hunt with Verne Huser
In cooperation with The National Wildlife Federation
1988, 256 pp., illustrations, glossary, index, bibliography
Cloth: $34.95 ISBN: 0-933280-48-3
Paper: $22.95 ISBN: 0-933280-47-5

Forest and the Trees: A Guide to Excellent Forestry
By Gordon Robinson, Introduction by Michael McCloskey
1988, 272 pp., indexes, appendices, glossary, tables, figures
Cloth: $34.95 ISBN: 0-933280-41-6
Paper: $19.95 ISBN: 0-933280-40-8

From THE LAND
Articles compiled from THE LAND, 1941–1954
Edited and compiled by Nancy P. Pittman
New Introduction by Wes Jackson, The Land Institute
Conservation Classic Edition 1988
459 pp., line drawings, index
Cloth: $34.95 ISBN: 0-933280-66-1
Paper: $19.95 ISBN: 0-933280-65-3

Holistic Resource Management
By Allan Savory
Center for Holistic Resource Management
1988, 512 pp., plates, diagrams, references, notes, index
Cloth: $39.95 ISBN: 0-933280-62-9
Paper: $24.95 ISBN: 0-933280-61-0

Our Common Lands: Defending the National Parks
Edited by David J. Simon
Foreword by Joseph L. Sax
In cooperation with the NPCA
1988, 575 pp., index, bibliography, appendices
Cloth: $45.00 ISBN: 0-933280-58-2
Paper: $24.95 ISBN: 0-933280-57-2

Reforming the Forest Service
By Randal O'Toole
1988, 250 pp., graphs, tables, notes
Cloth: $34.95 ISBN: 0-933280-49-1
Paper: $19.95 ISBN: 0-933280-45-9

Reserved Water Rights Settlement Manual
By Peter W. Sly, Director, Conference of Western Attorneys General
Preface by Jim Jones, Attorney General, State of Ohio
1988, 265 pp., index, appendices, bibliography
Cloth: $34.95 ISBN: 0-933280-72-6
Paper: $22.95 ISBN: 0-933280-71-8

Sierra Nevada: A Mountain Journey
By Tim Palmer
1988, 352 pp., illustrations, appendices, index
Cloth: $31.95 ISBN: 0-933280-54-8
Paper: $14.95 ISBN: 0-933280-53-X

Western Water Made Simple
By the Editors of *High Country News*
1987, 256 pp., illustrations, maps
Paper: $15.95 ISBN: 0-933280-39-4

Wildlife of the Florida Keys: A Natural History
By James D. Lazell, Jr.
1989, 225 pp., photographs, illustrations, index
Cloth: $31.95 ISBN: 0-933280-98-X
Paper: $19.95 ISBN: 0-933280-97-1

For a complete catalog of Island Press publications, please write:

Island Press
Box 7
Covelo, CA 95428